CONSTITUTIONAL
MYTHS

ALSO BY RAY RAPHAEL

FOUNDING ERA

A People's History of the American Revolution:
How Common People Shaped the Fight for Independence

The First American Revolution: Before Lexington and Concord

Founding Myths: Stories That Hide Our Patriotic Past

Founders: The People Who Brought You a Nation

The Complete Idiot's Guide to the Founding
Fathers and the Birth of Our Nation

Mr. President: How and Why the Founders Created a Chief Executive

Revolutionary Founders: Rebels, Radicals, and Reformers in the Making
of the Nation *(co-edited with Alfred F. Young and Gary B. Nash)*

CALIFORNIA HISTORY AND REGIONAL ISSUES

An Everyday History of Somewhere

Edges: Human Ecology of the Backcountry

Tree Talk: The People and Politics of Timber

Cash Crop: An American Dream

Little White Father: Redick McKee on the California Frontier

More Tree Talk: The People, Politics, and Economics of Timber

Two Peoples, One Place: Humboldt History,
volume 1 *(with Freeman House)*

EDUCATION AND SOCIOLOGY

The Teacher's Voice: A Sense of Who We Are

The Men from the Boys: Rites of Passage in Male America

CONSTITUTIONAL
MYTHS

What We Get Wrong and How to Get It Right

Ray Raphael

THE NEW PRESS

NEW YORK
LONDON

Requests for permission to reproduce selections from this book should be mailed to:
Permissions Department, The New Press, 38 Greene Street, New York, NY 10013.

Published in the United States by The New Press, New York, 2013
Distributed by Perseus Distribution

LIBRARY OF CONGRESS CATALOGING-IN-PUBLICATION DATA

Raphael, Ray.
  Constitutional myths : what we get wrong and how to get it right / Ray Raphael.
     pages   cm
  Includes bibliographical references and index.
  ISBN 978-1-59558-832-6 (hardcover)—ISBN 978-1-59558-838-8 (e-book) (print)   1. Constitutional
history—United States—18th century.   2. United States—History—1783–1815.   I. Title.
  KF4541.R375   2013
  342.7302'9—dc23   2012041849

The New Press publishes books that promote and enrich public discussion and understanding of
the issues vital to our democracy and to a more equitable world. These books are made possible by
the enthusiasm of our readers; the support of a committed group of donors, large and small; the
collaboration of our many partners in the independent media and the not-for-profit sector; booksellers,
who often hand-sell New Press books; librarians; and above all by our authors.

www.thenewpress.com

Composition by dix!
This book was set in Fournier MT

Printed in the United States of America

10   9   8   7   6   5   4   3   2   1

For George Washington, who wanted government to work.

For Benjamin Franklin, smarter than us all but
still doubting his own infallibility.

For the Constitution's framers,
who did not believe compromise a sin.

For the founding generation, who kept the framers on their toes.

And for Americans today—may we listen more, shout less,
and think to the future, as the framers did.

CONTENTS

PREFACE: THE HISTORICAL CONSTITUTION

On September 17, 1947, the United States Constitution was taken for a ride, transported by a red, white, and blue diesel-electric locomotive christened *The Spirit of Seventy-Six*. Starting in Philadelphia, the document's birthplace, and journeying for more than a year, it was viewed by reverential crowds at some three hundred stops in all forty-eight states.

The precious cargo aboard the "Freedom Train" included not only the Constitution but also the Magna Carta, Thomas Jefferson's draft of the Declaration of Independence, and 124 other documents deemed critical to establishing and preserving America's freedom. Some key amendments to the Constitution, however, failed to make the passenger list. The Fourteenth, with its promise of "equal protection," and the Fifteenth, which prohibits racial discrimination in voting, were denied passage. At some stops in the South, the Freedom Train played to segregated audiences, whites entering the mobile museum at one time and blacks at another.[1]

Today, traveling over the Internet and broadcast media, the Constitution is once again viewed by segregated audiences. The separation is voluntary this time, with the division following ideological lines that can be as uninformed and as stringent as bygone racial ones. People see in our governing document only what they wish to see. It is not a unifying force, as its authors had intended, but a wedge that widens the partisan divide.

Lost in our battle over the Constitution is the actual historical record. *Constitutional Myths* reintroduces that record and lays it alongside commonly accepted views. Based on in-depth accounts from founding times, not on later interpretations by interested citizens, professional historians, or even Supreme Court justices, it reveals how far our stories about the Constitution have strayed.

That historical record is both extensive and accessible. In the summer of 1787, as men we now call the framers conjured and debated evolving drafts of the Constitution, one of their number, James Madison, took meticulous notes. Seated immediately in front of the presiding officer, "with other members on my right & left hands," Madison did not miss "more than a casual fraction of an hour in any day, so that I could not have lost a single speech, unless a very short one." Other delegates to the Convention in Philadelphia took less comprehensive notes. After the framers released their handiwork and submitted it to the states for approval, thousands of other American citizens weighed in. These public debates, both written and oral, were recorded and preserved. Then, as the First Federal Congress struggled to put the Constitution to work, those proceedings were recorded as well. During this pivotal time in our nation's history, men who played key roles in writing, ratifying, and implementing the Constitution wrote privately and extensively to each other, discussing both broad ideas and specific provisions.[2]

To make sense of the abundant sources, *Constitutional Myths* constructs narrative timelines and sticks closely to them. Using the tried-and-true tool of basic chronology, it explores the context of what people said and did, for without context we have no history, just a jumble of things that happened. Citing the Constitution or the views of prominent founders without referring to context is great political sport, but it is also the quickest route to falsification. Political arguments are peppered with such phrases as "Hamilton believed . . .", "According to Madison . . .", or "As Jefferson says . . ." Even serious scholars and jurists fall into the trap when they try to integrate statements made by a particular founder at various times and differing contexts into a single, coherent philosophy. Jefferson, Madison, and Adams engaged in political life or commented on politics for over half a century each, Washington and Franklin for four decades, Hamilton for twenty-five years.

Was Hamilton really a monarchist? What did Jefferson think about slavery? These questions, without further definition, make little sense. History does not demand consistency.[3]

Nor can history be understood by treating the past as if it were the present. Much has happened since the founders' time: national expansion on a shrinking planet, nuclear and biological warfare, Internet and broadcast technologies, and so on—more than two centuries of subsequent history. Compare then and now. On October 15, 1789, President Washington set out from New York with only two aides and six servants to tour New England. In his diary, he chronicled the first day of his journey:

> The road for the greater part, indeed the whole way, was very rough and stoney, but the land strong, well covered with grass and a luxurient crop of Indian corn intermixed with pompions [pumpkins] which were ungathered in the fields. We met four droves of beef cattle for the New York market (about 30 in a drove) some of which were very fine—also a flock of sheep for the same place. We scarcely passed a farm house that did not abd. in geese.

Washington was traveling through what is now the Bronx, traversed by interstate highways and expressways, not stony roads, and home to some 1.4 million people packed tightly within apartments. If the country Washington observed was very different back then, so too was the manner in which he observed it, close up and literally on the ground, experiencing every stone on the road. He could meet his constituency directly, without intervention from an advance team, a press corps, or a small army of secret service agents.[4]

Some changes directly affect the Constitution. In the founding era, when nations went to war, they *declared* war, but the United States, despite extensive military engagements in Korea, Vietnam, Iraq, and Afghanistan, has not declared war since World War II, two-thirds of a century in the past. In today's world, in which military conflicts no longer feature armies of belligerent nations lining up and firing weapons at each other, declaring war can appear as anachronistic as fighting a duel. So how do we treat Article I, Section 8, Clause 11 of the Constitution, which stipulates that only Congress has the power to declare war? Is that provision simply obsolete, or if not, how can it be adapted to changing circumstances?

Historical changes include the evolution of language, the medium of the Constitution. When the founders used the word "Republican," they were not referring to a political party but to a governmental philosophy that most of them championed: people elect their own leaders at reasonably frequent intervals, and those leaders decide what's best for the country. "Democracy," meanwhile, had a somewhat negative connotation. While all the founders believed good government must be rooted in the people, most viewed direct popular control of government warily. Yet now we call ourselves Democrats or Republicans, and in the name of "the people," we try to influence every public act. In fact, the framers of the Constitution had hoped to keep *any* political party from manipulating or capturing the government.

The most fickle word is *federal*. Today, we speak of the national government located in Washington, DC, as the *federal* government, yet people claiming they are true to *federalist* principles resist central authority and demonize the city that houses the federal government. There is some historical precedent for this muddle. In 1787, twelve states sent delegates to a *federal* convention to address possible changes to the Articles of Confederation. During that convention, delegates who wanted to continue the old *Confederation*, with a few amendments, called themselves *federalists*, while those who wanted to abandon the Articles and create a stronger central government were considered nationalists. Afterward, proponents of the plan that emanated from the *Federal Convention* (that's what everybody called it, not the Constitutional Convention) assumed the term *federalist* for themselves, even though they had been nationalists at the Convention. Alexander Hamilton, James Madison, and John Jay, advocates of the new plan, wrote a series of essays they titled *The Federalist*, which many now call *The Federalist Papers*.

Opponents of the proposed plan fought back, signing their essays *A Democratic Federalist*, *A Republican Federalist*, or *Federal Farmer*, but the Constitution's supporters won the battle of words: *Federalists* they would be. The Constitution's opponents were thus denoted *Anti-Federalists*, even though few called themselves by that name.

Confusing? Of course, and *federal* is just one word. Imagine the linguistic problems created by the entire Constitution, written at a much different time but applied to situations today.[5]

Which is to say: if you want to know the historical Constitution, pay attention. Release for a moment what you think you know, and listen. "The past is a foreign country," people say. "They do things differently there." Although we all might agree with that statement on some level, this *particular* past—the framing and ratification of the Constitution—is our country too. Because it lives with us today and even determines our actions, it clouds the distinctions between past and present and tempts us to forget the most fundamental of all historical truths: that was then and this is now.[6]

In 1787, George Washington, James Madison, Alexander Hamilton, and others believed that government, such as it was under the Articles of Confederation, was broken. In response, they created an entirely new form.

Today, we hear from all sides that "government is broken," and we are again at a crossroads. We are not about to throw off the old rules this time—by and large they have served us well, and we have too much vested in them by now—but how can we make government work within our constitutional framework?

Many turn to the founders for guidance: what would *they* do if they were alive today?

We cannot even begin to address this question without considering a prior one: what did they do *during their own time*, not in our terms but theirs, when they wrote and ratified the Constitution? That is the primary inquiry of this book.

A second inquiry follows closely: how and why have Americans conjured phantom constitutions and substituted these for the historical one?

Finally, we come to the sweeping question that affects us all: what does the Constitution, written at a different time, mean for us today?

CONSTITUTIONAL
MYTHS

1

A REVOLUTION IN FAVOR
OF GOVERNMENT

Myth: The framers of the Constitution
opposed a strong federal government.

The Constitution is the fundamental law of the nation that limits government
and guarantees the rights and liberties of every American.
> —Website of the James Madison Memorial Fellowship Foundation,
> an independent agency of the executive branch of the federal government[1]

The Founders designed the federal government to be weak and inefficient to secure the sovereignty of the states and the people. The framers knew all too well
the abuse rendered by a large, centralized government.
> —Letter to the *Redwood Times*, a community newspaper in California[2]

Kernel of Truth

When citizens of thirteen colonies along North America's eastern seaboard
were still part of the British Empire, they considered themselves Virginians,
Pennsylvanians, or New Yorkers, not Americans. Once independent, each
of the former colonies created a distinct government that was empowered
to pass laws, tax citizens, and draft soldiers. These sovereign states formed
an alliance called the Articles of Confederation, but the "United States, in
Congress assembled," the body it charged with running the Confederation,
was *not* permitted to levy taxes, draft soldiers, or pass laws operating on
individual citizens. Having been oppressed so recently by a strong, distant
government, citizens were in no hurry to create a new central authority that
might pose the risk of subjugating its own people. Guarding against that

danger was a fundamental condition of the creation of the Confederation: each state must retain "the sole and exclusive right" to govern its internal affairs. The American revolutionaries, in short, jealously protected the rights of the states and of the citizens within each state.[3]

But . . .

That was plan A, but was it working? People like George Washington, James Madison, and Alexander Hamilton didn't think so. By 1787 the fledgling United States was under severe economic, political, and social duress, they felt. Congress was flat broke. Massachusetts was rocked by a major insurrection, and when called upon to put down that uprising, Congress balked, for it lacked money and commanded but a few soldiers, scattered in western outposts. Often, Congress did not even muster a quorum, conducting no business at all. Meanwhile, European powers were perched and ready, prepared to take advantage of what appeared to be the imminent implosion of the not-so-united states.

It was time to consider plan B, these prominent leaders determined. Perhaps the United States, to live up to its name, required not merely an *alliance* among sovereign and independent states, but an actual *government* that could make laws that operated on individuals, tax citizens, and raise armies. And so it was that delegates from twelve states gathered in Philadelphia in the summer of 1787 for what they called the Federal Convention. They would stage a new revolution, one that supported an "energetic" government with sufficient "vigor" (favorite words of the framers) to lead the United States from the brink. For almost four months, they labored to form its structure.[4]

On September 5, 1787, while the Federal Convention was still in session, a writer for the *Pennsylvania Gazette* put it this way: "The Year 1776 is celebrated for a revolution in favor of *Liberty*. The year 1787, it is expected, will be celebrated with equal joy, for a revolution in favor of *Government*."[5]

The Full Story

From the very beginning, Anglo American colonists were wedded to the idea of local self-government. "We, whose names are underwritten," wrote forty-one male passengers aboard the *Mayflower* in 1620, "do by these presents, solemnly and mutually, in the presence of God and one another, covenant and combine ourselves together into a civil Body Politick, for our better ordering and preservation." For "the general good of the Colony," these signers of the Mayflower Compact agreed to create "just and equal laws, ordinances, acts, constitutions, and officers . . . unto which we promise all due submission and obedience."[6]

For the next century and a half, English subjects in Massachusetts gathered in town meetings to decide for themselves how to prevent hogs from digging up the streets or keep cougars at bay. They also weighed in on issues affecting the whole province, such as deciding on a royal governor's salary or whether to tax the consumption of wine and spirits. Once the town meeting arrived at a decision, it instructed its representative to the provincial assembly to speak for the town. In 1766 Worcester told its representative to oppose tax-supported Latin schools, which were of no use to ordinary citizens, and the following year it commanded him to "use your influence to obtain a law to put an end to that unchristian and impolitick practice of making slaves of the humane species in this province." He should "adhere to these our instructions, and the spirit of them, as you regard our friendship, and would avoid our just resentment."[7]

Although colonists to the south of New England did not hold town meetings, free whites nonetheless established and benefited from representative government. In 1619 local communities in Virginia selected representatives who gathered as the House of Burgesses, a legislative assembly that passed laws and levied taxes. Other colonies created similar assemblies. Throughout the colonial era these bodies tussled with royal governors, who admitted that they represented the Crown first and the people second, as they naturally would in a monarchical empire. "My firm attachment to his majesty's person family & government challenges my first attention," said New Hampshire's governor Benning Wentworth. "My next pursuit shall be the peace & prosperity of his majesty's subjects of this Province."[8]

Preferring their own representative bodies and resenting the failure of authorities to recognize and defend English liberties, many colonists ignored or resisted the dictates of Crown and Parliament and the governors who administered them. In 1769, retaliating against Virginia legislators' expressed opposition to British colonial policies, Virginia's Lord Botetourt dissolved the House of Burgesses—to no avail. Members simply moved down the street to the Raleigh Tavern, where they continued to conduct business under their own authority. In 1774, in response to the Boston Tea Party, Parliament outlawed Massachusetts town meetings, but angry residents of Salem met just a block from the office of the royal governor, General Thomas Gage. When Gage arrested seven men for calling the meeting, three thousand local farmers showed up in an instant and forced him to set the prisoners free. After the successful defiance of Governor Gage in Salem, patriots in neighboring Danvers held another meeting "and continued it two or three howers longer than was necessary, to see if he [Gage] would interrupt 'em." He didn't. Town meetings would continue, Parliament and the royal governor notwithstanding.[9]

Insistence on local government was a major cause of the War for Independence. Long before the Second Continental Congress declared independence, local communities stated they were ready to make that definitive move. On October 4, 1774—exactly twenty-one months before the adoption of the congressional Declaration of Independence—the town meeting of Worcester, Massachusetts, instructed its representative to the provincial congress to push for a new and independent government. In the spring of 1776, immediately preceding the final break from British rule, local and state bodies passed at least ninety other declarations, each one stating that it was time for the United Colonies of America to rule themselves. These resolutions and declarations did not mean, however, that a new central government should call all the shots. Many of these earlier declarations of independence insisted that whereas Congress must assume new powers, the states must retain "the sole and exclusive right" to govern their own internal affairs. People were not about to relinquish any of their political independence, even to other Americans.[10]

So yes, absolutely, Americans in 1776 "knew all too well the abuse rendered by a large, centralized government" and did not wish to replicate the proto-British, top-down model. But that was 1776. By 1787, much had changed.[11]

• • •

Our national government, in embryonic form, began in September 1774, when delegates from twelve separate and distinct colonies assembled in Carpenters' Hall in Philadelphia. We call that initial meeting the First Continental Congress, but people didn't know what to call it then. Virginia's colonists spoke of "a general congress of deputies from all the colonies"; in Massachusetts people talked of "a meeting of committees from the several Colonies on this Continent"; and in Connecticut citizens referred, in a confused manner, to "such congress, or convention of commissioners, or committees of the several Colonies in British America." In any case, when rebellious colonists called this meeting a "congress," they did not mean an actual *government*, but something more akin to the county conventions of the Committees of Correspondence and the provincial congresses that had been trying to coordinate local resistance efforts. It passed resolutions, not laws. After less than two months, the "deputies" adjourned, and they would not meet again until the following spring, more than six months later.[12]

By the time that Second Continental Congress convened in May of 1775, British soldiers had marched on Lexington and Concord, local militiamen had driven them back, and a homegrown army of New Englanders had formed a cordon around Boston to keep British officers from staging any further assaults. The Massachusetts Provincial Congress, another makeshift group lacking governmental credentials, was running this army— unwillingly. It petitioned the Continental Congress: "As the army, collecting from different colonies, is for the general defence of the rights of America, we would beg leave to suggest to your consideration, the propriety of your taking the regulation and general direction of it." Delegates from Virginia, Pennsylvania, and other colonies outside New England could hardly refuse. The New England Army suddenly became the Continental Army, with George Washington, a Virginian, in command, appointed to that post by the Second Continental Congress.[13]

Suddenly in the business of administering an army, Congress needed to raise money, procure and deliver supplies, and perform other tasks generally undertaken by governments. It did this in two ways. It issued its own money (even though it was not even a government), and it *asked* (not required) each of the separate states to kick in.

Over a year later, on July 2, 1776, Congress resolved "that these United Colonies are, and of right ought to be, free and independent States" and "that a plan of confederation be prepared and transmitted to the respective Colonies for their consideration and approbation." Some states had already adopted permanent or provisional constitutions, some were in the process of doing so, and all assumed that since they were no longer under British authority, they would be forming their own new governments. Congress, though, was not contemplating a sovereign government but "a plan of confederation," to be submitted to the sovereign states. What form would that take? Indeed, what exactly *was* Congress or, for that matter, the United States of America, this newly created entity?

Nobody had clear answers to these questions, and all recognized that precise resolutions to sensitive issues might shatter the fragile consensus holding the states together. Nonetheless, Congress had to come up with a plan of some sort. It established a committee, which appointed John Dickinson, the celebrated author of *Letters from a Farmer in Pennsylvania*, a prewar critique of British imperial policies, to write an initial draft.

When Dickinson first presented his work, it contained a curious provision: "All charges of war and all other expences that shall be incurr'd for the general wellfare and allowed by the Union in General Congress, shall be defrayed out of a Common Treasury, which shall be supplied by the several Colonies in proportion to the number of [*blank*] in each Colony." How should that blank be filled in? If expenses were to be apportioned by population, should slaves be included? Northern states, which permitted slavery but had few slaves, said of course, while southern states, in which enslaved people counted for significant portions of the population, said never. If property were the base, should improvements be counted as well as land? Northern states, with more improvements, said never, while southern states thought it was a good idea. Since each colony had much to gain or lose according to how the mysterious blank would be filled in, members of Congress bickered.[14]

Other issues arose. Should Congress control western settlement? Maryland, with no state claims in the West, wanted that, but Virginia, which claimed land clear across the continent to the "South Sea" (Pacific Ocean), said it would never accept any plan that threatened its rights to those lands.

Should each state have an equal voice in Congress? Tiny Delaware, Dickinson's home state, said yes, but Virginia, Pennsylvania, and Massachusetts, the most populous states, said no.

Months passed and no settlement was reached. Local interests superceded the national interest. Not until November 1777, when France refused to lend the United States any money unless there *was* a United States, did Congress finally approve the Articles of Confederation and send it to the states for ratification. It would take more than three years for all thirteen states to sign on.

Throughout most of the Revolutionary War, the United States remained under the interim management of the Second Continental Congress. Although Congress was expected to administer the Continental Army, it possessed no means of raising money on its own. The state governments were Congress's milch cows, as people said in those days. When the army needed more soldiers, Congress asked each state to field a specific number of men. It also set quotas for beef, flour, gunpowder, blankets, tent canvas, and other supplies, but if a state did not come up with its fair share, there was no enforcement mechanism. Soldiers would simply go without.

As the war dragged on, the currency Congress issued lost more than 99 percent of its value, and by the end, in order to remain solvent, Congress granted full authority over the nation's finances to a single individual (see chapter 2). Only with considerable help from abroad and begrudging sacrifice by unpaid soldiers did Congress manage to keep an army in the field.

On March 1, 1781, after France threatened to withdraw military support unless the states pulled it together, the thirteenth state, Maryland, finally approved the Articles of Confederation. At last there was a nation of sorts, but calling "The United States of America" at that point an actual nation is a stretch, and few people at the time used that term. The Articles themselves did not use the word "nation," preferring the term "firm league of friendship." In structure this league of friendship differed little from a military alliance, and most of its provisions concerned either relations with other nations or mechanisms for refereeing disputes between the states. The Articles did grant Congress the power to establish a minimal national infrastructure—creating post offices, regulating the land and naval forces "when in service of the United States," and fixing standards for coinage, weights, and measures—but it provided no means to raise revenues other than requisitions issued to the states and no mechanisms to enforce compliance. In short, the Articles of Confederation tread lightly around the authority of the states, and Article II made this very clear: "Each state retains its sovereignty, freedom, and independence, and every power, jurisdiction, and right, which is not by this Confederation expressly delegated to the United States, in Congress assembled."

Could this system work? Would a "firm league of friendship" among otherwise sovereign and independent states with diverse and competing interests suffice?

In October of 1781, seven months after the Articles were ratified, a French fleet and a combined American and French land force trapped General Charles Cornwallis and seven thousand British soldiers at Yorktown, Virginia, forcing their surrender. Although Britain still had some forty thousand troops stationed in America and King George III wanted to continue the fight, its army and navy soon suffered other setbacks in what had become a global war against France, Spain, and the Netherlands. To preserve its empire elsewhere, Parliament finally decided to pull back from North America. However constrained and beleaguered, Congress and the army it supported had prevailed in a war of attrition.

Yet in the minds of some leading political figures, peace presented its own set of challenges. No longer facing a common enemy, Georgians and Virginians and Pennsylvanians and New Yorkers were less willing to sacrifice for the common good. "War is indeed a rude, rough nurse to infant states," said Gouverneur Morris in August 1782, fearful that a treaty of peace would prove a setback to nation building. Only "a continuation of the war" would "convince people of the necessity of obedience to common counsel for general purposes." [15]

George Washington also craved a dynamic federal government. He knew from firsthand experience how a disjointed administration by Congress and thirteen quarrelsome states had sapped the nation's strength for eight long wartime years, from 1775 to 1783. Throughout that time, he had begged Congress for money, men, and supplies, while Congress in turn begged the largely autonomous states to make good on the requisitions issued to them. If America continued on such a course, it would fail, he felt. Just before retiring from the military, while he still had the attention of his fellow countrymen, "The General," as everybody called him, offered strong words on the subject. On June 8, 1783, in a circular letter to the thirteen states, called at the time his "legacy," he sounded an urgent tone: "According to the system of policy the states shall adopt at this moment, they will stand or fall, and by their confirmation or lapse, it is yet to be decided, whether the Revolution must ultimately be considered as a blessing or a curse. With this conviction of the importance of the present crisis, silence in me would be a crime." [16]

Then, pulling no punches, in language that was emotional and persuasive, he presented his own "system of policy," a broad outline for "an indissoluble union of the states under one federal head." Americans must "forget their local prejudices and policies," he said, and "make those mutual concessions which are requisite to the general prosperity, and in some instances, to sacrifice their individual advantages to the interest of the community." That was the lecturing part, what the public might expect from the country's most exalted leader, but Washington went further: "There should be lodged somewhere a supreme power to regulate and govern the general concerns of the confederated republic, without which the union cannot long endure." By "supreme power" he meant neither God nor an individual executive, but a national government, a "supreme authority" over and above the separate states. With those words, Washington retired from public life. [17]

The nation did not heed Washington's advice. As Gouverneur Morris suspected, people saw less need for "common counsel for general purposes" when no external enemy threatened. As each state struggled to pay its debts and otherwise recover from wartime disruptions, politics turned local. Within the Confederation Congress, those favoring a stronger general government lost power to men who considered themselves true republicans— not that it really mattered, for Congress was conducting very little business in any case.

Regional interests came to a head when John Jay sought permission from Congress to negotiate an agreement with Spain that would win special trading status for the United States but relinquish American claims to shipping rights on the Mississippi River. The agreement, which would have benefited the commercially oriented northeastern states but hurt the westward-leaning southern states, bogged down in Congress. The United States could not settle on a uniform commercial policy.

Washington watched all this from the sidelines, and in October 1785, he grumbled in a private letter to James Warren: "Illiberality, jealousy, & local policy mix too much in all our public councils for the good government of the Union. In a word, the Confederation appears to me to be little more than an empty sound, and Congress a nugatory body. . . . [W]e are descending into the valleys of confusion and darkness. . . . The necessity therefore of a controuling power is obvious, and why it should be with-held is beyond comprehension."[18]

In Washington's view, the descent continued. Britain required that all American debts to British subjects be paid in specie, setting off a chain reaction that undercut the American economy. During the economic downturn that started in 1785, creditors and tax collectors demanded payment in hard-to-come-by coins of gold and silver. Unable to meet such demands, hard-pressed citizens, and primarily farmers, insisted that state governments relieve the burdens they faced. In some states, such as Rhode Island, they forced legislatures to print paper money, soften enforcement for the collection of debts, allow taxes to be paid in the form of old horses or small parcels of worthless pine barrens, and so on. Washington and his fellow nationalists feared that such maneuvers would jeopardize the nation's credit and its future. Indebted farmers, meanwhile, thought that some state governments were not acting quickly or vigorously enough to protect their interests. They rebelled.

The most notable insurrection was in Massachusetts, whose state legislature, dominated by eastern lawyers and merchants, resisted the pleas of farmers in the western part of the state for relief. In response, angry armed men who described themselves as "Regulators" converged on county seats to shut down the state's courts and prevent enforcement of debts and foreclosure actions. (Only their enemies labeled them "Shaysites" and the uprising "Shays' Rebellion," named after Revolutionary War veteran Captain Daniel Shays, one of the movement's several leaders.) Nor was unrest limited to Massachusetts. Farmers also closed courts in Virginia, Maryland, and New Jersey. After a court closure in Camden, South Carolina, Judge Aedanus Burke stated that not even "5,000 troops, the best in America or Europe, could enforce obedience to the Common Pleas." In York, Pennsylvania, 200 men armed with guns and clubs took back cattle that had been seized by the state government in lieu of taxes. Farmers in Connecticut, New Hampshire, and Vermont staged protests. The entire nation appeared at risk.[19]

The day after Christmas 1786, George Washington wrote to the Confederation's secretary of war Henry Knox, the man he had left in charge of the remnants of the Continental Army three years earlier: "I feel, my dear General Knox, infinitely more than I can express to you, for the disorders, which have arisen in these states. Good God! Who, besides a Tory, could have foreseen, or a Briton predicted them?" A few weeks later, Washington wrote to Knox again: "If government shrinks, or is unable to enforce its laws, . . . anarchy & confusion must prevail—and every thing will turn topsy turvey in that State." But with only a few hundred men to guard the western borderlands, Knox could do nothing to suppress the rebellions. In dire need of a national army, Congress once again requisitioned the states and once again came up short. Massachusetts could not even supply funds to put down its own rebels. In the end, it took a private army, hired by wealthy merchants, to restore order.[20]

For George Washington, Gouverneur Morris, John Jay, and Henry Knox, as for James Madison, Alexander Hamilton, and other prominent nationalists, the wave of unrest, however unwanted, provided a unique political opportunity. Over the previous decade, ever since the declaration of American independence, advocates of a stronger national government had lost out to deep-seated fears of a central authority that would be geographically distant from many Americans. Now, those fears were matched by others of equal power: economic collapse, social upheaval, and political disintegration, allegedly dragging the nation toward anarchy and a return to the state of nature, where no man's property would be secure. Historians to this day argue whether things were quite so bad as the nationalists made them out to be, but that is beside the question. This was the nationalists' political moment, their chance to reframe America's political dialogue by stressing such concerns. If they played their cards right, they might yet wind up with the centralization they thought was needed to give the United States a firm financial foundation and enduring governmental structure. In their minds, a drastically revised constitutional framework could protect the fruits of the Revolution: American independence and republican government.

On February 21, 1787, in the immediate wake of the insurrection in Massachusetts, the Confederation Congress called for a special interstate convention "for the sole and express purpose of revising the Articles of Confederation and reporting to Congress and the several legislatures such alterations and provisions therein as shall . . . render the federal Constitution adequate to the exigencies of Government and the preservation of the Union." Such a convention, Congress said, appeared to be "the most probable means of establishing in these states a firm national government." Such language—"firm national government"—would not have won much applause at an earlier date, but it was now deemed acceptable.[21]

Political leaders began to ponder: precisely what "alterations" would "render the federal Constitution [the Articles of Confederation] adequate to the exigencies of Government"? Separately, John Jay, Henry Knox, and James Madison each sketched ideas for a complete overhaul of the federal government and sent them to Washington, whom they hoped would attend the convention and play a key role in its deliberations. All three outlines diverted radically from the Articles of Confederation, and Knox, in particular, referred bluntly to the "imbecilities of the present government." He feared that the convention "might devise some expedients to brace up the present defective confederation so as just to keep us together." In his view, what was needed was "*one government* instead of an association of governments."[22]

Washington wrote back to Knox: "The system on which you seem disposed to build a national government is certainly more energetic, and I dare say, in every point of view is more desirable than the present one." Yet even if the forthcoming convention adopted such a scheme, could it ever gain the approval of the states? Washington feared it would not: "The darling Sovereignties of the States individually, the Governors, . . . the Legislators— with a long train of etcetra whose political consequence will be lessened, if not anihilated, would give their weight of opposition to such a revolution."[23]

Several of Washington's allies—Jay, Knox, Hamilton, and Madison— urged him to attend the convention, and he did understand that his presence would help legitimize this revolution in the making. To Knox, though, he expressed his misgivings. If several states chose *not* to send delegates, or if they "fettered" their delegates or "cramped" their options, he saw no reason "to be a sharer in this business." When Knox reported back that all states but one were sending delegates "with ample powers to point out radical cures for the present political evils," Washington finally agreed to go.[24]

Washington, Madison, and five other Virginians were the only out-of-state delegates to arrive on time, and while waiting for other delegations they prepared a new and radical scheme. On May 29, the first day of formal deliberations, Virginia's governor Edmund Randolph presented his state delegation's fifteen-point plan. The first article hinted at the nationalists' design: "Resolved that the Articles of Confederation ought to be so corrected & enlarged as to accomplish the objects proposed by their institution; namely, 'common defence, security of liberty and general welfare.' "[25]

Why only a hint, wondered Gouverneur Morris? Why not proclaim their actual design? At Morris's bidding, Randolph moved to strengthen the wording: "A *national* government ought to be established consisting of a *supreme* legislative, executive & judiciary." Madison's meticulous notes on the convention, the main source of what went on behind those closed doors, emphasized the words "national" and "supreme."[26]

This motion set off a spirited discussion "on the force and extent of the particular terms *national & supreme*." Some delegates declared that they were authorized by their state legislatures only to amend the Articles of Confederation, not to abolish them, but Gouverneur Morris countered, "In all communities, there must be one supreme power, and one only." A "federal" government was no more than "a mere compact resting on the good faith of the parties," he explained, while a "national, supreme" government implied "a compleat and compulsive operation."[27]

To our ears that language—"a compleat and compulsive operation"— might sound harsh, but not so to George Washington in 1787. Two years earlier, writing to James Warren, he had contended that the "necessity . . . of a controuling power is obvious," and in 1786 he had told John Jay he favored "the intervention of a coercive power . . . which will pervade the whole Union in as energetic a manner, as the authority of the different state governments extends over the several states." Now, among the delegates assembled in Pennsylvania's State House, this stance was common currency. Of the eight states then in attendance that voted that day, six approved the radical move to create a sovereign national government with supreme authority, one opposed it, and one was divided. In a single daring stroke, the convention scrapped the Articles of Confederation—a mere contract among sovereign states, each "supreme."[28]

The revolution in favor of government was under way, and this is where our book takes form: at the Federal Convention in Philadelphia on May 30, 1787, as the men we now call the framers discussed how to devise an energetic and vigorous new government for the United States. They wanted to institute a "coercive power" that would "pervade the whole Union," yet they had to do so carefully, always mindful that the people, in whom all authority resides, would have the last say.

2

TAXES

Myth: The framers hated taxes.

I just wondered that if our founders thought taxation without representation was bad, what would they think of representation *with* taxation?

—Representative Michele Bachmann, presidential candidate,
speaking to Conservative Political Action Conference, February 26, 2009[1]

The Founders, who framed a Constitution to protect us from government, did not dare consider an income tax.

—Thomas Del Beccaro, chairman, California Republican Party[2]

Kernel of Truth

"No taxation without representation" and "liberty and property" were the rallying cries of America's original patriots. Before the Revolution, British American colonists believed they were entitled to full rights as Englishmen, including (and especially) the right to keep their own property. The Crown, for all its powers, was not permitted to seize land, possessions, or money from its citizens; only the people themselves, acting through their elected representatives, could relinquish any share of what they rightfully owned. Because Americans did not have any representatives in Parliament, they were taxed instead by colonial assemblies, in which they were represented. This was the only legitimate form of taxation, in their minds.[3]

That's how the system operated before the end of the French and Indian War (known in Europe as the Seven Years' War), when Britain more than doubled its holdings in North America. After 1763, to finance the expanded empire, Parliament levied various taxes on the colonies. Colonists from

Massachusetts to Georgia resisted, Parliament and the Crown held firm, and Americans, refusing to cave in, eventually declared their independence.

In the wake of the American declaration of independence, only state legislatures had the power to levy taxes or duties. The Continental Congress lacked the authority to tax because congressmen represented their states, not the people themselves. After 1781, when the Articles of Confederation took effect, the Confederation Congress could not tax citizens directly, nor could it tax imported goods without approval from all thirteen state legislatures. People in any one state, the reasoning went, should not be taxed upon the authority of representatives from other states. Even when facing the expenses of fighting a protracted war, Americans refused to be taxed by anyone but their immediate representatives. They feared that a central government, if granted the power of taxation, might replicate the injustices that Parliament and Crown had inflicted on the colonists.

But . . .

After the Revolutionary War, without the power to tax, the Confederation Congress was unable to deliver two of the most fundamental government services: protection of property and national defense.

In the wake of the war, with states struggling to pay back their debts, citizens found themselves taxed more heavily than they had been before independence. Meanwhile, overseas merchants insisted on payment in specie, so the money supply shrank. Debt-ridden and overtaxed farmers pushed for various forms of relief. They wanted state governments to increase the money supply by issuing paper money so they wouldn't need specie to pay their debts and taxes. To lessen their tax burdens, they also wanted their state governments not to honor war bonds at face value, but rather to honor them only at the value that speculators had paid for them. Such measures displeased the men we now call the founders. The net effect of debtor relief, they believed, was to deprive creditors of what was rightfully theirs, thereby nullifying the obligation of contracts. Under normal conditions, creditors could rely on courts to help them collect debts owed to them, but in 1786 and 1787 debtors in some states actually closed the courts to prevent such proceedings. When rebels in Massachusetts shut down courts and threatened to seize arms so they could march on Boston, the penniless Congress, with just a few hundred soldiers stationed in the West, could do nothing about it. Political leaders who thought in national terms worried that debtor insurrections and laws favoring debtors over creditors would threaten all private property and in the end convulse the republic.

These troubles threatened national defense. With the American people embroiled in domestic turmoil and Congress lacking any means to raise an army, the fledgling nation was vulnerable to foreign attack. How might it defend itself? It would need to either tax its citizens (which it was not allowed to do), requisition the states for money (it had tried that many times, with at best mixed results), or borrow from creditors abroad (if it could find any investors willing to lend to a government with no means of raising money for repayment). All was in flux. In the minds of many prominent Americans, no property was safe and the nation as a whole lay exposed.

The only way out, they figured, was to revamp the rules under which the United States operated. First and foremost, Congress needed the authority to raise its own funds through taxation, and not just a few cents here and there. Without credit to borrow in case of emergency, the national government would always be vulnerable to foreign nations that *did* have the money to spend on warfare, or at least sufficient credit to raise armies and navies. But to secure credit, the United States would have to convince investors it could and would raise revenues so it could pay its bills. The government's tools could not be too constricted. Congress needed the sweeping authority to tax.

Such was the reasoning of George Washington, James Madison, Edmund Randolph, Alexander Hamilton, Robert Morris, Gouverneur Morris, and other committed nationalists who organized a convention in 1787 to strengthen the financial standing of the federal government. We might not want to hear it, but to taxes we owe our Constitution.[4]

The Full Story

The 1689 English Bill of Rights, a document dear to the hearts of British subjects in North America, stipulated that "the levying money for or to the use of the Crown by pretence of prerogative, without grant of Parliament

. . . is illegal" and "that election of members of Parliament ought to be free." Colonists interpreted these two provisions to mean "no taxation without representation," not only in England but also in America.

Here, colonists did not shirk taxation, so long as they were taxed by their own representatives. Colonial assemblies, elected by the people, raised funds in a variety of ways. They imposed retail licenses and excises, import duties, and tonnage fees. These were considered "indirect taxes" because they taxed activities, not people; in a sense they were voluntary because if you didn't want to pay a tax, you simply didn't engage in the activity being taxed. Indirect taxes rarely sufficed, however, which meant that citizens had to be taxed directly, either by a poll or head tax, applied evenly to all taxpaying citizens, or by some form of property tax, in which those with larger holdings assumed a greater share of the tax burden. One variation on the property tax, a "faculty tax," resembled the modern income tax. People were assessed not only on the basis of their property but also according to their ability, or faculty, to make money. Each profession was taxed according to its likely "returns and gains." Often, because specie was scarce, taxes could be paid in commodities such tobacco, corn, wheat, rice, beaver skins, whale oil, or turpentine.[5]

In times of war, when money had to be raised in a hurry, current taxes alone were never enough. Colonial governments had to purchase supplies for their fighting men with bills of credit, which would circulate as money. Typically, when a colonial government issued these bills, it would allocate taxes for the next few years to pay them off. If taxes were not allocated or if people lost faith in the government's ability to raise money, however, the bills would quickly lose their worth. Wars were thereby financed by a promise of future taxes, but this system of deficit spending worked only if the bills of credit were issued with restraint and backed by an adequate program of taxation. Such measures were common in colonial times because Britain, France, and Native nations fought frequently for control of eastern North America.[6]

The newly independent states inherited these precedents from their colonial predecessors. They needed to adapt such practices to pay for the Revolutionary War, but the systems they developed proved disastrous and almost led to the nation's ruin.

At the outset of the war in 1775, more than a year before declaring independence, the Continental Congress issued 2 million dollars in paper bills. (It denominated its currency in dollars, the unit used in Spain, rather than in pounds, as the British did.) In July, when George Washington assumed command of the army surrounding Boston, Congress followed with another million dollars, and by the end of 1775 it had issued 6 million. That was only the beginning. In 1776 it issued 19 million dollars, in 1777 another 13 million, in 1778 63 million, and in 1779 124 million. By then the dollar had fallen to only 3 percent of its original value, and two years later, in 1781, a dollar could not buy a penny's worth of goods. At the time, Americans mocked the national paper money as "not worth a Continental," a phrase still used today. The problem was that the currency was never backed by a revenue-producing plan that shored up its value. The public had no reason to believe that Congress could ever redeem the bills it issued.[7]

Congress was not directly at fault, for it was playing with a weak hand. How could it meet its obligations and buttress its credit when it lacked the authority to levy taxes? Nor could Congress ask states to meet their obligations and increase taxes ten- or twentyfold when state taxpayers had not yet recovered from the financial duress brought on by war. In colonial times, the assemblies had issued bills of credit, and the new state legislatures tried to do so again, but with the flood of paper money emitted by both the states and Congress, nobody dared take the money too seriously. State currency inflated along with federal currency, likewise dropping in value.

Who, then, *did* pay for the Revolutionary War? Apart from France, our helpful ally, and Dutch bankers willing to invest in American securities, farmers and others who sold supplies to the government bore the war's expense, although they did so unwittingly and indirectly. During the war years, suppliers had accepted Continental currency in exchange for goods and services, but when that currency lost the lion's share of its value, they had little hope of recompense. The losses, therefore, were distributed through the population as suppliers spent the depreciating money. As Benjamin Franklin commented wryly in 1779, "This currency, as we manage it, is a wonderful machine. It performs its office when we issue it; it pays and clothes troops, and provides victuals and ammunition; and when we are obliged to issue a quantity excessive, it pays itself off by depreciation."[8]

Although paper currency did finance the war effort for the first few years, running a nation with a continually depreciating currency was hardly sustainable. By 1781 nobody accepted Congress's paper in payment, suppliers refused to offer goods on credit, and investors shied from lending more funds. The army faced severe shortages of food and military wares. Congress told states to send supplies if they couldn't send money, but the returns were minimal. Meanwhile, soldiers threatened to return to their homes if they didn't get paid.

Flat broke, Congress urged the merchant-prince Robert Morris, reputedly the wealthiest man in America, to assume a newly created office, superintendent of finance. His assigned task was to shore up the nation's credit rating. "*The* Financier," as Morris was called, accepted the position in exchange for unprecedented powers: he could fire government employees at will, import or export goods on the nation's tab, and deal directly with foreign ministers, thereby running his own department of foreign affairs. Embracing the role, Morris created a national bank empowered to issue bills of credit, and beyond that, he offered his own personal credit, which was solid, to back the nation's credit, which had collapsed. He countersigned government notes, called "Morris Notes," which the public was willing to accept. People might not trust Congress, but they knew that Robert Morris would make good on his word.

These stopgap measures, however, were all "in anticipation of taxes," Morris informed Congress and the public. "It is possible the public credit might be restored," he said, but only if the states granted Congress authority to raise its own money. The problem, though, was that the Articles of Confederation prohibited Congress from levying taxes, and all thirteen states had to ratify any amendment revising that ban. In 1781, when Congress tried to amend the Articles to permit a 5 percent impost on imported goods, most states agreed, but tiny Rhode Island, a commercial state that preferred to levy its own imposts, refused. Two years later, in 1783, Congress tried again to amend the Articles of Confederation in order to levy an impost, and this time New York, another commercial state that taxed goods coming into its port, would not go along with the program except under conditions that Congress found unacceptable. The failure to grant Congress the power of taxation, Morris contended, would convince the nation's enemies "that we are unworthy of confidence" and "that our Union is a rope of sand."[9]

Unable to tax, Congress had to send requisitions to each state to pay its proportional share first of the war's expenses and then, after the fighting was over, of the accumulated wartime debt. The states responded unevenly and with diminishing payments. They came through with two-thirds of the requisitions of October 1781 and April 1784 but only one-third of the September 1782 requisition and one-fifth of the amount Congress requested in September 1785.

Those were the good times. After that, with a recession in full swing and memories of the war fading, the states lost the ability and the incentive to make good on the public debt. New Jersey and Connecticut announced boldly that they would not pay. (New Jersey later rescinded its defiant stance, but it still didn't offer any payment.) In February 1786, a committee of Congress bemoaned the lack of compliance: "The requisitions of Congress, for eight years past, have been so irregular in their operation, so uncertain in their collection, and so evidently unproductive, that a reliance on them in future as a source from whence moneys are to be drawn to discharge the engagements of the Confederacy . . . would be dangerous to the welfare and peace of the Union." If this was meant to instill fear and generate compliance, it failed. The August 1786 requisition generated a mere 2 percent return. From October 1786 through March 1787, the states turned over a grand total of $663 to the federal treasury to keep the Confederacy afloat. To use a modern idiom, the federal government, such as it was, had been shrunk to the size where it could drown in a bathtub.[10]

James Madison, among many others, thought he saw the handwriting on the wall. Unless the system of public finance was radically altered, "the United States, in Congress assembled" would soon go under, just as Robert Morris had predicted it would. In April 1787, when Madison compiled a memorandum listing the "Vices of the Political System of the United States," his very first item addressed the heart of the problem: "1. Failure of the States to comply with the Constitutional requisition." He elaborated: "This evil has been so fully experienced both during the war and since the peace, results so naturally from the number and independent authority of the

States, and has been so uniformly exemplified in every similar Confederacy, that it may be considered . . . fatal to the object of the present system." [11]

What was to be done? That's what the delegates to the Federal Convention in Philadelphia had to figure out. They all wanted to authorize Congress to raise its own funds by levying imposts—that was a major reason they were there—but they disagreed on two overlapping issues. Should federal taxes be exclusively indirect (imposts and excises), or could they also be direct (poll and property taxes)? And if direct taxes were permitted, before they went into effect, should Congress give the states the opportunity to come up with the money themselves? [12]

The delegates resolved both issues. On July 3, when Roger Sherman suggested that Congress be granted "the power of levying taxes on trade, but not the power of direct taxation," he was voted down, two states to eight. Direct taxes would be permitted. And on August 21, when Luther Martin moved that Congress not be allowed to collect taxes from citizens unless the states had tried to do so but failed, he too was voted down, one state to eight with one divided. Congress could bypass the states by levying its own taxes, whether direct or indirect, on individuals and their economic activities.

Overwhelmingly, the framers determined not to limit Congress's ability to raise funds any more than was necessary. In the final draft of the Constitution, when listing congressional powers in the first clause of Article I, Section 8, they started with the most basic one, without which all else would be meaningless: "The Congress shall have Power To lay and Collect Taxes, Duties, Imposts and Excises, to pay the Debts and provide for the common Defence and general Welfare of the United States; but all Duties and Imposts and Excises shall be uniform throughout the United States." Here, the generic term "taxes" neither included nor excluded direct taxation. The fourth clause of Article I, Section 9, clarified that point: "No Capitation [poll], or other direct, Tax shall be laid, unless in Proportion to the Census or Enumeration herein before directed to be taken." This revealed that taxes on individuals (capitation or poll taxes) and other direct taxes (the most common being on land) were to be included in Congress's revenue-raising arsenal, but only if they were apportioned among the states according to population—a stipulation that would prove unworkable and be overturned in 1913 by the Sixteenth Amendment, as shown below.

The framers did build two other qualifications into the Constitution. As stated in the first clause of Section 8, they insisted on keeping taxes "uniform" from state to state and from region to region. Some delegates worried that Congress might impose property taxes on slaves, for instance, which would burden the South more than the North. Also, in the fifth clause of Article I, Section 9, they declared, "No Tax or Duty shall be laid on Articles exported from any State." Again, their intention was to prevent taxes from falling unduly on one region; a federal export tax on tobacco, for instance, would affect Virginians but not New Englanders.

Beyond these caveats intended to ensure regional fairness, the framers gave Congress broad powers to tax as it saw fit. Although they assumed that Congress would prefer import taxes, the least intrusive means of raising revenue, they refused to place other measures off limits. The best way to put the new government on a firm financial footing was to grant Congress across-the-board powers of taxation, and they did so.

But would the public buy it?

Many Americans, perhaps most, did not. Capitalizing on the antitax sentiment that had triggered the Revolution, opponents of the Constitution painted horrific images of tax collectors fanning out across the land, commanding citizens to relinquish some of their treasure. These were the types of intrusions people could expect from a large, centralized government, critics warned. They had no problem with import duties that could be collected at a handful of seaports, but giving Congress the authority to tax as it pleased was simply too risky, they contended. They worried, too, that congressional taxing power would preempt or even preclude state taxing power, and without revenue state governments would wither.

The issue was hotly contested in the first major state to vote on ratification, Pennsylvania. Although supporters of the Constitution, calling themselves Federalists, prevailed at the state convention, opponents, who became known against their will as Anti-Federalists, issued a scathing dissent that highlighted Congress's sweeping powers of taxation. "By virtue of their power of taxation, Congress may command the whole, or any part of the property of the people," the dissenters wrote. "They may impose what imposts upon commerce; they may impose what land taxes, poll taxes, excises, duties of all written instruments, and duties on every other article that they may judge proper; in short, every species of taxation." To remedy this, they proposed an amendment that would have restricted national taxation to imposts, duties, and postage on letters. Although the ratifying convention rejected the dissenters' list of amendments, the naysaying delegates published their amendments, complete with explanatory statements, and circulated them widely throughout the nation.[13]

Resistance to federal powers of taxation continued at the Massachusetts ratifying convention, which officially proposed a different yet related amendment to the Constitution. Congress still would be able to levy direct taxes, the amendment said, but only after "the moneys arising from the impost and excise" proved "insufficient for the public exigencies." After that, Congress would have to requisition the states, asking them to come up with their apportioned quotas "in such way and manner as the legislatures of the states shall think best." Only if imposts proved insufficient *and* states did not come through with some or all of their requisitions could Congress "assess and levy" direct taxes to make up the difference. This amendment, as contorted as it was, served as a model for other states. Subsequently, all six ratification conventions that suggested amendments included tax overhauls similar to that of Massachusetts. On the ground, the vote was in: Congress should levy taxes only as a last resort.[14]

Federalist leaders like Madison believed that this multistep process was seriously flawed. No potential lender would trust such a time-consuming and unwieldy system to produce revenue. On paper, the proposed amendments did not strip Congress of any real power, since in the end it still could levy the taxes it needed. In real life, though, the national government once again would have to beg from the states, and if the states failed to come through, as appeared likely judging from past experience, much time would elapse before funds were raised. This was no way to run a government.

At the Virginia ratifying convention, Madison noted correctly that "the issue of direct taxation is most generally objected to," but he insisted that taxes were the key to a strong and energetic government. The Constitution's opponents countered that direct national taxation would lead inevitably to a government that was *too* strong and energetic. Patrick Henry led the crusade with flaming oratory. "Must I give my soul—my lungs—to Congress?" he demanded. "What powerful check is there here to prevent the most extravagant and profligate squandering of the public money?" To bring his argument home, Henry got more graphic yet:

> In this scheme of energetic government, the people will find two sets of tax-gatherers—the state and the federal sheriffs. This, it seems to me, will produce such dreadful oppression as the people cannot possibly bear. The federal sheriff may commit what oppression, make what distresses, he pleases, and ruin you with impunity; for how are you to tie his hands? Have you any sufficiently decided means of preventing him from sucking your blood by speculations, commissions, and fees? Thus thousands of your people will be most shamefully robbed.[15]

Less flamboyantly, but perhaps more persuasively, George Mason read aloud Robert Morris's proposal for national taxation: "six shillings on every hundred acres of land, six shillings per poll, and ninepence per gallon on all spirituous liquors distilled in the country." Such taxes would be manifestly unjust, Mason contended. An acre of land near Philadelphia or Boston might be worth one hundred pounds, compared with twenty shillings for an acre in Virginia—yet both landowners would be forced to pay the same amount in taxes. The poll tax was even more "grievous" because "it falls light on the rich and heavy on the poor." Virginia's poll tax was so "generally disliked in this state," Mason said, "that we were obliged to abolish it last year." The liquor tax, meanwhile, would "carry the exciseman to every farmer's house, who distils a little brandy, where he may search and ransack as he pleases." Such injustices would be inevitable if taxes were levied by "a government where the representatives will have no communication with the people." That is why Mason proposed an amendment similar to the one passed in Massachusetts, requiring Congress to requisition the states before passing any direct taxes. State governments, being closer to the people, were in a better position to tax fairly.[16]

Governor Edmund Randolph of Virginia, who had refused to sign the Constitution at the convention but who now supported it, argued vigorously on the other side. "Money is the nerve—the life and soul of a government," he began. "It is the utmost folly to say that a government could be carried on without this great agent of human affairs. Wars cannot be carried on without a full and uncontrolled discretionary power to raise money in an eligible manner." If the United States were suddenly attacked, where could Congress get the money to defend America? It would have to "divert the revenues, from the usual appropriations, to the defence of the Union," and that would destroy whatever remained of the public credit. "The interest on the public debt could not be paid; foreign and domestic creditors would be disappointed and irritated; and the displeasure of the former might lead to the most serious consequences. What could the general government do, in such a situation, without the power of providing money by taxation?" Granting Congress sweeping powers of immediate taxation was therefore necessary for national security, the foundation of liberty. Withholding or even delaying Congress's power to tax, Randolph concluded, would be "laying a train [of gunpowder] by which liberty is to be blown up."[17]

In the end, both sides of the Virginia debate got some of what they wanted. Henry, Mason, and their allies convinced the ratifying convention to approve a twenty-item "declaration of rights" that included the principle of no taxation without representation: "No aid, charge, tax, or fee, can be set, rated, or levied, upon the people without their own consent, or that of their representatives." In addition, among the twenty amendments it proposed for the body of the Constitution was this: "When Congress shall lay direct taxes or excises, they shall immediately inform the Executive power of each State of the quota of such state according to the Census herein directed, which is proposed to be thereby raised; And if the Legislature of any State shall pass a law which shall be effectual for raising such quota at the time required by Congress, the taxes and excises laid by Congress shall not be collected, in such State." The convention had spoken; these were the delegates' wishes.[18]

But they were wishes only, for the ratifying convention had no power to make any actual changes in the Constitution. Randolph, Madison, and their backers might have lost the battle over proposed amendments, but they won the war over ratification. The Virginia convention voted to approve the new Constitution by 89 to 79—and it was the tenth state to do so, one over the required minimum of nine. The Constitution would take effect, no matter what its critics did. Henceforth, Congress would possess the authority to levy whatever taxes it pleased, direct or indirect, except direct taxes not apportioned according to the census or taxes on exports. That was "the supreme Law of the Land," as the Constitution declared unequivocally in Article VI.

The hopes of the Constitution's opponents did not end there, however. In addition to the amendments that would qualify national powers of taxation, state ratifying conventions had proposed a variety of other amendments, and they pushed for a second constitutional convention to consider them. James Madison, though, feared that such a convention might undermine key features of the Constitution, including Congress's broad powers of taxation, and with the blessing of President George Washington he introduced in the First Federal Congress a list of amendments that presented no real threat to the structure of the Constitution. Madison reasoned that his amendments, which evolved into what we now call the Bill of Rights, would quell the movement for a full convention (see chapter 7).

Noticeably absent from Madison's list was any change to the system of national taxation along the lines proposed by several state ratifying conventions. Thomas Tudor Tucker, a representative from South Carolina who had opposed the Constitution, noticed the omission and introduced an amendment nearly identical to Luther Martin's defeated motion at the Federal Convention and to the amendments offered at the state conventions: Congress should first levy "duties, imposts, and excises," then requisition the states, and only if both of these failed to produce sufficient funds for "the public exigencies" would it be authorized to impose direct taxes. Samuel Livermore of New Hampshire declared that Tucker's amendment had proved extremely popular and was "of more importance" than all the others. The people, he predicted, "would not value" Madison's amendments "more than a pinch of snuff " if the taxation amendment were rejected.[19]

However popular the amendment might have been out-of-doors, only nine representatives supported Tucker's motion, while thirty-nine opposed it. The Senate turned down a similar measure without even a roll-call vote. This defeat dealt amendments seeking to limit congressional taxing power a mortal blow. Despite the efforts of the founding era's antitax crusaders, Congress's broad powers of taxation—the central concern of the framers—was firmly entrenched in the United States Constitution.[20]

• • •

Constitutionally, the matter was closed. Congress could enact both indirect and direct taxes if and when it pleased, provided that it apportion the direct taxes according to each state's population. Not surprisingly, Congress shied from direct taxes, knowing how unpopular they would be. In 1790, when it adopted Alexander Hamilton's plan to assume the states' wartime debts and begin to pay them off, it decided instead to place an excise tax on the sale of liquor, also Hamilton's idea.[21]

Yet even excise taxes could fall disproportionately on particular regions, contradicting the spirit (if not the letter) of the Constitution's command that "all Duties, Imposts, and Excises shall be uniform throughout the United States." Because domestic liquor was produced primarily in what was then the American West, and since western farmers depended heavily on the income from the sale of their liquor, they bore a disproportionate share of the federal tax burden. In 1794 farmers in western Pennsylvania and other trans-Appalachian regions attacked tax collectors and even considered secession, leading President Washington, again at Hamilton's urging, to ride at the head of an army headed westward. The Revolutionary cry of "taxation without representation" was simplified to the even more basic complaint of "unfair taxation."[22]

In 1794, to provide revenue for an array of defense measures (fortifying harbors, establishing armories, enlisting soldiers, and building or purchasing armed ships), Congress levied what we call today luxury and sin taxes on imported wines and spirits, refined sugar, and snuff. These excise taxes were clearly authorized by the Constitution, but when Congress levied a tax of sixteen dollars for every carriage, some argued that this was a tax on *ownership* rather than on economic activity; it was therefore a direct tax and would have to be apportioned among the states, they claimed. Massachusetts representative Theodore Sedgwick, a defender of the tax, countered: "It would astonish the people of America to learn that they had made a Constitution by which pleasure carriages and other objects of luxury were excepted from contributing to the public exigencies." Apportionment would not work, they continued, because several states "had few or no carriages." Daniel Hylton, a Virginian who owned 125 chariots for his personal use, refused to pay the tax, and his case went all the way to the Supreme Court. In 1796, for the first time, the High Court ruled on the constitutionality of a federal law. The justices determined the tax was an excise and did not have to be apportioned among the states, so it was indeed in accordance with the Constitution. Hylton had to pay the tax.[23]

In 1798 Congress levied its first avowedly direct tax. To pay for a military mobilization in anticipation of a war with France, it passed "An act to lay and collect a direct tax within the United States," to be "assessed upon dwelling-houses, lands, and slaves." The tax on slaves was straightforward: fifty cents per head, with no distinctions. The tax on houses and lands, though, was sharply graduated, starting at two-tenths of one percent for houses and land worth $100 to $500, then three-tenths of one percent for property valued at $500 to $1,000, and so on, ending at a full percent for holdings over $30,000.

The emphasis on taxing the wealthy was not motivated by class leveling. The tax was enacted by a Federalist-dominated Congress, in fact, and Federalists represented the interests of the well-to-do merchants, manufacturers, lawyers, and other professionals. Allowing the tax burden to fall more heavily on the rich was a long-standing tradition dating back to early colonial times. Because most citizens provided a good share of their own sustenance, they engaged in money transactions as seldom as possible and had little to give to the government beyond their minimal poll taxes. Property taxes, however, could depend on the extent of a person's holdings, for those with more property were better able to contribute to the public coffers. This position could be justified philosophically, since those with more property had a greater "stake" in protecting that property, a primary responsibility of government.[24]

Administration of the 1798 direct tax followed another long-standing custom. To assess the value of houses, government agents relied largely on the number and size of windows. Because windows had to be purchased whereas other primary building materials—wood, stone, or brick—could be obtained from the land, they were a better measure than square footage of the owner's ability to pay. In common parlance, the 1798 direct tax became known as the "window tax," even though the statute did not specifically mention windows.[25]

Dutifully abiding by the Constitution, Congress apportioned the two million dollars it demanded according to the population of each state, down to the tenth of a cent. Pennsylvania, for instance, was required to yield "two hundred and thirty-seven thousand one hundred and seventy-seven dollars, seventy-two cents, and three mills." If the enumerated taxes fell short of that figure, the tax rates would have to be increased until the state met its quota. Taxes were to be "collected by the supervisors, inspectors and collectors of the internal revenues of the United States"—an embryonic Internal Revenue Service. Government agents were empowered to "collect the said taxes, by distress and sale of the goods, chattels or effects of the persons delinquent" from those who refused to pay their due. A slave could thus be taken and sold in lieu of taxes. For a farmer without slaves, "all grass, or produce of farms, standing and growing thereon, shall and may be taken and sold for the said tax." Further, unless and until taxes were paid, the federal government would hold "a lien upon all lands, and other real estate, and all slaves, of the individuals who may be assessed for the same." [26]

Congress's foray into the world of direct taxation proved extremely unpopular among those opposed to a war with France. This time it was German-speaking farmers in eastern Pennsylvania who actually rebelled, bullying the tax collectors and causing President John Adams to order the suppression of the uprising by force. When the anticipated war with France never materialized, Congress soon repealed these direct taxes and Adams pardoned the leaders of the rebellion. Like the liquor tax before it, the direct tax of 1798 had severe political repercussions, even though it followed the letter of the law as laid down by the United States Constitution.

After the 1798 debacle, Congress tried its best to avoid direct taxation. It did pass a direct tax to finance the War of 1812, but this time, hoping to lessen resistance, it allowed each state to come up with the tax money according to its own scheme, much in the spirit of the tax amendments proposed during the ratification debates of 1788. Careful not to transgress the Constitution, Congress now stipulated the precise amounts to be paid not only state by state but also county by county; clearly, it took the concept of apportionment seriously.

The federal income tax made its debut in the Civil War. Faculty taxes, the predecessors to income taxes, had been used by several states during the Revolutionary War, and in the 1840s six states had experimented with income taxes, but those were all adjuncts, not central features of the states' taxation programs. By contrast, in 1862 Congress decided to tax "the annual gains, profits, or income of every person residing in the United States, whether derived from any kind of property, rents, interests, dividends, salaries, or from any profession, trade, employment, or vocation carried on in the United States or elsewhere." The rates were mildly progressive: 3 percent for incomes between $600 and $10,000, and 5 percent on incomes in excess of $10,000. Congress adopted an income tax instead of a property tax for two reasons. First, its reach was broader and could spread the tax burden throughout the population more evenly. Second, it was considered an indirect tax because it taxed an "activity"—making money—not the person himself or his property. Previously, the Supreme Court had ruled that the only direct taxes were poll taxes and property taxes, and that meant the income tax was not subject to the apportionment rule laid down by the Constitution.[27]

When the federal income tax made its next appearance in the mid-1890s, however, the U.S. Supreme Court, in *Pollock v. Farmers' Loan and Trust Company* (1895), overturned precedent and declared that any federal tax on income derived from real property (rents) and even on income derived from ownership of personal property (interest and dividends) was in fact a thinly veiled property tax. Given that taxes on rents, interest, and dividends functioned as property taxes, and given that property taxes were direct taxes, *portions* of the income tax under consideration—those accruing to these forms of income—needed to be apportioned among the states, as the Constitution required. Further, because the Income Tax Act of 1894 did not distinguish between the income from labor, which the Court still considered indirect, and income from rents, interest, and dividends, which it held were direct, the Court, by a five-to-four majority, declared that all sections of the bill that contained a direct tax were unconstitutional, even if some taxes within those sections were still constitutional.[28]

Theoretically, Congress could have responded at this point by levying a new indirect tax on wages and a separate direct tax on rents, interest, and dividends, to be apportioned state by state. Apportionment, however, triggered other problems that had become evident over the years. Any time that Congress tried to heed the apportionment requirement of Article I, Section 9, Clause 4, by setting a precise amount that each state must raise, it inevitably created variations in tax rates. Today, for instance, if Congress decided that each state must pay a share of income taxes proportionate to its population, citizens of Mississippi, the poorest state in the Union, would be taxed at a per capita average rate of 17.9 percent, whereas those residing in the rich state of Connecticut, who can better afford to pay taxes, would be charged an average rate of only 9.2 percent. Not only would this be bad policy, but it would also contradict at least the spirit of the "uniform throughout the United States" requirement set forth in Article I, Section 8, Clause 1 of the Constitution. Any form of property or income tax would produce a similar result because wealth and income are not evenly distributed from state to state. Unwittingly, the framers had created a situation in which strict adherence to one section of the Constitution contradicted the intent of another.[29]

The increasingly unworkable distinctions between direct and indirect taxation, and the different manners in which these were treated in the Constitution, were counterintuitive and counterproductive. A tax on wages, the direct product of a person's labor, was considered indirect, whereas income from interest was somehow linked to individual citizens in a more direct manner requiring greater constitutional protection. If the federal government were ever to establish a durable system of taxation that included income taxes, it would have to eliminate the cause of the confusion.

Politically, the narrow five-to-four decision in *Pollock* was a bombshell. Democrats were outraged that the Supreme Court required taxes on rent, interest, and dividends to be apportioned among the states but allowed Congress to tax income derived from labor without this restriction. Further, because the contradictions inherent in the apportionment of direct taxes had become apparent, the Supreme Court had effectively prohibited *any* federal tax related to property. At this point in time, as the Gilded Age collided with the growing Populist movement, the terms "property" and "labor" were particularly loaded, and it became increasingly more difficult to defend the notion that only labor, and not property, could be taxed. Progressive Republicans like Theodore Roosevelt eventually joined Democrats on the tax-reform bandwagon, and Congress finally responded to the widespread pressure for reform by proposing to amend the Constitution: "The Congress shall have power to lay and collect taxes on incomes, *from whatever source derived, without apportionment among the several States, and without regard to any census or enumeration.*" The latter part of the amendment, italicized here but normally overlooked, is actually the heart of the matter. The Sixteenth Amendment did not render income taxes suddenly constitutional, as is commonly assumed. *Some* income taxes were *already* deemed constitutional, even after the Supreme Court's decision in *Pollock*.

The Sixteenth Amendment solved the problem created by the distinctions of taxation within the Constitution and by the Supreme Court's rather bizarre interpretation of those distinctions. Income from wages should not be easier to tax than income deriving from ownership of property, most Americans believed, and the only way to resolve that disparity was to eliminate the strange and seemingly artificial disparity between direct taxes, which needed to be apportioned, and indirect taxes, which did not. The Sixteenth Amendment settled that matter by announcing clearly that any and all income taxes Congress levied did not have to be apportioned among the states. In today's parlance, it simplified the tax code.

The Sixteenth Amendment, ratified in 1913, was the first since Reconstruction and the first to address the vast inequities in wealth and income that had emerged in the Gilded Age. It was certainly in keeping with the larger goal of securing a reliable source of income for the federal government via the taxing power. In 1787, the framers of the Constitution wanted to create a workable and enduring tax structure that did not vary in its impact by region. True, they preferred indirect taxes such as imposts and excises, which were voluntary, but they correctly envisioned that these would not always produce the needed revenues, so they made certain that Congress possessed the power to levy direct taxes as well. They did not foresee that the distinction between direct and indirect taxes would cause such confusion and impede their goal. By altering the tax structure to eliminate unexpected and unwanted consequences, the Sixteenth Amendment completed the framers' work.

Why did the Federal Convention, when it was creating the taxing power, not *specifically* authorize Congress to levy taxes on income? The neglect was casual, not purposive. Because they lived in a predominantly agricultural society in which income was difficult to define or quantify, income taxes were incidental at that time. When levied at all, the predecessors to today's income taxes took the form of faculty taxes that focused on what a person was likely to earn, not on what he did earn—and that, by definition, was conjectural and therefore inexact. Property, on the other hand, was easy to define and quantify and therefore easy to tax. Even so, the distinction between property and income at that time was cloudy and not particularly significant. In fact, in the late eighteenth century, property often was valued according to the rent, or income, that it could produce. The framers neither authorized nor prohibited income taxes as we know them today because such taxes, made possible by industrial and post-industrial societies, were not within their known world. They did not imagine a time when nearly everyone would depend on income from wages and salaries.

From the framers' point of view, the central idea was to facilitate Congress's ability to tax, not to limit it. All taxes except those on exports were on the table, with the one restriction on apportionment. Once that restriction proved unworkable, however, would the framers have wanted all direct taxation to cease? It is highly doubtful that they would wish to weaken the hand of the national government, determined as they were to strengthen it. Would they have wanted to grant the federal government a reliable source of revenue, thereby ensuring its credit, through a broadly based system of taxation? Of course. That was the very heart of their mission in Philadelphia in 1787.

George Washington certainly thought that way. In September 1796, after serving two terms as president, he published his Farewell Address to the American people. In it, he told his fellow citizens as politely as he could to pay their taxes without too much complaint. "As a very important source of strength and security, cherish public credit," he told the nation. "It is necessary that public opinion should co-operate. . . . [I]t is essential that you should practically bear in mind that towards the payment of debts there must be revenue; that to have revenue there must be taxes; that no taxes can be devised which are not more or less inconvenient and unpleasant." Finally, he pleaded "for a spirit of acquiescence in the measures for obtaining revenue, which the public exigencies may at any time dictate." [30]

These might not be the words we want to hear, but that's why Washington said them. A strong and prosperous nation cannot exist without sound taxation, and that is precisely why the framers granted the people's representative in Congress such sweeping authority to raise revenues sufficient to meet "the public exigencies."

3

POLITICS

Myth: The framers were impartial statesmen, above interest-driven politics.

It is really an assembly of demigods.

—Thomas Jefferson to John Adams, referring to the
men appointed to the Federal Convention[1]

This convention, composed of men who possessed the confidence of the people, and many of whom had become highly distinguished by their patriotism, virtue and wisdom, in times which tried the minds and hearts of men, undertook the arduous task. In the mild season of peace, with minds unoccupied by other subjects, they passed many months in cool, uninterrupted, and daily consultation; and finally, without having been awed by power, or influenced by any passions except love for their country, they presented and recommended to the people the plan produced by their joint and very unanimous councils.

—John Jay, *The Federalist No. 2*

[The] framers [were] a race of statesmen—patriots, with the good of the whole country at the bottom of every act—not politicians merely, not men representing and fighting for State, local, or party, or individual interests.

—John Robert Irelan, *The Republic, or, A History of the
United States of America*, an 18-volume text from 1888[2]

They [the well-known founders] were America's first and, in many respects, its only natural aristocracy. . . .

—Joseph J. Ellis, *Founding Brothers: The Revolutionary Generation* (2000)[3]

Kernel of Truth

Every one of the framers of the United States Constitution had the good of the nation at heart. They had come to Philadelphia in 1787 with a common purpose: to improve the workings of government. The Articles of Confederation, said Edmund Randolph in his speech introducing the Virginia Plan, had been written at a time "when the inefficiency of requisitions was unknown—no commercial discord had arisen among any states—no rebellion had appeared as in Massts.—foreign debts had not become urgent—the havoc of paper money had not been foreseen—treaties had not been violated." To deal with problems such as these, he declared, Americans would have to alter the rules of the game so the "jealousy of the states" did not impede governing for the common good. Not a single framer disagreed with this basic sentiment.[4]

If ever a group of men were equipped to accomplish such a task, it was this particular assemblage. They were well versed in the writings of Locke, Hume, Montesquieu, and other European philosophers who had given much thought to the nature of government. Unlike these Europeans, though, they were not unduly burdened by deeply ingrained traditions, such as deference to aristocratic privilege, running counter to the ideals of the transatlantic Enlightenment. They could take the best of their British heritage and leave the worst. They were also seasoned by two decades of Revolutionary experience; several had helped write their state constitutions, and all had taken part in deliberative bodies that grappled with difficult issues and made consequential decisions. They knew how to express their ideas, for in Revolutionary America, legislative debate was a highly developed art form and even something of a sport. They knew, too, how to listen to others and how to work collectively, not only in floor debates but also within committees that generated practical solutions. Never again would there be a group of Americans so learned, experienced, and motivated. All wanted to enshrine republican principles within a set of rules intended to govern a large and still-growing nation.

This was their moment, and the framers knew it. Once Randolph had presented the set of resolutions prepared by the Virginia delegation and known to posterity as the Virginia Plan, "he concluded with an exhortation, not to suffer the present opportunity of establishing general peace, harmony, happiness and liberty in the U. S. to pass away unimproved." To a man, they determined not to squander their unique "opportunity."

But . . .

Whereas each of the framers had the good of the nation in mind, each also represented his own state and constituents. Given that interests differed state by state and region by region, interest-driven haggling often interrupted more philosophical and high-minded debate. Delegates from Delaware were determined to ensure that each state should be equally represented in Congress, a position that significantly increased the influence of their small state. Southern delegates argued that slaves be treated as people for purposes of apportioning representation, which would increase their influence, while northern delegates, with fewer slaves in their states, thought they should not. The resulting three-fifths compromise was a convenient if embarrassing settlement, the price of keeping the Union together. It did not reflect some great canon of republican law.

Although textbooks routinely outline the Convention's major compromises, they seldom acknowledge fully the implications of these debates and the horse trading that resolved them, nor do they pay sufficient attention to lesser-known contests between competing interest groups. The "original intent" of the framers sometimes was shaped by philosophy, but as often as not provisions within the Constitution reveal another, more pragmatic, original intent: to secure the votes of a majority of the states' delegations.

Understandably sensitive to how no-nonsense debate within the Convention might appear to those outside, the framers did not want blow-by-blow accounts of their dealings to leak out. That is one reason they pledged to keep records secret. As James Madison later put it, "As a guide in expounding and applying the provisions of the Constitution, the debates and incidental decisions of the Convention can have no authoritative character. . . . The legitimate meaning of the instrument must be derived from the text itself." Any attempt to find "legitimate meaning" in the Convention's debates and compromises might "compromise" the authority of the Constitution.[5]

Thomas Jefferson, in France at the time as the American minister, complained to John Adams about the secrecy of the proceedings. In the same letter in which he called delegates to the Federal Convention "an assembly of demigods," he wrote: "I am sorry they began their deliberations by so abominable a precedent as that of tying up the tongues of their members. Nothing can justify this example but the innocence of their intentions, & ignorance of the value of public discussions. I have no doubt that all their other measures will be good & wise." It was one thing to reach this conclusion from 3,000 miles away, but had Jefferson participated in the Convention, in all likelihood he too would have seen that public disclosure would undermine the mystique and hinder prospects for ratification.[6]

It is not Jefferson's reservations that survive in the public mind, but his calling the framers "demigods." We idolize the framers, we assume the nation would be better off in their hands, and we continually ask, "What would our founders do?" Although the answer to that question will of course vary issue by issue, and although we often inquire about issues that the framers and their contemporaries could not possibly have understood, if we choose to answer honestly, we would discover a surprisingly consistent methodology: the framers would create workable compromises that might not be ideologically pure but appeared the least objectionable.

When introducing the New Jersey Plan in mid-June, William Paterson said, "I believe that a little practical virtue is to be preferred to the finest theoretical principles, which cannot be carried into effect." Oliver Ellsworth of Connecticut, while speaking on behalf of what would become the Great Compromise, said, "Let not too much be attempted; by which all may be lost." He was not, he confessed, "in general a half-way man," yet he "preferred doing half the good we could, rather than do nothing at all. The other half may be added, when the necessity shall be more fully experienced." Like other framers, Paterson and Ellsworth treated the daily juggling of interests, grounded in lived experience, as key to the art of politics, not to be shunned but embraced. The Federal Convention featured humans living in the real world, not gods on some ethereal planet.[7]

The Full Story

On Friday, May 25, 1787, twenty-nine delegates from nine states (three additional states would be represented later) gathered in the Pennsylvania State House with credentials and instructions from their respective legislatures. The instructions authorized delegates to join with their peers "in devising, deliberating on, and discussing, such alterations and further provisions as may be necessary to render the Fœderal Constitution adequate to the exigencies of the Union," or, more simply, to meet "for the purpose of revising the Fœderal Constitution." The wording varied slightly, but the messages were similar. All twelve state legislatures that dispatched delegates told them to build on the existing Constitution, the Articles of Confederation. Delegates were empowered to make suggestions for altering it or for adding "further provisions," but no state instructed its delegates to devise an entirely new plan.[8]

One set of instructions stood out from the rest. The Delaware legislature added a significant caveat: "provided, that such alterations or further provisions, or any of them, do not extend to that part of the Fifth Article of the Confederation of the said States, . . . which declares that 'In determining questions in the United States in Congress Assembled each State shall have one vote.' " The motive was obvious: the 1790 census, taken three years later, counted 11,783 free white males in Delaware, while Virginia had 110,936 free white males. Under the existing rules, the Articles of Confederation, both states were entitled to one vote in Congress. This meant that each citizen of Delaware had nine times as much influence in Congress as a citizen of Virginia possessed. Understandably, the Delaware assembly did not wish to lose this advantage.[9]

Not surprisingly, on May 30, the first day of debating Virginia's initial resolutions, James Madison challenged Delaware's special status and moved "that the equality of suffrage established by the Articles of Confederation ought not to prevail in the national Legislature, and that an equitable ratio of representation ought to be substituted." This was precisely what the Delaware assembly had worried might happen, so George Read, a delegate from Delaware, quickly moved "that the whole clause relating to the point of Representation be postponed; reminding the Come. [Committee of the

Whole] that the deputies from Delaware were restrained by their commission from assenting to any change of the rule of suffrage, and in case such a change should be fixed on, it might become their duty to retire from the Convention."[10]

"Retire from the Convention"—would Read and his delegation really walk out at the outset? On the one hand, tiny Delaware was hardly in a position to go it alone should the rest of the states decide on a new set of rules to govern the Union, but on the other hand, Delaware's delegates could force the issue by boarding boats and floating home, just a few miles down the river that bore their state's name. Few delegates from other states wanted to chance the embarrassment of Delaware's early departure. Moreover, because the Articles of Confederation could not be altered without unanimous approval from the constituent states, Delaware could potentially abort any plan the Convention submitted.

Unwilling to cede the point, Madison argued: "Whatever reason might have existed for the equality of suffrage when the Union was a federal one among sovereign States, it must cease when a national Govermt. should be put into the place." But Read and the rest of the delegation from Delaware were engaging in politics, pure and simple. "This did not appear to satisfy Mr. Read," Madison observed caustically in his notes. Read's motion to postpone carried the floor with no further debate. The smallest state, playing tough, carried the day.

Delaware's delegates were seemingly obstinate, but just three days later, on June 2, John Dickinson conceded that some alteration of the equal-voting provision in the Articles of Confederation might be in order, despite his instructions to hold firm. The controversy over representation, he predicted, "must probably end in mutual concession." In particular, Dickinson "hoped that each State would retain an equal voice at least in one branch of the National Legislature," while "either the number of inhabitants or the quantum of property" could form the basis for proportional representation in the other branch.

And so, on the fourth day of debates, the broad outlines of the Great Compromise were already on the floor, yet delegates from large states and small states would continue to do battle for six more weeks before settling up. Intellectually, the solution was obvious, but politically it proved difficult. As Alexander Hamilton observed on June 29, the debate over representation was a "contest for power, not for liberty." [11]

As delegates tussled, interest and philosophy tangled. Large-state advocates of proportional representation argued that for the national government to be "supreme," as they had already decided (see chapter 1), it must act directly on citizens, without the interference of states. Conveniently, bypassing the states meant there was no reason for them to be represented equally. Pennsylvania's James Wilson commented, "The Genl. Govt. is not an assemblage of States, but of individuals for certain political purposes—it is not meant for the States, but for the individuals composing them; the individuals therefore not the States, ought to be represented in it: A proportion in this representation can be preserved in the 2d. as well as in the 1st." [12]

Opponents of proportional representation turned this argument on its head. To prevent domination by a potentially oppressive national government, state governments *must* be represented in Congress, and what better way than to be represented equally? Maryland's Luther Martin "contended at great length and with great eagerness that the General Govt. was meant merely to preserve the State Governts.: not to govern individuals." Thirteen states, joining together in common cause, remained "equal" parties to the Union, and they could not "give up an equality of votes without giving up their liberty." The Virginia Plan was "a system of slavery for 10 States," since Virginia, Massachusetts, and Pennsylvania, with half the votes, could easily "do as they please." [13]

The fight was furious. Delaware's Gunning Bedford Jr. warned that if the large states succeeded in overturning the one-state, one-vote provision of the Articles of Confederation, "the small ones will find some foreign ally of more honor and good faith, who will take them by the hand and do them justice." He then added he "did not mean by this to intimidate or alarm," but of course he did. That was the very purpose of his remarks. [14]

On the other side, Pennsylvania's Gouverneur Morris envisioned apocalyptic consequences should "state attachments" prevail: "This Country must be united. If persuasion does not unite it, the sword will. . . . The scenes of horror attending civil commotion can not be described, and the conclusion of them will be worse than the term of their continuance. The stronger party will then make traytors of the weaker; and the Gallows & Halter will finish the work of the sword." [15]

This hyperbolic war of words was not for the timid. With each side pushing to the limits, Elbridge Gerry "lamented that instead of coming here like a band of brothers, belonging to the same family, we seemed to have brought with us the spirit of political negociators." [16]

By June 28 Benjamin Franklin had heard enough. "We indeed seem to feel our own want of political wisdom," he lamented, "since we have been running about in search of it." A month of "close attendance & continual reasonings with each other" had produced but "small progress." Unless the bickering ceased, "We shall be divided by our little partial local interests" and "our projects will be confounded."

Was there any way out? "In this situation of this Assembly, groping as it were in the dark to find political truth, and scarce able to distinguish it when presented to us, how has it happened, Sir, that we have not hitherto once thought of humbly applying to the Father of lights to illuminate our understandings?" Franklin then suggested they start each day's proceedings with "prayers imploring the assistance of Heaven, and its blessings on our deliberations." Delegates could not agree even on this, and his motion was tabled. [17]

Tempers rose yet higher. Positions rigidified. *Never* was the operative word. James Wilson proclaimed "he never could listen to an equality of votes," while Luther Martin declared he would "never confederate if it could not be done on just principles." Increasingly, debate followed the standard lines of interest-driven politics—we have to defend *our* interests to prevent *others*, who defend theirs, from destroying us. Gunning Bedford claimed that because the large states were "dictated by interest, by ambition" and sought "to aggrandize themselves at the expense of the small," it was unrealistic for the small states to submit to their "proposed degradation" and act "from pure disinterestedness." [18]

On July 2, after the Convention deadlocked on a motion for equal representation in the second branch, South Carolina's Charles Cotesworth Pinckney "proposed that a Committee consisting of a member from each State should be appointed to devise & report some compromise." Most delegates agreed, but diehards on each extreme were not ready to settle. James Wilson objected to a committee that replicated the one-state, one-vote mechanism that his side opposed. Luther Martin, his opponent, did not object to the matter being assigned to a committee but declared his position on the committee's deliberations in advance; he insisted that "no modifications whatever could reconcile the smaller States to the least diminution of their equal Sovereignty." It was a classic response: compromise is fine, but only on my terms.

In the circuitous maneuverings typical of the Convention, the committee embraced a suggestion John Dickinson had made a month earlier: equal representation in one house, proportional representation in the other. At the suggestion of Benjamin Franklin, it sweetened the deal for the large states— all money bills would originate in the house with proportional representation because citizens could be taxed only by their direct representatives. The provision had the sanction of history. The more popular house of all colonial and state legislatures, as well as the House of Commons in the British Parliament, similarly held the exclusive power to introduce money bills.[19]

This compromise did not satisfy James Wilson, James Madison, or Gouverneur Morris.

Wilson complained that "the Committee had exceeded their powers," even though it had merely suggested grounds for a compromise, as it had been instructed to do.[20]

Madison insisted that "the enlightened and impartial part of America" should not be held hostage to "the minority," as he called delegates from the small states. "If the principal States comprehending a majority of the people of the U. S. should concur in a just & judicious plan, he had the firmest hopes, that all the other States would by degrees accede to it." *Principal States*—so long as Virginians and Pennsylvanians spoke of themselves in that manner and expected those from lesser states to "accede," they were unlikely to calm the fears of delegates from Delaware and New Jersey.[21]

Morris raised the ante. He had come to the Convention not only as "a Representative of America" but also "in some degree as a Representative of the whole human race; for the whole human race will be affected by the proceedings of this Convention." Others, he said, had not been so principled. All the talk of protecting the interests of small states made him "suppose that we were assembled to truck and bargain for our particular States." Voting by states in the second branch would only perpetuate this sad state of affairs, producing "constant disputes & appeals to the States which will undermine the Genl. Government." This was precisely the evil the Convention had hoped to remedy, for "State attachments, and State importance have been the bane of this Country. We can not annihilate; but we may perhaps take out the teeth of the serpents."[22]

As delegates debated the committee's report, the devil was in the details. Setting aside for the moment the report's most controversial provision, equal votes for all states in the second house of Congress, delegates tried to calculate the "equitable ratio of representation" in the first house. Should representation be determined by population, by property, or by tax contributions to the federal treasury? And whatever method they adopted, until a census could be taken, how should they allocate representatives in the first Congress to convene under the new Constitution?

No state wanted to be shortchanged, so delegates resumed their bickering. Gouverneur Morris again voiced displeasure with the blatantly self-serving debates. The states, he said, "had many representatives on the floor," while few deemed themselves "representatives of America."[23]

George Washington, as the Convention's president, could not express his views openly, but he did grouse in private. To his former aide-de-camp Alexander Hamilton, who had abandoned the Convention in frustration, he complained that "narrow minded politicians . . . under the influence of local views" were impeding all progress. "The state of the Councils," he reported, was spiraling downward, leaving "little ground on which the hope of a good establishment can be formed." The parochial interests within the Convention left him uncharacteristically despondent: "I *almost* despair of seeing a favourable issue to the proceedings of our Convention, and do therefore repent having had any agency in the business."[24]

Even more trouble lay ahead.

On July 11, the day after Washington complained to Hamilton, with the committee's compromise still on the table, South Carolina's Pierce Butler and Charles Cotesworth Pinckney moved "that blacks be included in the rule of representation, equally with the whites." It was a bold maneuver. One month earlier, on June 11, delegates had decided that representation should be "in proportion to the whole number of white & other free Citizens & inhabitants of every age sex & condition including those bound to servitude for a term of years and three fifths of all other persons not comprehended in the foregoing description, except Indians not paying taxes, in each State"— the now-famous three-fifths compromise. They had not settled on that fraction arbitrarily. Back in 1783, the Confederation Congress had decided to count each slave as three-fifths of a free person in fixing a state's quota for the requisition of funds, so delegates had used the same fraction, "this being the rule in the Act of Congress agreed to by eleven States, for apportioning quotas of revenue on the States" four years earlier. Yet now, suddenly, three-fifths no longer satisfied delegates from South Carolina and Georgia. Butler explained their reasoning: "the labour of a slave in S. Carola. was as productive & valuable as that of a freeman in Massts., . . . and consequently an equal representation ought to be allowed for them in a Government which was instituted principally for the protection of property." [25]

Nathaniel Gorham, a Massachusetts delegate who presided over the Convention when it met in the informal Committee of the Whole House, reminded the southerners that in 1783, when Congress was trying to figure out who should bear the burden of taxation, "the delegates representing the States having slaves" had argued "that the blacks were still more inferior to freemen." Now, "when the ratio of representation is to be established, we are assured that they are equal to freemen."

In response, North Carolina's Hugh Williamson immediately "reminded Mr. Ghorum [Gorham] that if the Southn. States contended for the inferiority of blacks to whites when taxation was in view, the Eastern States on the same occasion contended for their equality." *Both* sides had reversed their positions. Williamson was content with preserving the three-fifths compromise, as were all those who did not want yet another round of argumentation. [26]

Butler's and Pinckney's motion was voted down, but Butler would not give up. The next day, July 12, he pushed once again for representation "according to the full number of inhabts. including all the blacks," and the day after that he expressed in a forthright manner why this was so important:

"The security the Southn. States want is that their negroes may not be taken from them, which some gentlemen within or without doors, have a very good mind to do."

Gouverneur Morris noted that the southern states were not the only ones fearful of future incursions on their rights. He imagined a time when the southern states, with room to expand, "will in a little time have a majority of the people of America" and perhaps trample on the rights of northeastern states, which depended on their fisheries and on commerce.[27]

As delegates with various interests jockeyed for position on these inter-related issues—slave states and free, small states versus large, northeastern states versus those looking to expand westward, plantation-based agriculture versus fishing and commerce—some drew lines in the sand. Luther Martin said he would prefer the nation split into "two Confederacies" if states were not equally represented in the second branch. North Carolina's William Richardson Davie issued a new ultimatum on behalf of the three-fifths compromise: if blacks were not counted in at least that proportion, his state "would never confederate" and "the business [of the Convention] was at an end." Insults were hurled back and forth. "The States that please to call themselves large, are the weekest in the Union," Martin pronounced. "Look at Masts. Look at Virga." We are left to imagine Gerry's heated, and per-haps undignified, response; Madison reported only that he "animadverted on Mr. L. Martins remarks on the weakness of Masts."[28]

When would this end, and how?

On Sunday delegates observed the Sabbath, and then on Monday, July 16, without any further debate, they voted on the entire compromise, in-cluding both "equality of votes in the second branch" and counting each slave as three-fifths of a free person for purposes of representation in the first branch. The package passed by the slimmest of margins: five states in favor, four states opposed, with Massachusetts divided.[29]

Even after the final vote, delegates from large states refused to concede. Virginia's Edmund Randolph moved that the convention adjourn for the day "that the large States might consider the steps proper to be taken in the present solemn crisis of the business." New Jersey's William Paterson called his bluff: why just for the day? Perhaps it was time to adjourn for good, re-scind "the rule of secrecy," and consult "our Constituents." That would be the end of any compromise, all delegates realized. The Convention granted Randolph's request to allow the large states to caucus, but the caucus found no alternative solution the small states would accept.

To no great fanfare, and with more ill will than good, delegates had given us the now celebrated Great Compromise.

While the broad outlines of representation seemed settled, controversy continued. The three-fifths compromise still had not fully resolved the controversy over "all other persons," the Constitution's euphemism for slaves. On August 6, in its fleshed-out draft of a constitution, the Committee of Detail gave Congress the power "to regulate commerce with foreign nations, and among the several States." Did this mean that the eight northern states, if they so wished, could curtail slavery either by a ban on slave importation or by a prohibitive impost? To reassure the southern states, the committee stipulated that Congress would not be allowed to tax or prohibit "the migration or importation of such persons as the several States shall think proper to admit." [30]

On August 21, Maryland's Luther Martin, a slave owner himself, moved to strike that provision. Since each imported slave would add to a state's representation, states would be rewarded politically for engaging in the slave trade, he argued. "It was inconsistent with the principles of the revolution and dishonorable to the American character to have such a feature in the Constitution." The following day George Mason, whose large plantation, near Washington's Mount Vernon, was worked by slaves, denounced slavery for both practical and moral reasons. It impeded "the immigration of Whites, who really enrich & strengthen a Country," while it produced "the most pernicious effect on manners." In words that are now often quoted, he boldly pronounced: "Every master of slaves is born a petty tyrant. They bring the judgment of heaven on a Country. As nations can not be rewarded or punished in the next world they must be in this." [31]

Did these slaveholders seriously oppose the very institution that supported them?

South Carolina's Charles Cotesworth Pinckney challenged Mason's high-toned stance, alleging baser motives: "As to Virginia she will gain by stopping the importations. Her slaves will rise in value, & she has more than she wants." This surplus of slaves would allow Virginians to establish "a monopoly in their favor," setting "their own terms for such as they might sell." Mason's moralizing merely protected Virginia's local industry—breeding slaves for the market—which foreign imports would impair.[32]

Other delegates from South Carolina and neighboring Georgia chimed in to defend the "right" to own slaves. Charles Pinckney (Charles Cotesworth Pinckney's cousin) argued from history: "If slavery be wrong, it is justified by the example of all the world." Pinckney "cited the case of Greece Rome & other antient States; the sanction given by France England, Holland & other modern States. In all ages one half of mankind have been slaves."

Georgia's Abraham Baldwin (a transplanted son of Connecticut) offered an argument that defenders of slavery would repeat many times before the Civil War: slavery was "a local matter," not a "national object," and Georgia would refuse to accept any attempt "to abridge one of her favorite prerogatives." Charles Pinckney offered a similar threat: "South Carolina can never receive the plan if it prohibits the slave trade." There must be no "meddling with the importation of negroes."

South Carolina's John Rutledge was particularly blunt: "Religion & humanity had nothing to do with this question—interest alone is the governing principle with nations." It was perhaps the brashest, and most honest, statement of the summer.[33]

We might think that the New England delegates, who opposed slavery, would fight to ban slave importation, but they did not. "Let us not intermeddle" in the dispute between the Upper and Lower South, said Connecticut's Oliver Ellsworth. "The morality or wisdom of slavery are considerations belonging to the States themselves." Further, because slaves "multiply so fast in Virginia & Maryland that it is cheaper to raise than import them, whilst in the sickly rice swamps foreign supplies are necessary," it would "be unjust towards S. Carolina & Georgia" to limit their importation.[34]

Of course politics was in play. Just as the South depended on slavery, New England could not survive without commerce. Because commerce could not flourish if each state had separate navigation laws and imposts, the Committee of Detail had assigned the power of commercial regulation to Congress in its draft of the Constitution—but it added that no navigation act could be passed without a two-thirds supermajority in both houses. This restriction bothered New Englanders, who worried that a minority of states could impede commerce, but it pleased southerners because it prevented northerners, who would enjoy a slight majority in Congress, from passing laws that hurt southern interests. Further, as many New England shipowners and merchants took part in the foreign and interstate slave trade, attempts to limit that trade would cut against their states' interests.[35]

Many delegates recognized that the issues represented by the navigation controversy and slave importation were linked, so the Convention sent both to a committee. Two days later, on August 24, the committee issued its report: Congress could not prohibit slave importation until the year 1800; it could levy import duties on slaves "not exceeding the average" of other duties, and the requirement for a congressional supermajority to pass commercial regulation would be dropped. Although there were gains and losses across the board, the contingent from the Deep South insisted on two other concessions: an extension of the allowance for slave importation until 1808 and a fugitive slave clause that in the nineteenth century would give rise to poisonous controversy: "If any person bound to service or labor in any of the U. States shall escape into another State, he . . . shall be delivered up to the person justly claiming their service or labor."

All of these matters were decided on the basis of interests, not of philosophy. Although delegates had brought abstract notions of sovereignty and representation to bear on the interest-driven battles leading to the Great Compromise, political motivations in the multifaceted compromises over slavery (both the deal struck in late August and the better-known three-fifths compromise) were more difficult to disguise. In the thick of the debate over slave importation, Rufus King of Massachusetts commented, "the subject should be considered in a political light only," and that is exactly the way delegates to the Federal Convention dispatched the embarrassing matter of slavery. Philosophical talk of liberty and human rights gave way in the end to legislative deal making.[36]

On August 24, in an unexpected and unlikely manner, the small-state, large-state division resurfaced. Delegates had debated the method of selecting the president several times, and the broad outlines of a solution seemed settled: the president would be "elected by ballot by the Legislature" and serve a single seven-year term. But how, exactly, would Congress choose the president? Would the House and Senate meet separately and would each have to approve the choice, as they did with legislative acts? If so, what if they disagreed? Or should they meet together in a special joint session, even though that would not happen in any other context? And if they met jointly, would each member have an equal vote, even though House members outnumbered senators?

Again, small-state concerns emerged. New Jersey's Jonathan Dayton (the Convention's youngest delegate) warned that if the two chambers met in joint session, the Senate, in which each state had an equal say, would be overwhelmed in the voting by the much larger House, dominated by large-state representatives. "A joint ballot would in fact give the appointment to one House," Dayton complained. The two chambers should vote separately, he concluded, so small states in the Senate could check the large states in the House, as with normal legislation.[37]

Though Dayton lost, he and his New Jersey colleague David Brearly countered with another proposal: Congress would choose the president in a joint session, but the entire delegation from each state would cast a single vote, as in the old Articles of Confederation. This blatantly small-state measure also failed.

All along, Gouverneur Morris had vigorously opposed congressional selection of the president because he believed that method would make the executive branch too dependent on the legislature. Although Morris represented a large state, he now viewed the small-state delegates as potential allies; working together, they might be able to revamp the system of presidential selection. In a manner typical of the Convention's proceedings, Morris, Dayton, and Brearly got the matter sent to a committee consisting of one member from each state. Brearly was its president and Gouverneur Morris a member.[38]

On September 4, the committee presented its report to a stunned Convention. What had been previously decided was overturned. The president was allowed to repeat in office, his term was shortened from seven years to four, and congressional selection was scrapped altogether. Instead, state legislatures would arrange for the selection of special electors who would choose the president. What we now call the Electoral College was born, the direct result of political finagling by a handful of delegates.

When trying to explain the committee's highly original method of presidential selection, Gouverneur Morris admitted, "It had been agreed to in the Committee on the ground of compromise." The number of electors for each state would equal that state's number of representatives and senators; large states would derive an advantage, but even the smallest state would be guaranteed three electors. Electors were to cast ballots for two candidates, one of whom could not be from the elector's home state, and the winner would need a majority, not just a plurality, of the electors' votes; taken together, these measures prevented large states from electing favorite sons and thereby offered some protection to small states. Further, because many or most elections were not expected to produce a clear winner (George Mason grumpily suggested that the Electoral College would fail to choose a president nineteen times out of twenty), runoffs featuring the five leading contenders would be determined in the Senate, where small states and large states had equal votes. The Convention later reassigned the determination of this runoff from the Senate to the House, but with members voting by state delegations—one state, one vote—to satisfy the small states.[39]

The compromise on presidential selection included a recommendation that only the House could initiate money bills. Although delegates had overturned this component of the Great Compromise on August 8, and although the measure was totally unrelated to electing the president, it was reintroduced to win the votes of delegates from large states. The elector compromise, because it awarded votes in large measure according to representation in the House, also reenforced the three-fifths compromise, thereby giving added heft to the South and gaining the support of delegates from slaveholding states.[40]

This drama, played on a small stage within a committee, was part of a larger one. Most framers did not trust the people enough to put the choice of president in their hands (see chapter 4), but they did not think Congress should make that decision either. Meanwhile, delegates from small states insisted that any system of presidential selection be tilted, at least slightly, in their favor. No coherent philosophy could encompass such divergent suspicions or impulses. What we have, in place of coherence, is the Electoral College, shaped at the Federal Convention amidst extravagant wheeling and dealing. This convoluted institution, which few Americans have ever understood, has granted the presidency to the loser of the popular vote on four occasions. Forged through compromise, it is ours to this day.[41]

Representation in Congress, slavery, commercial regulations, election of the president—these contentious issues were hotly debated by delegates with vested interests in the outcomes. They argued, cajoled, and bluffed, just as politicians do now, and in the end no delegate received all of what he wanted.

A few delegates left before the end. Maryland's Luther Martin and John Francis Mercer and New York's Robert Yates and John Lansing Jr. had wanted only to perfect the Confederation, leaving the states still in charge. Once they realized that other delegates would not bend their way, they returned to their home states to whip up opposition amongst the populace.

George Mason, Elbridge Gerry, and Edmund Randolph stayed to the end but refused to sign the document, and Mason and Gerry, like Martin, Mercer, Yates, and Lansing, actively opposed its ratification. For these men, missing or destructive elements undermined the entire project. Even before the Federal Convention had adjourned, Mason determined to push for changes among the people "out-of-doors"—a common contemporary term. On the back of his copy of the Constitution's almost-final draft, he "drew up some general Objections . . . by way of protest," as he reported to Thomas Jefferson. Mason was "discouraged" from reading his objections on the floor "by the precipitate, & intemperate, not to say indecent Manner, in which the Business was conducted, during the last Week of the Convention, after the Patrons of this new plan found they had a decided Majority in their Favour." Instead, he sent copies to friends and allies, those recipients sent them on to others, and Mason's list of "Objections to the Constitution" became a core document for the Constitution's opponents.[42]

Mason's opposition, it is generally said, stemmed from a principled concern: he bemoaned the absence of a "Declaration of Rights." This is partly correct, yet he also listed more than a dozen other faults of the proposed new plan, including the Constitution's failure to require a congressional supermajority to enact "commercial and navigation laws":

> By requiring only a majority to make all commercial and navigation laws, the five Southern States, whose produce and circumstances are totally different from that of the eight Northern and Eastern States, may be ruined, for such rigid and premature regulations may be made as will enable the merchants of the Northern and Eastern States not only to demand an exhorbitant freight, but to monopolize the purchase of the commodities at their own price, for many years, to the great injury of the landed interest, and impoverishment of the people; and the danger is the greater as the gain on one side will be in proportion to the loss on the other.

As at the Federal Convention, such avowedly regional interests would influence the ratification debates. This rankled George Washington, Mason's neighbor and, for most of their lives, a good friend and trusted political ally. Mason, he said, was one of those who refused "to make those mutual concessions which are requisite to the general prosperity, and in some instances, to sacrifice their individual advantages to the interest of the community." [43]

Randolph, the other nonsigner from Virginia, shared Mason's concern. Toward the end of the Convention, he had declared there were "features so odious in the constitution as it now stands, that he doubted whether he should be able to agree to it," and failure to require a supermajority for navigation laws "would compleat the deformity of the system." Randolph was not above compromise, but he had been left out of this one, which had been struck in committee between New Englanders, who opposed a supermajority for navigation acts, and delegates from the Deep South, who wanted to continue slave importation. Each side granted the other its desire, while Virginia, which opposed both measures, had been left out entirely. How could Randolph affix his name to a document so deformed that it did not even consider the interests of the largest state in the union? [44]

All other delegates still present at the end of the Convention signed the document. Despite the cantankerous debates that characterized the summer, they accepted the compromises that were forged and agreed to support the entire package, including measures with which they still disagreed. On the very last day, shortly before the Convention adjourned, Alexander Hamilton attempted to persuade the last handful of wavering and reluctant colleagues. Although "no man's ideas were more remote from the plan" than his own, he declared, the choice "between anarchy and Convulsion on one side, and the chance of good to be expected from the plan on the other," was obvious.[45]

In a similar vein, Gouverneur Morris said that he continued to have "objections," but "considering the present plan as the best that was to be attained," he would "take it with all its faults." The majority of delegates, he concluded, "had determined in its favor and by that determination he should abide. The moment this plan goes forth all other considerations will be laid aside, and the great question will be, shall there be a national Government or not?"

Benjamin Franklin, with characteristic modesty and shrewdness, wrote an elegant, inspiring, and sometimes humorous speech that he asked James Wilson to read: "Thus I consent, Sir, to this Constitution because I expect no better, and because I am not sure, that it is not the best. The opinions I have had of its errors, I sacrifice to the public good." He freely acknowledged the inevitable self-interest of the delegates, but ever the optimist, he managed to give even that a positive spin: "When you assemble a number of men to have the advantage of their joint wisdom, you inevitably assemble with those men, all their prejudices, their passions, their errors of opinion, their local interests, and their selfish views. From such an assembly can a perfect production be expected? It therefore astonishes me, Sir, to find this system approaching so near to perfection as it does."

George Washington knew all too well how imperfect the proposed Constitution was and how it had been shaped by "local interests" and "selfish views," but he endorsed it nonetheless. One week after the Convention adjourned, he wrote to three former governors of Virginia, appealing for their support: "I wish the Constitution which is offered had been made more perfect, but I sincerely believe it is the best that could be obtained at this time; and, as a Constitutional door is opened for amendment hereafter, the adoption of it under the present circumstances of the Union is in my opinion desirable."[46]

Not perfect but workable, that was the tone—and it was also the strongest argument for ratification. A national government was needed, and here were the outlines for one. The Constitution could be fine-tuned later. Even the official letter the Federal Convention sent to the Confederation Congress, which transmitted the proposed Constitution, struck that chord. The "consolidation of our Union," the letter stated, was so "seriously and deeply impressed on our minds" that each state delegation was "less rigid on points of inferior magnitude, than might have been otherwise expected; and thus the Constitution, which we now present, is the result of a spirit of amity, and of that mutual deference and concession which the peculiarity of our political situation rendered indispensable." [47]

Many Americans today find it difficult to treat the so-called Constitutional Convention (a name applied with historical hindsight) as a rough-and-tumble political affair. Such honesty, they fear, would undermine the participants' credibility and the almost scriptural sanctity of the resulting document. We need not be so timid. By altering our perspective only slightly, we might even view the contentious proceedings, and the eventual compromises, as a fitting model for the interest-driven constitutional democracy that soon emerged and flourished with time.

Downplaying the political nature of our government's creation is well meant but misguided. It creates too much distance between our world and that of the framers. If we see the men who wrote the Constitution as above politics, we cannot see them as models for how we might resolve our differences today. They become less relevant, not more so.

Historically, if we fail to acknowledge the dynamic politics of the Federal Convention, we are left with myth and fabrication. On the word of Franklin, Washington, and others, we know that interest played its part, and thanks to the fastidious work of James Madison, we see it in practice. Whereas the gentlemen who gathered in the Pennsylvania State House in 1787 fully understood the historic nature of their enterprise and did their best to ground the overall structure of their plan on solid republican theory, their philosophical arguments were thoroughly entwined with push-and-pull politics, as such arguments always are in real historical circumstances. There is no reason this should surprise us.

4

PRINCIPLES

Myth: The framers were guided by clear principles of limited government.

Analyze how the U.S. Constitution reflects the principles of limited government, republicanism, checks and balances, federalism, separation of powers, popular sovereignty, and individual rights.

—Texas History Standards, grade 8[1]

The 7 principles of the US constitution are: Popular Sovereignty . . . Separation of Powers . . . Checks and Balances . . . Limited Government . . . Republicanism . . . Federalism . . . Individual Rights.

—Answers.com/WikiAnswers[2]

Kernel of Truth

The men who wrote the Constitution thought deeply about the nature of government and did their best to base the document on what they called first principles. As avid students of and participants in the transatlantic Enlightenment, they found no shortage of principles to choose from: the social contract theory of government, associated most often with the British philosopher John Locke; separation of powers, a core feature of Britain's unwritten constitution; and so on. They cited often Montesquieu's *The Spirit of the Laws*, which noted that laws should be adapted to the conditions of each country—its people, customs, religion, and geographic characteristics. Of the varieties of government Montesquieu outlined, they all believed that the United States was better suited to a purely republican form in which the people are sovereign than to an aristocratic, monarchical, or despotic government. They were also steeped in the British Whig tradition, which viewed concentrated governmental power as the eternal enemy of liberty.

The framers embraced the opportunity to embody these ideas in a real-life national republic. To prevent Old World tyranny from being replicated here in America, they based their new plan on republican ideals that delineated governmental authority. The enduring power of the Constitution stems in no small measure from the ability of the framers to fashion rules that defined the reach of the new central government and its relationship to the existing states.

But . . .

The lists of principles we learn to memorize in civics classes, like those in the quotations above, focus on restraining government, and the matter-of-fact presentation implies that the principles are clear and the lists are exclusive. In fact, the principles the framers embraced were not so simple and concise, and these men, though wary of governmental power, did not focus solely or even principally on limiting it.

What's missing from these tidy lists of founding principles is the motive force, the reason the framers decided to tackle the difficult task of forming new rules in the first place. If all they cared about was restraining power, they would have stuck with the Articles of Confederation, which restrained government quite effectively by never really creating one. Instead, they tossed out the old agreement and started from scratch.

The indispensable question is: Why?

Whereas the framers believed that government without restraint would inevitably lead to tyranny, they also thought that government without strength would lead to chaos and anarchy—a fair description, in their view, of what was happening to the United States. To turn the nation around, they needed to fashion a strong central government, and to justify that brazen move, they would have to base their new government on sound civic principles.

Government, the framers held, was necessary both to promote the common good and to keep people from reverting to a state of nature, where neither life nor property is secure. (The English philosopher Thomas Hobbes had espoused this philosophy in the mid-seventeenth century, and the framers, though adhering to the Whig view of liberty, did not dispute Hobbes's central claim.) For a government to possess sufficient "vigor" or "energy" to promote these worthy goals, it must be granted the powers to levy taxes, to raise an army, and to regulate commerce. Further, at the risk of becoming inconsequential and even of falling apart, a central government must be able to operate directly on its citizens, without intervention from state governments, and its actions must be respected as the law of the land. These principles of strong and effective government deserve equal billing with others that guard against government overreach; in fact, they should be listed side by side.

Finding the proper balance between competing principles—between grants of power and restraints on power—was a major challenge facing the framers. Each of these principles, on inspection, is more complex than it seems. Is liberty hindered or helped by a government strong enough to protect the weak from the strong? How can state and federal governments both be sovereign when only one is ultimately "supreme"? Does popular sovereignty imply that the people should have a direct role in their government? If one branch of government checks another, how can those two branches really be considered separate?

None of these quandaries can be resolved by sloganeering, yet they all need to be examined if we wish to fathom the framers' daring attempt to devise workable rules that did justice to their principles.

The Full Story

The framers' thinking about government was shaped in part by the signature events of seventeenth-century English history: the midcentury civil wars and the so-called Glorious Revolution of 1688, which firmly established the role of Parliament within a mixed monarchical republic. In the wake of that revolution, and continuing through the American Revolution nearly a century later, British Whigs, whose first principle was liberty, tussled politically with British Tories, who emphasized the need for stability. Most eighteenth-century Americans, including the framers in their formative years, considered themselves Whigs—but Whigs whose ideas soon took on a peculiarly

American flavor. They grew up with liberty on their minds, ever suspicious of monarchical prerogatives, the abuses of royal governors and judges, and even the overreach of Parliament, generally regarded in England as the ultimate Whig political institution. In Americans' eyes, imperial government was always suspect, and in the years leading up to independence, Americans concluded that the British Empire was so unredeemably corrupted as to spell the end of English liberty.

Locally, though, American colonials saw government as a positive force. Because citizens elected their representatives annually, the colonial legislatures expressed what could be viewed as the people's will. Save for governors appointed by the Crown and the officials they appointed, American colonies functioned like small republics.

After declaring independence, when Americans formalized those republics by framing and adopting new state constitutions, constitution writers in each state studied how best to effectuate republican principles. Most argued that power should be assigned to separated branches. Pennsylvania chose instead to keep all power within one branch, the legislative branch, but it instituted a host of democratic safeguards to keep the people in charge of their government; all bills, for instance, could not be voted on until after the following election, giving the people an opportunity to weigh in. In either case, that the people now *owned* their government undermined, or at least transformed, the central axiom of Whig thought: government is the natural antagonist of the people's liberty. Such writers as Thomas Paine declared that when government is a creature of the people, people cannot be their own enemies—at least in theory, and at least for *small* governments.

What about a federal government with authority extending throughout the nation? Would such a government be a natural friend of the people or an ever-present threat to their liberty?

Americans in 1787 differed on this. Some said that "no government formed on the principles of freedom can pervade all North America." Because "it is impossible for one code of laws to suit Georgia and Massachusetts," enforcement of the law would have to rely on "military coercion."[3]

The men who wrote the Constitution and their supporters in the ratification controversy thought otherwise. If they grounded the federal government, like the state governments, on frequent popular elections, that government, like the state governments, would be an embodiment of the people. Because rulers and the people would no longer be "contending interests," there would be "no quarrel between government and liberty." Government, in fact, would be the "shield and protector" of liberty.[4]

Both predictions were conjectural because no nation the size of the United States had yet demonstrated whether a purely republican government could endure. Historically, though, the framers prevailed and the Constitution was ratified. The experiment with a national republic was under way, and it was grounded on the assumption that government and liberty did not have to work at cross-purposes.

The framers did not totally abandon Whig principles, which had been formulated to check magisterial rule, but they adjusted them to suit a republic. Government was still suspect but, following Montesquieu, they created mechanisms within government that would keep liberty secure. They did not think at the outset, "Let's see how we can restrain government," but rather, "Let's see how we can create a strong government with some set of internal checks, so it won't tyrannize."

Strengthening and restraining principles are woven throughout the Constitution's text. The Preamble contains a forthright declaration of popular sovereignty: "We the people of the United States . . . do ordain and establish this Constitution." Then, in broad strokes, it states the reasons for creating the Constitution: "in order to form a more perfect Union, establish Justice, insure domestic Tranquility, provide for the common defence, promote the general Welfare, and secure the Blessings of Liberty to ourselves and our Posterity." Article I, Section 8 lists eighteen federal powers to be used in achieving these goals. The first authorizes Congress to levy taxes to "provide for the common Defence and general Welfare of the United States," and the last allows Congress to "make all Laws which shall be necessary and proper for carrying into Execution the foregoing Powers, and all other Powers vested by this Constitution in the Government of the United States."

Though textbooks rarely summarize these key provisions by a named principle, they should. We might call this the "government needs to be strong enough to do its job" principle, or, more economically, we could combine it with a commonly listed principle, turning the lopsided "limited government" into "strong government with defined powers," but one way or another, we need to include in any catalogue of principles a positive as-sertion of federal constitutional power. The Constitution would not be the same if the framers hadn't embraced the ideal of strong and effective gov-ernment—in fact, it would not even exist.

The restraint principles embedded within the text also need rebranding. "Separation of powers" and "checks and balances" are not distinct princi-ples, and if treated that way, they contradict each other. To check one an-other's powers, the allegedly separate branches actually intermingle. The president, an executive officer, has the power to veto legislative acts of Congress; the vice president presides over the Senate; the Senate approves appointments made by the president, clearly an executive function. In fact, separation of powers and checks and balances aren't exactly principles but strategies in service of a more general goal: diffusion of authority to prevent concentrations of power.[5]

Whatever we call these principles, they are generally considered re-straints or limitations, although in fact they serve the opposite purpose. By distributing authority within the federal government, the framers were able to give that government *greater* powers than it dared grant to a single body. As protections grew, more powers could be added—that was the framers' basic strategy and crowning achievement.

On the other hand, the strengthening of government in Article I was si-multaneously a restraining principle. Yes, the federal government could commit citizens to the expenditure of blood and treasure through war and taxation, but first the people's direct representatives had to approve, and if representatives approved but the people didn't, the people could remove those representatives through free and frequent elections. In every case, the relationship between strength and restraint was complementary, not contradictory.

All principles embedded within the Constitution's text must be treated in relation to one another and to the whole. When viewed in this broader con-text, each principle in itself becomes more complex, in some sense contain-ing what appears to be its opposite. If at first this seems counterintuitive, consider how three cherished principles that appear on every list—limited powers, individual rights, and popular sovereignty—were treated within the

Constitution. Whereas these are generally viewed as restraints on government, the full story is deeper and richer.

Limited Powers: Strict Versus Loose Construction

At first glance, the case for strictly limited powers seems so obvious. The purpose of a written constitution is to state what government is permitted to do and how it should go about doing it. Powers are to be listed, but the list would be meaningless if *other* powers, not listed, were also permitted. When the framers enumerated the powers of Congress in Article I, Section 8 of the United States Constitution, they intended their list to be exhaustive. Should there be any doubt, the Tenth Amendment cleared that up: "The powers not delegated to the United States by the Constitution, nor prohibited by it to the States, are reserved to the States respectively, or to the people." Case closed.[6]

Yet this was not so obvious to George Washington, and the case was hardly closed. Early in 1791, less than two years into his first presidential term, Congress authorized the creation of a national bank, a public-private partnership that was the brainchild of Alexander Hamilton, Washington's treasury secretary. Washington liked Hamilton's scheme. The bank's notes, backed by substantial private investors, would hold their value better than the government's paper currency, and these notes would pump money into the sagging economy without endangering public credit. There was one problem, however. The United States Constitution did not specifically authorize the federal government to charter banks, a power that had been the province of the states, and it made no provision for granting one group of investors special status in United States law. These seeming gaps in constitutional authorization for the bank bill presented the president with a dilemma: should he sign the bill that Congress had sent him, which he believed would help the nation, or should he veto it because it exerted powers not explicitly authorized by the Constitution?

Washington asked his attorney general, Edmund Randolph, for a legal opinion, and Randolph gave a decisive answer: Congress did not possess a constitutional authority to incorporate the Bank of the United States. There was no specific clause empowering it to do so, he said, and the final clause of Article I, Section 8, which allowed it to "make all laws that shall be necessary and proper for carrying into execution the foregoing powers," might be subject to dangerous abuse. If that clause were given too much "latitude," wouldn't it "terminate in an unlimited power in Congress"?[7]

Washington then consulted Thomas Jefferson, his secretary of state, and Jefferson agreed with Randolph. He understood the practical reasons for preferring bank notes to paper money, but that did not justify bypassing the Constitution. "Perhaps indeed bank bills may be a more *convenient* vehicle than treasury orders," Jefferson said, "but a little *difference* in the degree of *convenience*, cannot constitute the necessity which the constitution makes the ground for assuming any non-enumerated power."[8]

Next, Washington asked his close friend and political confidant James Madison, who had opposed the bill in the House of Representatives, to draft a veto message. Madison's draft stated point-blank: "I object to the Bill because it is an essential principle of the Government that powers not delegated by the Constitution cannot be rightfully exercised; because the power proposed by the bill to be received is not expressly delegated; and because I cannot satisfy myself that it results from any express power by fair and safe rules of implication."[9]

Finally, before delivering that message, Washington asked Hamilton to respond to the arguments proffered by the bank's opponents. Working quickly, Hamilton drafted a lengthy and powerful defense of his measure. "Every power vested in a government," he proclaimed, "includes . . . a right to employ all the *means* requisite, and *fairly applicable* to the attainment of the *ends* of such power, and which are not precluded by restrictions and exceptions specified in the Constitution, or not immoral, or not contrary to the ends of political society." Here, Hamilton reversed the burden of proof: the exceptions, not the precise powers, needed to be specified. This was exactly the all-encompassing interpretation Randolph warned against, but Hamilton argued that Randolph, Jefferson, and Madison, in their narrow interpretation of "necessary and proper," would "beget endless uncertainty and embarrassment" and cripple the legitimate functioning of government. Were "light houses, beacons, buoys & public piers" absolutely necessary to governmental operations? No, a country could exist without them—and the

United States would have to do without them, if his opponents had their way, because the construction of these public works was not included in the eighteen powers relegated to Congress in Article I, Section 8 of the Constitution. Wouldn't it be foolhardy to deem a government-supported lighthouse unconstitutional? Weren't such powers implied by "general Welfare," which does lie within the province of the Constitution?[10]

Hamilton also applied his broad construction of "necessary and proper" to national security concerns:

A nation is threatened with a war, large sums are wanted on a sudden to make the requisite preparations. Taxes are laid for the purpose, but it requires time to obtain the benefit of them. Anticipation is indispensable. If there be a bank the supply can at once be had. If there be none, loans from individuals must be sought. The progress of these is often too slow for the exigency; in some situations they are not practicable at all. Frequently when they are, it is of great consequence to be able to anticipate the product of them by advance from a bank.

If Washington vetoed the bank bill, Hamilton concluded, he would be undermining the overarching goal of the framers: "To suppose, then, that the government is precluded from the employment of so usual and so important an instrument for the administration of its finances as that of a bank, is to suppose what does not coincide with the general tenor and complexion of the constitution."[11]

In the end, the president sided with Hamilton. Washington had been pushing for a strong, efficient national government for years, and a veto based on a limited interpretation of the "necessary and proper" powers of Congress would have ceded much of the ground he and his fellow nationalists had gained by framing, ratifying, and implementing the Constitution. It was a truly momentous decision. Had Washington declared for the other side, the entire trajectory of the federal government would likely have been altered.[12]

In truth, both sides of the debate were partly right. The principle of enumerated powers is indispensable to the Constitution, but so too is the principle of implied powers, embodied in the "necessary and proper" clause of Article I, Section 8. At the Federal Convention, when the Committee of

Detail originally proposed a list of congressional powers, delegates debated most of these, altered a few, and occasionally proposed new ones. They wanted to grant the federal government immense powers it lacked under the Articles of Confederation, but they listed them very carefully so as to preclude avenues for abuse. Even though the last of the powers the committee suggested was singularly different and admittedly sweeping—"to make all laws that shall be necessary and proper for carrying into execution the foregoing powers, and all other powers vested, by this Constitution, in the government of the United States, or in any department or officer thereof"—it caused no stir, discussion, or debate. The framers viewed this clause as an essential complement to the rest. Without it, administration of all the other powers might be compromised.

Outside the closed doors of the Pennsylvania State House, however, once the Constitution was before the American people, many saw this matter differently. During the ratification debates, skeptics worried that the "necessary and proper" clause, as well as the supremacy clause and the two mentions of "general Welfare," might open the door to federal powers not specifically enumerated in Article I, Section 8. To forestall this possibility, they proposed an amendment to the proposed Constitution that would explicitly confine federal authority to the listed powers. Massachusetts was the first state whose ratifying convention proposed amendments (see chapter 7), and here is its first proposal: "That it be explicitly declared, that all Powers not expressly delegated by the aforesaid Constitution are reserved to the several States to be by them exercised." The Articles of Confederation had declared that each state retain powers "not by this confederation expressly delegated to the United States, in Congress assembled," and citizens of Massachusetts wanted a similar security in the new Constitution. Other state conventions proposed identical or similar amendments.[13]

"Expressly" was the vital word in the minds of the Constitution's detractors. Saying that powers not *delegated* to the federal government were reserved to the states was not enough; adding *expressly* eliminated wiggle room, with all its attendant hazards. In retrospect, their worries were not unfounded. Without that definitive limitation, proponents of a strong federal government could argue (and later did argue) that even questionable powers can be implied, though not explicitly stated.

The Constitution was ratified without any of the amendments opponents proposed at the state ratification conventions. The push for a forthright limitation of federal power did not end there, however. In the First Federal Congress, when James Madison proposed constitutional amendments that would later evolve into the Bill of Rights (see chapter 7), he included a clear statement of the principle of enumerated powers: "The powers not delegated by this constitution, nor prohibited by it to the States, are reserved to the States respectively." That statement, though, was not clear enough for South Carolina representative Thomas Tudor Tucker, who moved to insert the key word "expressly" before "delegated." That would keep any so-called implied powers from ever sneaking in.[14]

Madison opposed the explicit limitation. "It was impossible to confine a Government to the exercise of express powers; there must necessarily be admitted powers by implication, unless the Constitution descended to recount every minutia." Tucker's motion was "negatived" by a voice vote. Three days later, Elbridge Gerry, a Massachusetts representative who had helped write the Constitution but then refused to sign it, reintroduced Tucker's motion, this time demanding a roll-call vote. Once more the motion failed, seventeen to thirty-two by the official count. All federal powers did not need to be "expressly" stipulated, the First Federal Congress *expressly* decided.[15]

Madison's proposal, slightly modified, turned into the Tenth Amendment: "The powers not delegated to the United States by the Constitution, nor prohibited by it to the States, are reserved to the States respectively, or to the people." Although some treat this provision as a definitive declaration of limited government, the Tenth Amendment was in fact a compromise. Federalists, although accepting the principle of enumerated powers, would have preferred to keep that principle implicit, while critics of the Constitution had wanted a stronger statement. Both sides bent, but both also won. This is not the way it has been used politically. For over two centuries, states' rights advocates have treated the Tenth Amendment as if it *did* contain the word "expressly," even though the amendment's authors, Madison and the First Federal Congress, had made certain it would not. Purposely, the wiggle room remained. The government should not be too closely confined, Madison argued, and his view prevailed. "Powers by implication," as he called them, should be allowed.[16]

Today, we still quarrel over "strict" versus "broad" constructions of the Constitution, much as Americans did in the 1790s. We do so because the Constitution signals mixed messages, and that is neither an accident nor a mistake. The framers refused to declare unfalteringly for "strict" or for "broad" because either choice, unmodified, would have been untenable. Without enumerating powers, the Constitution would permit the indefinite expansion of federal authority, yet without the flexibility inherent in implied powers, Congress could allocate no funds to help build dikes, dams, or airports; monitor weather to warn people of tornadoes; finance research for the eradication of smallpox (one of the great scourges of the founding generation); operate the Library of Congress and the Smithsonian Institution; or stage celebrations on the centennial and bicentennial anniversaries of the framing and ratification of the Constitution. Admittedly, *all* would not be lost. Even now, under Article I, Section 8, Clauses 10 and 11, Congress would still possess the authority to "punish Piracies" and "grant Letters of Marque and Reprisal."

Individual Rights and the Common Good

The framers inserted a handful of individual guarantees in the Constitution, such as a writ of habeas corpus, but they did not assert the basic principle of individual rights. Because the new government did not take rights away, veterans of the Federal Convention explained, all rights still resided with the people, without question. Out-of-doors, however, the people were not convinced. Many of their state constitutions had assured them of their rights in written declarations, and in this time of momentous constitutional change they were on their guard. The clamor for rights continued until ratification in 1791 of the first ten amendments to the Constitution (see chapter 7).

The framers' neglect was not incidental if seen in the context of those times. Most believed that rights were more threatened by the absence of strong government than by its presence. They observed the Regulators' rebellion in Massachusetts and moves by state legislatures to abrogate contracts and print paper money with grave misgivings. Neither people nor property was safe. Should such trends continue, anarchy would reign and liberty would be lost. Without the rule of law, minorities would be subject to the tyranny of the majority. One key reason to create a new and stronger federal government was to "secure the Blessings of Liberty to ourselves and our Posterity." Government *was* the solution.

Through the founding era, Americans across the political spectrum held these convictions in common. The Declaration of Independence stated that "governments are instituted among Men" to "secure" the rights of "Life, Liberty, and the Pursuit of Happiness." According to the Articles of Confederation, the states needed to form "a firm league of friendship . . . for their common defense, the security of their liberties, and their mutual and general welfare." In both the Articles and the Constitution, note the proximity of three terms: common defense, liberties, and general welfare. These were all of a piece, reinforcing one another.

In colonial times, before the major incursions of British imperial authority in the mid-1760s, liberty and authority on the local level were not antagonists, but coupled. American colonials enjoyed a degree of home rule unparalleled in Europe at the time and scarcely imaginable to us today. Particularly in the New England colonies, where citizens gathered to make decisions as a corporate body, government was perceived not as an external force exerting authority and endangering liberties but as a vehicle for promoting the common good. People could better secure their liberties by coming together than by trying to do so separately.

Local governments enacted regulations that restricted individual behavior but protected the public, which included everybody. The "blessings of liberty"—being safe from a fire started by one's neighbor, for instance—were more secure with regulations than without them. Consider these ordinances adopted in Albany, New York, in 1773. As in other late colonial towns and cities, Albany required houses to be inspected by "viewers of hearths" and leather buckets to be kept at the ready, and it also placed a limit of twenty-eight pounds on gunpowder that could stored in a private building. All powder in excess of that amount needed to be stored at the community magazine, for a price. The city also imposed traffic laws: "Any horse or horses with coaches, chairs, waggons, carts, sleds, or other carriages" found to be driving "immoderate or fast" was fined three shillings. Beyond promoting safety, regulations prompted responsible behavior, thereby reducing day-to-day apprehensions and making life more pleasant. Property owners were required to pave the streets in front of their houses with "good and sufficient stones." A baker needed to "plainly mark the two initial letters of his Christian name and sirname upon every loaf of bread he shall expose to sale within the said city, upon pain of forfeiting all such bread . . . to be distributed to the poor." Meat prices were controlled, and meat from sick or injured animals "so poor and emaciated as to be unfit for eating" could not be sold. Other health regulations included prohibitions against throwing "any carrion, garbage, oyster shells, ashes, ordure, rubbish, or any other kinds of filth or dirt whatsoever" or dumping "any tubs or pots of ordure any where but in the river." Although most medical practices were unregulated, there was one notable exception. Any "midwife or man-midwife" needed to take this oath: "That you will be diligent, faithful and ready, to help every woman labouring of child, as well the poor as the rich, and that, in time of necessity you will not forsake or leave one woman to go to another. . . . That as often as you shall perceive any peril or danger, either in the woman or child, and you shall be in doubt, you shall thenceforth, in due time, send for other midwives, or except [accept] women in that family, and use their advice, counsel, and assistance, in that behalf." [17]

In the colonists' fight against British imperial policies, the public good often trumped concerns for individual rights. Patriots boycotted British goods, but that ban could succeed only if merchants went along. When some didn't, claiming that they were at liberty to buy and sell as they pleased, Samuel Adams responded: "Have you not a right if you please, to set fire to your own houses, because they are your own, tho in probability it will destroy a whole neighborhood, perhaps a whole city! Where did you learn that in a state or society you had a right to do as you please? And that it was an infringement of that right to restrain you?" [18]

Individual rights were sacrificed again when resistance turned to warfare. Citizens were drafted and prices were regulated. Merchants complained that they should be able to sell food and goods at whatever price the market would bear, but others insisted that the needs of society forced limitations on personal liberty, as often happens in times of war or scarcity. [19]

For more than a decade following independence, from 1776 to the Federal Convention in 1787, states legislatures tried to codify all aspects of public life, regulating the activities of individuals for the betterment of society. In colonial times, many laws had been enforced at the discretion of unaccountable officials such as customs inspectors; now, in reaction, laws were written in such exactitude as to eliminate discretion and thereby corruption. By 1787, in a private memorandum titled "Vices of the Political System of the United States," James Madison argued that "the multiplicity of laws in several states" had progressed too far, but he did not mean that he was against legal regulation per se. Instead, he complained about the "want of concert in matters where common interest requires it." Regulations for the common good were not bad, but piecemeal legislation, often pandering to special interests, rendered more meaningful federal measures "abortive." [20]

Concern for the common good was foremost in the minds of the framers when they gathered in the late spring and summer of 1787. On June 11, Benjamin Franklin implored his colleagues to display less rancor in their disagreements over representation in Congress, which was interfering with their larger goal, "promoting & securing the common good." On June 22, speaking against multiple office holding for sitting members of Congress, Alexander Hamilton warned that the "prevailing passions" of "ambition and interest" driving human behavior should be made "subservient to the public good." On August 24, when considering whether the president should be selected by a joint meeting of Congress or by separate ballots of the House and Senate, Nathaniel Gorham urged delegates to forget their concerns for political gain in making their decision; "the public good," he said, "was the true object to be kept in view." And so it went. Even Luther Martin, the Convention's most vocal opponent of strong central authority, tempered his preference for individual rights. Whereas the "first principle of government is founded on the natural rights of individuals," he said, "I am willing to give up private interest for the public good—but I must be satisfied first, that it is the public interest—and who can decide this point? A majority only of the union." Like politicians today who habitually appeal to the "will of the American people," the framers alluded to the "public good" to affirm whatever point they happened to be making. The term had universal appeal. [21]

Within the Constitution, the term "general welfare," connoting the public good, appears twice. In the Preamble, "promote the general Welfare" immediately precedes "secure the Blessings of Liberty"; there is no hint of conflict between the two. The second mention comes in the first clause of

Article I, Section 8, the hard-hitting passage that gives Congress the power to tax (see chapter 2). Taxes, the framers said, would be used to "provide for the common defence and general Welfare of the United States." When this positive grant of power was proposed by the Committee of Eleven on September 4, not a single delegate objected. "General Welfare" was not a contentious concept, nor was it placed in opposition to liberty or seen as a threat to individual rights.

Today liberty, like so much else, has been privatized. It frequently translates to a person doing as he or she pleases without regulation—a blasphemous word in the mouths of many—or without regard for the common good. Much of what the framers intended, hoped, or expected is lost in that distorted translation. In those times, government did not necessarily drive a wedge between liberty and authority. A monarchical government might do so, an imperial government might do so, or too weak a government might do so, but a republican government, carefully conceived and rooted in the collective will of the people, could protect liberty by exerting authority. People were safest under the management of a vigorous and effective government, imbued with sufficient powers to keep the ambitious few or the mindless many from trampling their rights.[22]

Popular Sovereignty, Representation, and Filtration

We generally assume that the phrase "popular sovereignty," like "individual rights," connotes limited government; if governmental authority ultimately rests with the people, the people, it seems, will want to circumscribe the powers their government has over them. That's not exactly how the framers treated the idea, however. They did believe that governments derive "their just powers from the consent of the governed," as the Declaration of Independence succinctly proclaimed. To get a seat at the table in Revolutionary and post-Revolutionary America, a political figure had to subscribe to that principle, and to the last man, each of the framers did. Yet the framers used popular sovereignty to strengthen government as well as to limit it. To imbue the new government with sufficient energy to lead the nation from the brink—in their minds, their fundamental object—they needed to base that government firmly on the people's consent. Popular sovereignty was a prerequisite for strong government. Without it, critics would be correct: only coercion could keep the nation together.[23]

Yet the learned delegates gathered at the Federal Convention did not believe the people could be trusted with the actual operations of government, and some trusted the people far less than others. "The people," Roger Sherman contended, "immediately should have as little to do as may be about the Government. They want information and are constantly liable to be misled." Elbridge Gerry agreed. "The evils we experience flow from the excess of democracy," he famously pronounced. While not all delegates were so blunt, most were wary of democratic forms in which the people either rule directly or control the acts of their representatives. Had they not seen state legislatures succumb to popular pressures for paper money and debtor relief? And wasn't that a major cause for their coming together?[24]

The framers faced a quandary. Their commitment to popular sovereignty suggested they should let the people rule, but if the people actually ran the government, the framers could not vest that government with much power. Democracy was a fearful concept and a powerful democracy even more so.

The framers' solution lay in the principle of representation. The people, the ultimate source of authority, would delegate that authority to others for defined amounts of time. Conceptually, representatives linked the people with their government while simultaneously placing them at some remove—often a considerable remove. In the federal edifice the framers constructed, only members of the House of Representatives, or the "first branch" of the legislature, would be elected by the people directly. Senators were to be chosen by state legislatures, the president by a special group of electors, and Supreme Court justices, federal judges, ambassadors, and "other public Ministers and Consuls" by the president, with the consent of the Senate. Through this system of "successive filtrations," as James Madison called it, a "great fabric" could be raised—but it needed to "rest on the solid foundation of the people themselves," who would elect representatives to the first branch. James Wilson, too, "was for raising the federal pyramid to a considerable altitude, and for that reason wished to give it as broad a basis as possible. No government could long subsist without the confidence of the people."[25]

Through representation and filtration, popular sovereignty would be preserved yet popular control prevented. The "federal pyramid"—that is to say, the federal government—would protect minorities from being abused by a democratically elected majority. The particular job of the Senate, or second branch, was to check the popularly elected House. Edmund Randolph, who introduced the Virginia Plan, explained the reasoning: "The democratic licentiousness of the State Legislatures proved the necessity of a firm Senate. The object of this 2d. branch is to controul the democratic branch of the Natl. Legislature." Gouverneur Morris echoed this rationale. "The propensity in the 1st. branch to legislate too much [and] to run into projects of paper money & similar expedients," he said, needed to be countered by the Senate. James Madison was even more direct. The task of the Senate, he pronounced, was "to protect the people agst. the transient impressions into which they themselves might be led." The existence of the United States Senate was predicated on the notion that people must be protected from their own ill-conceived notions.[26]

The framers tried not to push their distancing maneuvers too far. At almost every turn, they looked over their shoulders at the people out-of-doors. Eventually, in the state ratifying conventions, delegates chosen by the people would accept or reject the document, and the framers could not overstep boundaries those people drew. It was a delicate balancing act. On the one hand, they treated the document as a contract agreed to by "We the People," and they insisted that the people of the several states, not the state legislatures, approve that contract. On the other hand, they expected the people to select wise and temperate leaders and then leave the act of governing to them.[27]

Today, though we point with great pride to the framers' endorsement of popular sovereignty, our interpretation of that term does not correspond to theirs. We like to emphasize the *popular*, shade it toward *populist*, and proclaim that the people own their government, pure and simple. The framers believed the relationship worked both ways. Sometimes, as Madison argued, government needs to protect the people from themselves—and 1787 was one of those times, he and his colleagues believed. The people, and the state legislatures that were responding to popular pressures, had to be reined in, and the Constitution provided a mechanism for doing just that. What the nation needed, they thought, was a strong and stable federal government, rooted in the people but not directly influenced by them, one that could counteract transient popular passions. Their job was to create such an instrument.[28]

Federalism, republicanism, separation of powers, checks and balances—exploring each of these so-called principles of limited government would reveal similarly nuanced intonations. Understandably, many Americans would prefer not to take that route. That our Constitution is written in plain language hints that its absolute meaning might be easy to comprehend and within our grasp, but history has demonstrated otherwise. If the Constitution were as transparent as ideologues make it out to be, the founding generation would not have haggled incessantly over what it really says.[29]

Today, Americans on the far ends of the political spectrum proclaim with certainty that they know precisely what the framers intended and the Constitution means. These facile readings mistake the part for the whole. The framers were not nearly so one-dimensional as many of their putative fans make them out to be. Indeed, if we are to locate the plain truth somewhere, it would likely appear not on the extreme edges, where so many claim they find it, but somewhere toward the middle, where the framers preferred to tread. Our founding document did not declare firmly for individual rights over the common good (or vice versa), and it gave plenty of fuel for advocates of both strict and loose constructions of the documents. In each case the framers explored the tensions between extremes and tried to find some balance. The discovery of the "true" principles behind the Constitution lies in the discussion, not on a multiple-choice answer sheet, and this discussion does not end. No simple algorithm can or will determine the Constitution's meaning. If we pretend that one exists—or even worse, that we know precisely what it is—we transform the multilayered document that forms the basis for our government into a high school text: linear, lifeless, and incomplete.

5

THE FATHER

Myth: James Madison sired the Constitution.

James Madison . . . is hailed as the "Father of the Constitution" for being the primary author of the United States Constitution.

—Wikipedia biography[1]

Each time an assembly of citizens gathers to deliberate and make decisions concerning the good of the community, the thinking and dedication of James Madison—"Father of the Constitution," Secretary of State, and President of the United States—live again.

—Website of the James Madison Memorial Fellowship Foundation, an independent agency of the executive branch of the federal government[2]

Kernel of Truth

James Madison played a prominent role in the initial conception, meticulous drafting, and final adoption of the United States Constitution. In 1786 he was a delegate to the Annapolis Convention, where he had hoped to discuss possible changes to the Articles of Confederation. That convention failed to get off the ground because of poor attendance, but it did set the national agenda by recommending a broader convention, to be held in Philadelphia the following summer, to consider ideas for rendering the Articles "adequate to the exigencies of the Union." In the spring of 1787, as Madison looked forward to that second convention, he outlined his ideas for a new government in a private memorandum and in letters to such men as George Washington. Then, arriving early in Philadelphia, he met with other delegates from Virginia to outline a plan that embodied some of his basic ideas and served as the initial working draft. Although modified over the course of the summer, the Virginia Plan was never abandoned and the Constitution evolved from this initial set of resolutions.

At the Convention Madison spoke fluently and often, second only to the voluble Gouverneur Morris of Pennsylvania. He viewed the document from the broadest possible perspective, based his suggestions on republican principles, and supported them with historical evidence. "Every Person seems to acknowledge his greatness," wrote William Pierce, from Georgia, in his thumbnail sketches of the Convention's delegates. "In the management of every great question he evidently took the lead in the Convention, and tho' he cannot be called an Orator, he is a most agreable, eloquent, and convincing Speaker . . . [and] he always comes forward the best informed Man of any point in debate."[3]

Madison also took careful and detailed notes, without which we would know little about what transpired in the secret sessions. Whether or not he was the "father" of the Constitution, he was certainly its scribe.[4]

After the Convention, Madison campaigned for ratification. He coauthored *The Federalist* essays (see chapter 6), and in his initial contribution, *The Federalist No. 10*, he presented an innovative argument for a republican form of government for a large nation such as the United States. Previously, people believed that republics only worked in small realms, but Madison reasoned that an extended republic, such as that promised by the proposed Constitution, could neutralize parochial interests, prevent any one leader or group from tyrannizing others, and afford greater protections for liberty and property. Finally, once the Constitution was ratified, it was James Madison who presented a series of amendments that evolved into what we now call the Bill of Rights (see chapter 7).

Deeply committed to constitutionalism, Madison worked tirelessly to establish written rules for a government that would both secure the nation and protect the rights of its people.

But . . .

In truth, nobody can be called the Father of the Constitution. Not George Washington, who presided over the proceedings and whose popularity influenced eventual passage, nor Alexander Hamilton, who shaped the

Constitution's execution during Washington's first administration. Not Gouverneur Morris, who insisted on scrapping the Articles of Confederation at the outset of the Convention, who spoke more often and offered more motions than anybody else, who engineered the transformation of the presidency, and who polished the final draft. Not John Adams, who did not attend the Federal Convention but did write extensively about constitutions and was principal draftsman of the Massachusetts Constitution of 1780, one of the models the framers looked to. Not the French philosopher Montesquieu, whose influential writings helped form the philosophical basis of the document. Not South Carolina's Pierce Butler or Delaware's George Read or New Jersey's Jonathan Dayton or any of the other delegates who enshrined their states' interests in the final document (see chapter 3). And not James Madison.[5]

Our nation's governing plan resulted from an amazing collaboration, and anything that belies this fact, such as labeling one person the "father," undermines the essence of the enterprise. Madison understood this better than we do today. In later years, when the mythology of his authorship was beginning to take hold, he warned off a friend: "You give me a credit to which I have no claim, in calling me '*The* writer of the Constitution of the U.S.' This was not like the fabled Goddess of Wisdom, the offspring of a single brain. It ought to be regarded as the work of many heads and many hands."[6]

Madison did not always get his way at the Convention. By one tabulation, he offered an opinion on seventy-one motions but lost out on forty of these. If Madison *had* had his way, the Constitution would look very different than it does. Senators would serve for nine years, not just six. The president would be advised not by his own cabinet but by an independent council. This council, not the Senate, would check presidential appointments. If impeached, the president would be tried by the Supreme Court, not the Senate. Members of the Supreme Court would join the president in a revisionary council empowered to veto acts of Congress, but Congress could override their veto by a three-quarters vote. The president would not hold the exclusive authority to negotiate treaties; because a president derived "so much power and importance from a state of war," Madison contended, the Senate should be able to conclude a treaty of peace without his assent.[7]

Whereas every framer suffered defeat on many matters, and whereas

Madison conceded the point in most of his losing battles, he stood firm on two issues critical to his overall vision: proportional representation in both houses of Congress and congressional veto power over *all* state legislation. Near the close of the Convention, when he realized he would not prevail on these points, he complained to Thomas Jefferson that the new Constitution, if adopted, would not "effectively answer its national object." The framers fell short, he believed, because they would not heed his advice.[8]

On a strictly pragmatic level, it is just as well they didn't. Never would state populations have accepted an absolute federal veto, nor would small states have ceded to proportional representation in both houses of Congress. Had Madison prevailed, he might have doomed the entire enterprise—but he did not prevail, so we do have a Constitution. That document does not bear the exclusive stamp of Madison's DNA, nor can its paternity be assigned to him.

The Full Story

In the spring of 1787 James Madison gave considerable thought to the forthcoming meeting in Philadelphia. Whereas some delegates, following the instructions they received from their states, sought only to make adjustments to the Articles of Confederation, Madison had grander designs. The whole plan of government needed to be overhauled, he believed. In letters to his friend Thomas Jefferson (in France at the time), Edmund Randolph (who, as Virginia's governor, would be the leader of Madison's delegation), and George Washington (who would undoubtedly be chosen president of the Convention), he presented "some outlines of a new system."[9]

The "individual independence of the States" must cease, he believed. Whereas "local authorities" could continue to exist "wherever they can be subordinately useful," state and local bodies must respect "a due supremacy of the national authority." This meant that a national government must operate on individual citizens "without the intervention of the State legislatures." Because a citizen of a small state like Delaware should have the same say in the national government as one from the most populous state, Virginia, representation in all branches had to be strictly according to population. The special privilege of small states under the Articles of Confederation must cease, and "the lesser States must in every event yield to the predominant will."

Next, the newly constituted national government "should be armed with positive and compleat authority in all cases which require uniformity; such as the regulation of trade, including the right of taxing both exports & imports, the fixing the terms and forms of naturalization, &c &c." Madison was not alone in this view; almost all delegates favored these extensions of authority.

But Madison went one step further: "Over and above this positive power, a negative *in all cases whatsoever* [Madison's emphasis] on the legislative acts of the States, as heretofore exercised by the Kingly prerogative, appears to me to be absolutely necessary, and to be the least possible encroachment on the State jurisdictions. Without this defensive power, every positive power that can be given on paper will be evaded & defeated." For Madison, this federal veto was key to the success of any new plan. If the national government could negate state laws, states would not be able to issue paper money or trample on the rights of creditors. "There has not been any moment since the peace at which the representatives of the union would have given an assent to paper money or any other measure of a kindred nature," he stated confidently (see chapter 2).

But what if states resisted national authority? "The right of coercion should be expressly declared," Madison wrote. The federal veto would keep states from acting independently, he hoped, and if not, commercial regulations might bring errant states to bay. Yet in case nothing else worked, and despite "the difficulty & awkwardness of operating by force on the collective will of a State," armed intervention must be permitted.[10]

Would the Convention agree with Madison?

The Virginia delegation did, but Madison's leadership within that elite group is often overstated. Arriving in Philadelphia before delegates from the other states, the Virginians worked together to draw up a preliminary draft for a new form of government. Madison was the junior member in a group that included luminaries George Washington, Governor Edmund Randolph, George Mason (who had played a large hand in drafting Virginia's Constitution of 1776), and George Wythe (the most respected jurist in the state, and perhaps the nation, and a legal mentor to Thomas Jefferson, future chief justice John Marshall, and virtually every legal scholar in Virginia). Whereas the Virginia Plan emerging from this cadre's deliberations embraced ideas that Madison embraced, it does not follow that the delegation simply rubber-stamped his suggestions. The structure proposed by the Virginia Plan—a strong national government composed of three separate branches, including a bicameral legislature—was not novel. Henry Knox and John Jay had proposed similar outlines for a new government to George Washington five months earlier, four months before Madison did. Washington copied the suggestions from Madison, Knox, and Jay, and carried them to Philadelphia, where he likely shared them with the Virginia caucus. Other members no doubt chimed in as well. What emerged from that caucus was not "Madison's Plan," as it is sometimes called.[11]

Within the caucus, Madison's view prevailed. According to the Virginia Plan, Congress could "negative all laws passed by the several States, contravening in the opinion of the National Legislature the articles of Union; and to call forth the force of the Union agst. any member of the Union failing to fulfill its duty under the articles thereof."[12]

On May 31 the Convention affirmed that provision, and on June 8 Charles Pinckney moved to strengthen it. Why limit a veto to laws "contravening in the opinion of the National Legislature the articles of Union"? What if some state passed a law that was highly destructive but did not expressly contradict the "articles of Union"? Congress, on its own authority, should decide whether a state law was proper and in the interests of the nation as a whole, Pinckney argued, and he moved "that the National Legislature shd. have authority to negative all laws which they shd. judge to be improper." This "universality of the power," he argued, was "indispensably necessary" to keep states "in due subordination to the nation." Madison seconded Pinckney's motion while noting that states had demonstrated a "constant tendency . . . to encroach on the federal authority; to violate national Treaties; to infringe the rights & interests of each other; to oppress the weaker party within their respective jurisdictions." To prevent such abuses of state power, the national government's "negative" over the states "must extend to all cases." The national government, he concluded, was like the sun, and the states were its planets. "This prerogative of the General Govt. is the great pervading principle that must controul the centrifugal tendency of the

States; which, without it, will continually fly out of their proper orbits and destroy the order & harmony of the political System."

Elbridge Gerry objected. Although he conceded that a national veto over state legislation would be useful in some cases—"to authorize a negative to paper money and similar measures," for instance—its unrestricted use was unjustified. States were "ignorant of each other's interests," he insisted, and the internal matters of any state should not be regulated by lawmakers from other states.

In the end the question was decided more by politics than by reason. Delaware's Gunning Bedford Jr. galvanized the opposition by appealing to fears of large-state overreach. "Delaware would have about 1/90 for its share in the General Councils, whilst Pa. & Va. would posses 1/3 of the whole," he observed. "Will not these large States crush the small ones whenever they stand in the way of their ambitious or interested views. This shews the impossibility of adopting such a system as that on the table, or any other founded on a change in the principle of representation." The Pinckney-Madison motion to strengthen the national veto failed, with only the three largest states, Virginia, Pennsylvania, and Massachusetts, voting for it. Yet as of that moment, the working draft still allowed Congress to veto state laws it deemed incompatible with "the articles of Union."

From mid-June to mid-July the battle between small states and large states over representation in Congress dominated the proceedings, and James Madison was a strong advocate for the large-state position. On July 2 a deadlocked Convention sent the matter to a committee composed of one delegate from each state, and three days later that committee reported to the full Convention a three-part compromise: the lower house would be apportioned by population; in the upper house "each state shall have an equal vote"; and "all bills for raising and appropriating money" must originate in the lower house and not be "altered or amended" by the upper house (see chapter 3).

Madison rejected the compromise. He insisted that its money bill provision was meaningless because a member of the Senate could always persuade some like-minded member in the House to initiate a money bill or amendment, and once a bill was introduced it still required Senate approval. This "left in force all the objections which had prevailed agst. allowing each State an equal voice." There were only two choices, he argued: "The Convention was reduced to the alternative of either departing from justice in order to conciliate the smaller States, and the minority of the people of the U. S., or of displeasing these by justly gratifying the larger States and the majority of the people." In the classic logic of a noncompromiser, Madison created a stark dichotomy and then ruled out the opposition's choice.[13]

On July 16, despite Madison's objections, the Convention approved by a razor-thin margin the Great Compromise that gave small states an equal say in the Senate. Would Madison finally accept defeat? On a motion by Edmund Randolph, the Convention adjourned to allow delegates from the large states to caucus and perhaps suggest a new course (see chapter 3). In his notes, Madison described that meeting in regretful, dismissive terms: "The time was wasted in vague conversation on the subject, without any specific proposition or agreement." Some delegates, he reported, wanted "the side comprising the principal States, and a majority of the people of America" to propose a new "scheme of Government," whereas others "seemed inclined to yield to the smaller States" in the interests of unity. Madison clearly was discontented with the meeting's failure to unite behind his position. He had wanted both proportional representation in each house of Congress *and* a federal government that would serve as a unifying force. Philosophically, he believed these two major goals were of a piece, but politically he failed to see that they worked at cross-purposes. Proportional representation in both branches of Congress was too divisive an issue.

Lacking the support to continue resistance, Madison and other disgruntled proponents of proportional representation reluctantly turned to other matters—but Madison did not move far. The following afternoon he defended once again the national veto of state legislation: "The necessity of a general Govt. proceeds from the propensity of the States to pursue their particular interests in opposition to the general interest. This propensity will continue to disturb the system, unless effectually controuled. Nothing short of a negative on their laws will controul it. They can pass laws which will accomplish their injurious objects before they can be repealed by the Genl. Legislre. or be set aside by the National Tribunals." Strangely, to buttress his argument, he cited admiringly the example of the British Crown: "A power of negativing the improper laws of the States is at once the most mild & certain means of preserving the harmony of the system. Its utility is sufficiently displayed in the British System. Nothing could maintain the harmony & subordination of the various parts of the empire, but the prerogative by which the Crown, stifles in the birth every Act of every part tending to discord or encroachment."

Americans, though, had rebelled in the 1760s and '70s against this "British System" and its harsh methods of preserving "harmony & subordination." Madison's argument had a dangerously Tory ring that would not play well out-of-doors, and Gouverneur Morris called him on his tone-deafness. "The proposal of it would disgust all the States," he predicted. Others argued that an explicit national veto was impractical because communication was slow and Congress did not sit year-round. The veto clause was stricken from the working draft of the Constitution.[14]

In two days, July 16 and 17, James Madison watched two of his most cherished features go down to defeat, but even so, he fought on. On August 23, perhaps after consulting with Madison, Charles Pinckney proposed a new version of the veto clause. He moved that Congress have the authority "to negative all laws passed by the several States interfering in the opinion of the Legislature with the general interests and harmony of the Union; provided that two thirds of the members of each House assent to the same." Pinckney and Madison reasoned that requiring a supermajority would make the veto measure more palatable to small states and slave states fearful of domination by Congress. Cleverly, though, they also strengthened the national negative by lowering the hurdle. Congress could veto any measure that ran counter to "the general interests and harmony of the Union," not just one that directly contradicted the "articles of Union."[15]

Knowing the measure still faced an uphill battle, Madison made a tactical move. With delegates wearied by continued debates, the best chance of adding any new provision at this point was to send the issue to committee, so he proposed that a committee work out the "modification." But even that suggestion stirred opposition. Although Wilson called the national veto "the key-stone wanted to compleat the wide arch of Government," Hugh Williamson called it "unnecessary" and John Rutledge declared, "If nothing else, this alone would damn and ought to damn the Constitution." No state would "ever agree to be bound hand & foot in this manner." By a vote of five states to six, the Convention refused to reconsider a national veto over all state laws, even in committee. The issue was finally resolved, and not to Madison's satisfaction.

When Madison wrote to Washington before the Convention, he had much to say about the national legislature and the national judiciary, but very little to say about a national executive: "I have scarcely ventured as yet to form my opinion either of the manner in which it ought to be constituted or of the authorities with which it ought to be cloathed," he confessed.[16]

The Virginia Plan reflected Madison's lack of clarity. It stated that "a National Executive" should be chosen by the national legislature, receive a fixed salary, and serve only one term, but it did not specify whether there would be one chief executive or several, how long he or they would serve, or what his or their powers would be, except in the broadest possible terms: "Besides a general authority to execute the National laws, it ought to enjoy the Executive rights vested in Congress by the Confederation."

On June 1, when the Convention first considered these questions, some delegates wanted a single executive, but others thought executive authority should be shared. Only when the Convention appeared at an impasse did Madison join the discussion, suggesting that delegates "fix the extent of the Executive authority"—in other words, define what he or they should do. Madison's "definition" of executive authority, however, clarified nothing. The executive or executives, he moved, should have "power to carry into effect the national laws, to appoint to offices in cases not otherwise provided for, and to execute such other powers as may from time to time be delegated by the national Legislature."

Three days later, on June 4, the Convention decided on a single chief executive, not several. But should this official have the power to "negative" acts of the legislature? Some thought yes, others thought no, and Madison suggested a middle ground: the executive could veto laws (to use a later term), but "a proper proportion of each branch" could "overrule the objections of the Executive." The idea wasn't new—it had first appeared in New York's 1777 constitution, which Madison had studied with care—and it struck a chord with the delegates. The Convention set the "proper proportion" at two-thirds (the New York formula), later changed it to three-quarters, and finally returned it to two-thirds, but the basic idea of an executive veto with a possibility of legislative override made it into the final Constitution and is often credited to Madison.

Even so, Madison's version of the veto differed markedly from the one that prevailed. In his mind, the chief executive should not exercise "revisionary" powers by himself but with "a convenient number of the National Judiciary"—again, an adaptation of New York's constitution. James Wilson joined Madison in this matter, yet despite strong arguments from two of the best minds of the Convention, when "the question for joining the Judges to the Executive in the revisionary business" came to a vote on June 6, their side lost out, three states to seven.

Madison did not consider this matter settled. Over six weeks later, on July 21, he and Wilson brought it once again to the Convention's floor. "This proposition had been before made and failed," Wilson admitted, "but he was so confirmed by reflection in the opinion of its utility, that he thought it incumbent on him to make another effort." Adding to the sense of gravity, Madison said he "considered the object of the motion as of great importance to the meditated Constitution." At issue was a great point of law—should judges have a say in legislation before cases involving that legislation come before them? It was also a question of balance—should two branches of government be aligned against a third? And a question of power—would judicial participation in the veto strengthen or weaken the executive? It was one of the great philosophical debates of the Convention, with the balance of power in the new government at stake. Despite speaking powerfully on behalf of a joint executive-judicial revisionary council, Madison did not get his way. The vote was closer this time, but on a matter that seriously affected governmental operations, the so-called Father of the Constitution lost yet again.

Characteristically, Madison refused to concede. On August 15, he raised the issue a third time, but now in a new form. Instead of a joint executive-judicial revisionary council, in which the president could be outvoted, the president and the Supreme Court would *each* have to approve any act of Congress. If either vetoed the bill, it would take a two-thirds vote in each house of Congress to override that veto; if both cast vetoes, the override threshold would rise to three-quarters. It was an ingenious scheme, but it went nowhere. Delegates still were wary of "any interference of the Judges in the Legislative business," as Charles Pinckney put it. True, they would have to evaluate laws after the fact when infractions came before the Court, but to do so beforehand, Pinckney observed, would "involve them in parties, and give a previous tincture to their opinions." Elbridge Gerry added dismissively, "This motion comes to the same thing with what had been already negatived," referring to the votes on June 6 and July 21. Madison's motion failed handily, three states to eight.[17]

On September 4, less than two weeks before the Convention would adjourn, the Committee of Eleven, charged with suggesting solutions to unresolved issues, revamped the executive department (see chapter 3). Though he served on that committee, Madison disagreed with some of its suggestions. Before, the Senate had held the power of appointments, but now the president would, pending the Senate's approval. Madison did not think a legislative body should concern itself with appointments, and when the issue came to the floor of the Convention, he favored transferring that authority to a separate executive council, again invoking a feature of New York's constitution. Only three states, though, agreed even to consider such a council.[18]

The Committee of Eleven report also moved treaty-making authority from the Senate to the president, although two-thirds of the Senate was required for ratification. Here, Madison took issue with the need for a supermajority. Shouldn't there be an exception for treaties concluding peace, he posited, "allowing these to be made with less difficulty than other treaties"? Pushing this theme one step farther, he moved that the Senate, with a two-thirds vote, could conclude a treaty of peace *without the consent of the president.* "The President," he argued, "would necessarily derive so much power and importance from a state of war that he might be tempted, if authorised, to impede a treaty of peace." It was a novel argument and perhaps a good one, but most delegates were not willing to undercut the chief executive's authority. Madison lost out on both counts.[19]

Madison also differed with the Committee of Eleven on the manner of impeachment. Perhaps to offset the Senate's partial loss of appointive and treaty-making powers, the committee gave that body the power to try all impeachments. Madison thought this made the president "improperly dependent" on Congress, but his suggestion that the Supreme Court try impeachments lost handily, two states to nine.[20]

Madison's views on the presidency cannot be neatly classified. Some appear to favor a strong executive, others seem geared to keep executive power in check. Yet this much is clear: he did not take the lead in fashioning the broad outlines of the office, nor did many of his particular ideas take hold. The Father of the Presidency he was not.

On September 17, the last day of the Convention, Benjamin Franklin, Alexander Hamilton, and Gouverneur Morris urged their fellow delegates to endorse the proposed Constitution, even if they disagreed with some of its provisions (see chapter 3). Franklin's modesty was memorable: "I confess that there are several parts of this constitution which I do not at present approve, but I am not sure I shall never approve them: For having lived long, I have experienced many instances of being obliged by better information, or fuller consideration, to change opinions even on important subjects, which I once thought right, but found to be otherwise. It is therefore that the older I grow, the more apt I am to doubt my own judgment, and to pay more respect to the judgment of others."

Madison, however, said nothing on that final day. Although he signed the Constitution, he was deeply disappointed with the Convention's outcome. Eleven days before the Convention adjourned, he sent a letter to Thomas Jefferson complaining that "the plan should it be adopted will neither effectually answer its national object nor prevent the local mischiefs which every where excite disgusts agst the state governments." Madison remained more attached to his nationalist views than Franklin was to his own defeated positions. In the words of constitutional historian and Madison scholar Jack N. Rakove, Madison "viewed all the decisions that had diluted his system not as necessary compromises but as fundamental errors in judgment."[21]

Weeks later, after Congress had referred the proposed new plan to the states, Madison complained again to Jefferson about the rejection of the national veto. He opened by claiming that the veto had been rejected by "a bare majority" at the Convention, although this was not true. (The final vote, on July 17, resulted in a solid three-to-seven defeat; the "bare majority" referred to a five-to-six vote on August 23 that merely would have referred the issue to committee.) In methodical fashion, citing lessons from ancient confederacies, recent struggles of the United Netherlands and the German Empire, and "our own experience both during the war and since the peace," he argued that without a central authority capable of nullifying local law, there would always be "a continual struggle between the head and inferior members" of government. Even though Madison could no longer affect the outcome of the Convention, he continued his argument for 2,583 words—comparable in length to essays he would soon publish in *The Federalist*.[22]

While Madison complained in private, in public he put on a different face. Although the proposed national government created by the Constitution turned out weaker than he wanted it to be, at least the Constitution provided for a national government, and that was a vast improvement over the Articles of Confederation. The Constitution needed to be ratified at all costs, and Madison would do whatever he could to make that happen.

Late in the fall of 1788, Alexander Hamilton invited Madison to contribute to a series of essays titled *The Federalist*, now often called *The Federalist Papers* (see chapter 6). Four weeks after penning his long letter to Jefferson, Madison published his first contribution to *The Federalist*. Today, we know Madison for the arguments he made in the twenty-six essays that he contributed to *The Federalist*, not for his unsuccessful attempts to create a stronger national government at the Federal Convention. We see him as the spokesman for the *"federal principle"* (his emphasis) and the balance of powers within the national government. In *The Federalist No. 39*, which many scholars treat as a definitive exposition and defense of America's unique federal system, Madison explained that the new plan was "neither a national nor a federal Constitution, but a composition of both." The House of Representatives was purely national in character, because people elected individuals to represent them in the national government without any interposition by the states. The Senate, by contrast, was federal in character, not national, because senators were chosen by state legislatures to represent the states, not the people, and each state had an equal say. This, in large measure, was what made the system so balanced, he boasted. Ironically, he was able to make such a claim only because he had failed to secure proportional representation in both houses of Congress at the Convention in Philadelphia the previous summer.[23]

Under the "federalist principle," powers were distributed between state and national governments, each supreme "within its own sphere." Even though balancing state and national authority was always central to Madison's philosophy, his weighting of those two spheres changed with time. At the Federal Convention, he gave preference to the national government, but in *The Federalist* he assuaged readers' fears of centralization by giving states the nod. In *The Federalist No. 39*, he noted that the jurisdiction of the national government "extends to certain enumerated objects only, and leaves to the several States a residuary and inviolable sovereignty over all other objects." Congress would have no more say over state and municipal matters than the states had over national policy. In *The Federalist No. 45*, Madison spoke more strongly yet for the residual rights of states: "The powers delegated by the proposed Constitution to the federal government are few and defined. Those which are to remain in the State governments are numerous and indefinite. The former will be exercised principally on external objects, as war, peace, negotiation, and foreign commerce. . . . The powers reserved to the several States will extend to all the objects which in the ordinary course of affairs, concern the lives and liberties, and properties of the people, and the internal order, improvement and prosperity of the State."

Although this tidy separation worked well for his purpose, it masked Madison's earlier view of what would be best for the nation, which he succinctly expressed in his defeated motion on June 8 at the Federal Convention: "the National Legislature shd. have authority to negative all laws which they shd. judge to be improper." *All* laws, by any interpretation, would include even those within the "sphere" supposedly reserved to the states. Imagine for the moment that Madison's motion had prevailed and then, in his essays for *The Federalist*, he had justified the national veto in the language he used when writing to Washington: "A negative *in all cases whatsoever* on the legislative acts of the States, as heretofore exercised by the Kingly prerogative, appears to me to be absolutely necessary." The prospect of such a "Kingly prerogative," unchecked and ever expansive, would likely have undone the framers' work. The so-called Father of the Constitution would have killed his own child.[24]

Madison's most famous argument in *The Federalist*, put forth in *The Federalist Nos. 10, 14,* and *51,* stated that individual rights were safer under a large or extended republic than under a small one. According to traditional wisdom, voiced most influentially by Montesquieu in his *The Spirit of the Laws*, republican governments worked best in small, self-contained states with homogeneous populations, whereas in large nations, where rulers were distanced from the people, republicanism inevitably broke down. Madison turned this argument on its head, transforming what most theorists viewed as a disease of republican government—factionalism—into a cure. In an extensive country, he insisted, a multiplicity of interests and factions can cancel one another out, making it more difficult for any single faction to form a majority and commandeer the government for its own purposes. "It is no less certain than it is important, notwithstanding the contrary opinions which have been entertained," he concluded in *The Federalist No. 51*, "that the larger the society, provided it lie within a practical sphere, the more duly capable it will be of self-government."

Today, we know this argument by reading *The Federalist*, but Madison had expressed it at least three previous times: immediately before the Federal Convention, during the Convention's proceedings, and in a letter to Thomas Jefferson dated October 24, 1787, five weeks after the Convention's end. The first two versions of his argument, however, included an element lacking from the argument's recapitulation in *The Federalist*: the need for a national veto to suppress state laws produced by factions. Because the new Constitution failed to provide that mechanism, Madison was forced to soften his argument. The lighter, gentler version of the argument survives in *The Federalist*, eclipsing the strident, harsher one.[25]

Many, perhaps most, educated Americans have been instructed by teachers to read either *The Federalist No. 10* or *51*, and apparently the diligent ones did. In 2004, when the National Archives, National History Day, and *U.S. News & World Report* asked the public to vote on which of one hundred documents were the most influential in American history, "Federalist Papers No. 10 & No. 51" came in twentieth, just below the Marshall Plan and the 1965 Voting Rights Act, but narrowly edging out the United Nations

Charter, the 1783 Treaty of Paris, in which Britain recognized American independence, and Thomas Edison's patent application for the lightbulb.[26]

Although Madison's clever thesis intrigues us today, it attracted little notice at the time. In *The Federalist No. 11*, published two days later, Alexander Hamilton promoted the commercial benefits of the proposed Constitution, and apparently that practical argument resonated better than Madison's theoretical one; Hamilton's essay was reprinted in six newspapers outside New York State, Madison's in only one. *The Federalist No. 51* was not picked up by any newspaper outside New York City, and by the time it appeared in the second bound volume of *The Federalist* on May 28, 1788, eight states had already ratified the Constitution, only one shy of the number required to place it in effect, and delegates to the ratification conventions in the remaining states had already been selected (see chapter 6). If people of those times had been asked to list the most influential essays penned during the ratification debates, *The Federalist Nos. 10* and *51* would not have made the grade.[27]

Circulation aside, other Federalist leaders did not use or cite Madison's argument. In debates at the states' ratifying conventions, when the Constitution's opponents argued that republican government could work only for small self-contained states, Federalists responded by pointing to the proposed system of representation, to the manageable size of Congress, to the deficiencies of confederacies, and so on—but they did not incorporate Madison's thoughts on offsetting factions.[28]

Not until the twentieth century did Madison's argument receive particular attention. *The Federalist No. 10* entered public debate in 1913 when progressive historians cited Madison's denunciation of debtor relief: "a rage for paper money, for an abolition of debts, for an equal division of property, or for any other improper or wicked project." This single passage, with its provocative wording, seemed to support their controversial and much-publicized economic interpretation of the Constitution, which held that most framers owned government securities and wanted to kill measures that would devalue them. Whether or not readers understood or embraced Madison's argument, they did take note.[29]

Decades later, with the promotion of pluralism in midcentury and the attention to diversity in the decades following, Madison's thinking on counteracting factions finally took hold. The Supreme Court cited *The Federalist*

No. 10 only once before 1974, although by then its judicial opinions had referenced other *Federalist* essays more than two hundred times. Justices rarely cited *The Federalist No. 51* before 1960, but after that they cited it more than any of the other eighty-four *Federalist* essays. Times had changed, and by reading history backwards, modern commentators attributed Madison's creative argument not only to him but also to "the Founding Fathers" (from Justice Byron White's *Storer v. Brown* ruling) or to "the Framers" (from Justice Clarence Thomas's 2007 dissent in *Nixon v. Shrink Missouri Government PAC*). The popular notion that Madison was somehow *the* framer helped justify this unwarranted leap.[30]

Fast-forward a decade, from the winter of 1787–88, when Madison penned his *Federalist* essays, to December 21, 1798. The political climate was far different, and many Americans were uneasy with recent extensions of federal authority. The government had formed a national army in anticipation of a full-scale war with France, and when some Americans opposed that move, Congress enacted the Alien and Sedition Acts to suppress dissent. James Madison, an early proponent of federal supremacy, now questioned Congress's authority to take such actions. In a series of dramatic resolutions he presented to the Virginia House of Delegates, he declared that when Congress exercised powers not granted to it under the Constitution, any state, as a contractual party to the original agreement, had the right to step in. The Virginia Resolutions, as they are now called, declared:

> That this Assembly doth explicitly and peremptorily declare, that it views the powers of the federal government, as resulting from the compact, to which the states are parties; as limited by the plain sense and intention of the instrument constituting the compact; as no further valid than they are authorized by the grants enumerated in that compact; and that in case of a deliberate, palpable, and dangerous exercise of other powers not granted by the said compact, the states who are parties thereto, have the right, and are in duty bound, to interpose for arresting the progress of the evil, and for maintaining within their respective limits, the authorities, rights and liberties appertaining to them.

Madison had come full circle. In 1787, if some delegate to the Federal Convention had moved that a state legislature could "interpose" its authority between its citizens and the execution of a national law and declare it "no further valid," he would have declared such a motion destructive to the entire project.[31]

Madison's striking transformation did not proceed along a linear path. Whereas he had argued during the ratification debates that federal powers would be "few and defined," when he traveled to New York to serve in the first House of Representatives he took a broader view. On April 20, 1789, ten days before George Washington's presidential inauguration, two men asked Congress to support a private scientific expedition to Baffin's Bay to investigate the magnetic north pole. Despite the Constitution's silence on such matters, Madison was willing to endorse the measure:

Well aware as I am that public bodies are liable to be assailed by visionary projectors, I nevertheless wish to ascertain the probability of the magnetic theory. If there is any considerable probability that the projected voyage would be successful, or throw any valuable light on the discovery of longitude, it certainly comports with the honor and dignity of Government to give it their countenance and support. . . . I am also well aware that the deranged situation of our treasury would not warrant us in spending considerable sums in visionary pursuits; but if an inconsiderable sum will answer on this occasion, and there is a probability of improving the science of navigation, I see no reason against it.

Support for scientific investigations was not included in the framers' carefully honed list of congressional powers in Article I, Section 8. At the Federal Convention, on August 18, Madison had suggested adding to that list the power "to encourage by premiums & provisions, the advancement of useful knowledge and discoveries," but his proposal had been sent to committee and was never reported out. That defeat did not matter to Madison now. Congress still had the authority to "provide for the common Defence and general Welfare of the United States," and those general words would have to suffice.[32]

The next day, Madison spoke in support of a six-cents-per-ton duty on commercial vessels, which he argued would be "necessary for the support of light-houses, hospitals for disabled seamen, and other establishments incident to commerce." At the Federal Convention, on September 15, he had stated that an "object for tonnage Duties" was to provide for "support of Seamen etc." and that this would be covered under Congress's power "to regulate commerce." It was an expansive interpretation of the often contested "commerce clause" (Article I, Section 8, Clause 3), a view we usually associate with Hamilton, the broad constructionist, not Madison, the soon-to-be strict constructionist (see chapter 4).[33]

In 1790, when Congress established the first federal census to apportion representation among the states, Madison suggested that it take advantage of "the present opportunity" to gather valuable information that went well beyond "the bare enumeration of the inhabitants," the express purpose of the census as stated in the Constitution. If the census provided a "description of the several classes [occupations] into which the community is divided," he said, that information would prove "extremely useful, when we come to pass laws, affecting any particular description of people." It was a good measure, he felt, and that was reason enough to pass it. Stretching the census past its specified constitutional function did not trouble him.[34]

Despite his writings in *The Federalist*, Madison, as a lawmaker, did not turn into a strict constructionist until his break with Hamilton over the national bank, early in 1791. Madison was no great fan of national banks, with their "concentration of wealth and influence," and he feared that such an institution in America would threaten republican government, as the Bank of England had corrupted politics in the former mother country. Leading the opposition to Hamilton's bill in the House of Representatives, Madison based his argument on constitutional grounds. "Is the power of establishing an incorporated Bank among the powers vested by the Constitution in the Legislature of the United States?" he asked rhetorically. It was not in the Preamble, which "only states the objects of the Confederation" and does not "designate the express powers by which those objects are to be obtained." (Note the reference to the Union as a "Confederation," a curious retreat from his nationalism at the Federal Convention.) Nor was it to be found in any of the eighteen clauses in Article 1, Section 8, he argued. True, granting a charter was a means to forming a bank, a bank was a means to accumulating capital, and accumulating capital was a means to borrowing money, a power that *was* granted to Congress in the second clause of Article I, Section 8. But "if implications, thus remote and thus multiplied, can be linked together, a chain may be formed that will reach every object of legislation, every object within the whole compass of political economy." Nor could the "necessary and proper" catchall justify the bank, he concluded. "The proposed bank could not even be called necessary to the Government; at most it could be but convenient." The expedition to Baffin's Bay, federal support for disabled seamen, and questioning people about their "class" in the census were no more "necessary to the Government" than a national bank, but Madison had not dismissed those nonenumerated measures on that account. Something deeper was at stake.[35]

The debate over the national bank, although argued on constitutional grounds, reflected diverging visions of nationalism. At the Federal Convention and during the ratification debates, Madison and Hamilton had both considered themselves "nationalists," but for very different reasons. Hamilton had wanted to create a strong nation-state, a commercial powerhouse capable of exerting international influence through a military force financed by national credit and national taxation. To achieve these goals, he argued, the constitutional powers granted to the national government should be interpreted in the broadest possible manner. By contrast, Madison envisioned a more self-sufficient nation not reliant on international commerce, an expensive military, or a large federal infrastructure. While Hamilton envisioned the United States as a growing empire, Madison hoped to create an exemplary republic. In his mind, the national government should be strengthened to achieve justice, not conquest; it needed power to neutralize parochial parties and to adjudicate quarrels between them. Although both visions seemed "nationalist" in the political climate of the late 1780s, the differences became painfully evident in the 1790s. Starting with the debate over the national bank, Madison's strict construction of the Constitution became the centerpiece of his resistance to Hamilton's version of nationalism.[36]

Madison's evolution, though understandable, is problematic if we declare him "the acknowledged Father of the Constitution." Which Constitution did he supposedly sire? The pronationalist one he would have preferred in

1787? The one proposed by the Federal Convention in 1787 and ratified by the states in 1788, despite his complaints but with his support? The one he interpreted rather loosely while serving in Congress in 1789 and 1790? Or the less centralized and more strictly interpreted version first touted in *The Federalist*, the one that came to define his political views from 1791 onward?

This confusion has been exploited and placed in the service of ideology. Madison's line in *The Federalist No. 45*—"The powers delegated by the proposed Constitution to the federal government are few and defined"—is among the most quoted sentences by a founder on the Internet today, with close to half a million entries turning up on a Google search. By contrast, his dramatic one-line advocacy of national supremacy in 1787—"A negative *in all cases whatsoever* on the legislative acts of the States, as heretofore exercised by the Kingly prerogative, appears to me to be absolutely necessary"—yields only ninety-three. True, the first comes from the much-publicized *The Federalist* and the second from a little-known source, but Google demonstrates that obscurity doesn't preclude popularity. In 1794, during a little-known debate in Congress over a motion to provide relief for refugees from the revolution in San Domingo, Madison said this: "I cannot undertake to lay my finger on that article of the Constitution which granted a right to Congress of expending, on objects of benevolence, the money of their constituents." That quotation, according to Google, is repeated over half a million times on the Internet. Conveniently, writers who prefer a minimal role for the federal government cite things Madison said years after the writing of the Constitution to demonstrate that document's meaning, while they ignore his attempts before and during the framing of the Constitution to expand its powers.[37]

For over two centuries Americans have cherry-picked statements made by various founders, but because Madison was allegedly the Constitution's "primary author" and the best single authority on its meaning, the stakes are higher in his case. What Madison says must be so, no matter when he said it. This assumption has played favorably to opponents of federal authority. Select a half dozen of Madison's quotations favoring states' rights or strict limitations on powers of the national government. Did Madison make any of these pronouncements in 1787? Good luck finding any from that magical year.

Now compare those quotations with any statements he *did* make during the summer of 1787. Did he at that time promote the rights of states or suggest strict limits on the powers of the federal government? Or did he wish to grant greater powers to the federal government and place tighter reins on the states?

A close look at the record will answer these questions. Even after the broader issues of proportional representation in the Senate and a national veto of state laws had been decided against him, Madison argued for specific expansions of national authority and contractions of state authority. The powers of the national legislature were first enumerated in the Committee of Detail report on August 6, and delegates spent the remainder of that month combing over the report. During these debates, when the nuts and bolts of the Constitution were being determined, Madison had much to say on several matters pertaining to the powers granted to the national government and the states.

- August 16: He argued unsuccessfully to allow Congress to tax exports.

- August 18: He suggested granting nine additional powers to Congress. The national legislature, he said, should be empowered to "establish an University," to "encourage by premiums & provisions, the advancement of useful knowledge and discoveries," to "exercise exclusively Legislative authority at the Seat of the General Government," and in order to provide an infrastructure for westward expansion, to "grant charters of incorporation in cases where the public good may require them, and the authority of a single State may be incompetent." His list was referred to committee but never reported out.

- August 18 and 23: He argued that the national government, not the states, should regulate, control, and discipline the militia, including the appointment of top officers. "The regulation of the Militia," he said, "did not seem in its nature to be divisible between two distinct authorities. If the States would trust the Genl. Govt. with a power over the public treasure, they would from the same consideration of necessity grant it the direction of the public force."

- August 20: He tried to clarify and expand what we now call the "elastic" clause—"And to make all laws necessary and proper for carrying into execution the foregoing powers, and all other powers vested, by this Constitution, in the Government of the U. S. or any department or officer thereof "—by adding "and establish all offices" after the word "laws."

- August 28: He argued for three new restrictions on state governments: prohibiting state legislatures from laying embargoes, ensuring that new states would not pass laws interfering with private contracts, and making an absolute prohibition against state duties and imposts.

- August 29: To strengthen the clause requiring each state to give "full faith and credit" to the laws of every other state, he proposed that Congress be "authorized to provide for the *execution* of Judgments in other States" so it could take an active role in preserving the union (emphasis in original).

- September 4: The Committee of Eleven, to which Madison belonged, greatly expanded the first power granted to Congress by the Committee of Detail. The original said, "The Legislature shall have power to lay and collect taxes duties imposts & excises," after which Madison's committee inserted, "to pay the debts and provide for the common defence & general welfare, of the U. S." In later years, the words "general welfare," like the term "necessary and proper" in the elastic clause, would place Madison and other strict constructionists in a defensive posture, but during the Convention he had a hand in framing both of these clauses. Each one was necessary to ensure that the national government possessed sufficient powers to do its job.

- September 14: He revived two of his suggestions from August 18: granting Congress the power to grant charters of incorporation and establish a nondenominational university. Both motions were rejected.[38]

In presenting these arguments, Madison produced sound bites you are not likely to find on Internet blogs. Consider this gem from the August 23 debate over organizing the militia: "The Discipline of the Militia is evidently a *National* concern, and ought to be provided for in the *National* Constitution" (emphases in original). Unsurprisingly, this appeal to place state militias under national control has been bypassed by states' rights advocates, gun rights enthusiasts, and the modern-day militia movement.

Or this one-liner that distills Madison's perspective at the Federal Convention: "As the greatest danger is that of disunion of the States, it is necessary to guard agat. it by sufficient powers to the Common Govt." We might expect to see this quotation often, but instead we find the words that immediately follow: "the greatest danger to liberty is from large standing armies."[39]

Even in this tighter game, Madison often did not get his way. On some occasions, he faced opposition even from such fellow nationalists as Gouverneur Morris, who argued that Madison's suggestions were not necessary, might alienate the public, and could endanger ratification. On every contested issue, Madison's voice was but one of many. He was not the sole protagonist.

In the end, the notion that the Constitution had an identifiable father, and that that man was James Madison, is not some innocent metaphor, as its proponents might contend, but a dangerous error with two interpretative consequences. First, by downgrading the collaborative process, it shelters us from disputed issues at the Federal Convention and the political jockeying that resolved them. The idea that we should pay attention to James Madison over all the rest of the Convention's delegates is an unwarranted shortcut, an unfortunate habit that belittles the complex process of constitution writing the framers conducted and the multilayered meanings of the document they produced.

And second, because of Madison's political and ideological evolution, the father metaphor leads to a distorted view of the Constitution's meaning. It turns the framer who most soured on the Constitution because it wasn't sufficiently "national" into the perfect standard-bearer for anti-national ideologies. If the author of the Constitution said the powers of the federal government are "few and defined" and those of the states are "numerous and indefinite," enemies of legitimate federal constitutional power see these words, taken at face value, as proof positive that the Constitution favored the states.

This unwarranted notion has penetrated to the core of our public discourse. It informs constitutional jurisprudence at the highest levels and affects national policy. The "power to tax and spend for the general welfare," Justices Antonin Scalia, Anthony Kennedy, Clarence Thomas, and Samuel Alito complained in their dissent in the 2012 Affordable Care Act decision, has unfortunately come to extend "beyond (what Madison thought it meant) taxing and spending for those aspects of the general welfare that were within the Federal Government's enumerated powers." The words within parentheses speak volumes. "What Madison thought it meant," in this context, stands for "what the founders thought it meant" and finally "what the Constitution really means." Because Madison supposedly wanted a strictly limited government, that is what the document must prescribe. However misguided, Madison-the-Father mythology is embedded within the default logic of constitutional reasoning.[40]

There is a simple remedy for this interpretative malady: we must take pains to date and contextualize historically every Madison quotation. A state can "interpose" in the execution of a federal law and declare it "no further valid"—yes, Madison did write those words in 1798, when the political party he opposed tried to outlaw dissent. Federal powers were "few and defined"—he made that forthright statement when trying to sell the Constitution, with its greatly enhanced federal powers, to a wary public in 1788. "As the greatest danger is that of disunion of the States, it is necessary to guard agat. it by sufficient powers to the Common Govt."—yes, these are Madison's own words, uttered in defense of nationalizing the militia *in 1787*, the critical year when our government was being formed. If we wish to discover what one of fifty-five framers, James Madison, thought when he and his colleagues wrote the Constitution, this quotation trumps the others.

6

THE FEDERALIST PAPERS

Myth: *The Federalist Papers* tell us what the Constitution really means.

Educate yourself on the Constitution and the Federalist Papers (which illustrate the original intent of the Founders in drafting the Constitution).

—Save Our Country Now website[1]

In deciding these cases, which I have found closer than I had anticipated, it is *The Federalist* that finally determines my position.

—Supreme Court Justice David Souter, dissenting opinion in
Printz v. the United States (1997)[2]

Kernel of Truth

During the ratification debates, Alexander Hamilton, James Madison, and John Jay penned eighty-five essays under the single pseudonym "Publius," a founder of the Roman Republic. Although authorship for several of these has been disputed, most scholars now agree that Hamilton wrote at least fifty, Madison most of the rest, and Jay only five. In Hamilton's home state of New York, opponents of the proposed Constitution, led by Governor George Clinton, held power, and critics were continually pressing their arguments in New York City's newspapers. Joining the fray as Publius, Hamilton wrote an essay addressed, "To the People of the State of New York," first published in the *Independent Journal* on October 27, 1787, under the heading "The Federalist." In this targeted attempt to change public opinion in New York, Publius promised to give readers a comprehensive explanation and defense of the new federal Constitution, which he compared "to your own State constitution."[3]

To share the writing effort, Hamilton invited John Jay, Gouverneur Morris, and William Duer to write other letters under Publius's name. Morris declined and Jay fell ill after contributing four letters. Hamilton judged Duer's efforts not up to the standard he was trying to set, and he next turned to James Madison, who was in New York at the time representing Virginia in the Confederation Congress. Because Congress rarely met for lack of a quorum, Madison agreed to take part. Like the New Yorkers Hamilton and Jay, Madison addressed his letters "To the People of the State of New York."[4]

Publius's essays, first appearing in newspapers but later published in two bound volumes titled *The Federalist*, treat the Constitution as a multifaceted but cohesive whole, a logically consistent implementation of republican theory. Initially, the essays circulated among supporters of the Constitution and helped them refine their arguments. Once the ratification controversy ended, *The Federalist* had a significant impact on subsequent American jurisprudence and political philosophy, continuing to this day. Commonly viewed as an expansion of the ideas expressed in the Constitution and the most thorough contemporaneous presentation of its philosophical underpinnings, *The Federalist* is regularly assigned to college students; studied by legal and constitutional scholars, historians, and political scientists; and cited frequently in the opinions of Supreme Court justices. *The Federalist* has become the Constitution's Talmud, an explanatory adjunct to scripture.

But . . .

Publius's remarkable essays were effective arguments, not disinterested and authoritative commentaries. These are very different genres, and right from the start, Hamilton made it clear which he intended. In *The Federalist No. 1*, Publius announced without apology that he would offer "arguments" to convince readers that "the safest course for your liberty, your dignity, and your happiness" was to adopt the new plan of government. "Yes, my countrymen, I own to you that, after having given it an attentive consideration, I am clearly of opinion it is your interest to adopt it," he wrote. "I will not amuse you with an appearance of deliberation when I have decided. I frankly acknowledge to you my convictions, and I will freely lay before you the reasons on which they are founded." Hamilton promised he would "not disgrace the cause of truth," but his tone was certainly combative. Many of the Constitution's opponents, he charged, were driven by "perverted ambition," hoping either "to aggrandize themselves by the confusions of their country" or to "divide the empire into several partial confederacies." [5]

James Madison also conceded motive, although in friendlier terms. "The ultimate object of these papers is to determine clearly and fully the merits of this Constitution, and the expediency of adopting it," he wrote in *The Federalist No. 37*, introducing a series of twenty-two consecutive essays under his authorship. Madison argued that he could not explain or defend the Constitution "without taking a more critical and thorough survey of the work of the convention, without examining it on all its sides, comparing it in all its parts, and calculating its probable effects." Madison's "survey" highlighted what he described as the Constitution's balance between federal and state authority, although he himself had pushed for a much stronger national government at the Federal Convention (see chapter 5).

In its historical context, *The Federalist* was a political document— certainly an impressive one, but no more "authoritative" than other attempts by the Constitution's supporters and opponents to persuade contemporaries to vote for or against the Constitution. In pamphlets and newspapers and oral debates, supporters and opponents had at it for the better part of a year. Though the eighty-five *Federalist* essays were part of this grand debate, they were scarcely the whole of it. The State Historical Society of Wisconsin has collected and reproduced these arguments in twenty-two hefty volumes and multiple microform supplements entitled *The Documentary History of the Ratification of the Constitution*. As five of the original thirteen states are not yet covered, editors project six more volumes on ratification and still more on the framing and adoption of the Bill of Rights. *The Federalist* essays fill less than one of these volumes.[6]

Hamilton, Madison, and Jay faced a daunting task. On the one hand, they needed to convince a wary public of the need to create a federal government with "supreme" authority over the states, and they had to gain acceptance for several controversial provisions: a standing army, Congress's power to levy direct taxes, and trusting all executive authority to one man, the president. On the other hand, they could not scare people off by painting the new powers of the federal government in stark colors. They had to push both hard and gently, and to understand *The Federalist* we must view its arguments in this light.

This is not the way *The Federalist* is treated in our national narrative. Instead, despite its conflicting tasks and sometimes contradictory messages, we accept it at face value and enshrine it as a quasi-official founding document. This authority is not warranted. *The Federalist* offers one possible reading of the Constitution offered by exceedingly intelligent writers pushing for ratification, but this is not in some mystical sense the certifiably *authoritative* reading.

The Full Story

Founding-era Americans knew nothing of a work called *The Federalist Papers*. In the winter and spring of 1787–88, as the proposed Constitution was being debated, citizens in New York City, and a few elsewhere, might be found reading newspaper articles under the heading "The Federalist." Mathew Carey's magazine *The American Museum* published a few of the early essays, and a select group of readers had access to the two bound volumes, the first appearing in March 1788 and the second late in May. The initial printing of this now-famous work was only 500 copies, and "several hundred" of these were still unsold in the fall of 1788, after the Constitution had been ratified. Nationally, the readership was exceedingly small.[7]

Eleven years later, unsold books from the first printing were placed back on the market, and in 1802 George F. Hopkins republished *The Federalist* in a new edition, this time naming the authors. After that, once or twice a decade, *The Federalist* was repackaged for a new audience.

The Federalist did not become *The Federalist Papers* until the mid-twentieth century. In 1944, the noted scholar Douglass Adair wrote an article entitled, "The Authorship of the Disputed Federalist Papers." He did not call the entire work *The Federalist Papers*; rather, he used "Federalist" to denote which "papers" he was discussing. Within the text of the article Adair, like all other scholars at the time and most scholars today, referred only to *The Federalist*.[8]

Four years later, perhaps borrowing from the title of Adair's article, the newly established Great Books Foundation, in "Session 16" of its "First Year Course," featured eighteen of the eighty-five "Federalist Papers," followed by the text of the Constitution. (Session 1 included the Declaration of Independence and selections from the Old Testament; Sessions 17 and 18 concluded the course with Adam Smith's *Wealth of Nations* and Karl Marx's *Communist Manifesto*.) The foundation's rebranding was tentative. The title head on each page remained "The Federalist," and each essay was introduced by the name and date of the newspaper in which it first appeared, seeming to justify the word "papers."

In 1961 the New American Library, under its Mentor imprint, picked up on the Great Books Foundation's title and ran with it in its new edition, offering neither explanation nor apology. The title head on its pages said "The Federalist Papers," as did its cover and title page. "Good reading for the millions" was Mentor's slogan, but the editors likely felt that "the millions" might have some trouble with eighty-five ponderous essays written for a very different audience. The original, obscure title only compounded that problem. Was "The Federalist" a person? a political party? a document? a philosophy? The reifying, self-reflexive new title, *The Federalist Papers*, provided clarity and gave the work a physical stamp.[9]

The Mentor edition of *The Federalist Papers* circulated widely, and the name swiftly took hold. To this day, Publius's essays bear the label bequeathed to them by mid-twentieth-century commercial publishers. Try asking a seemingly informed American citizen what *The Federalist* refers to and you will most likely get a blank stare; *The Federalist Papers*, on the other hand, might induce a response—a vague memory of a high school civics class, a reading assignment in college, or possibly a reasonable description of Publius's essays. Even Justice Clarence Thomas, the Supreme Court's ardent originalist who insists on sticking to the historical record in all instances (see chapter 8), refers casually to Publius's essays by a name the authors never knew.[10]

The subtitle as well as the title has changed over time. Here is the title page for volume 1 of the original collection, published by John and Archibald M'Lean of New York in March 1788:

THE

FEDERALIST:

A COLLECTION

OF

ESSAYS,

WRITTEN IN FAVOUR OF

THE NEW CONSTITUTION,

AS AGREED UPON BY THE FEDERAL CONVENTION, SEPTEMBER 17, 1787[11]

In 1802, Hopkins's revised edition condensed the descriptive but bulky original into a neat and tidy version that eliminated any suggestion of argumentation:

THE

FEDERALIST:

ON THE NEW CONSTITUTION

BY PUBLIUS.

Subsequent editions over the next six decades adopted that simplified version, but in 1863 Henry B. Dawson opted to return to the original. A year later John C. Hamilton, the primary author's son, plucked the document from its historical context to sound an entirely different note:

THE

FEDERALIST:

A COMMENTARY

ON THE

CONSTITUTION OF THE UNITED STATES.

A Collection of Essays,

BY

ALEXANDER HAMILTON,

JAY AND MADISON

Without changing a word of the text, Hamilton's son managed to editorialize. Most obviously, he promoted his father over the other authors, but he also lifted *The Federalist* to higher ground. Essays the authors had written "in favour of" the Constitution were now abstracted observations, with no admission of bias. The neutralizing word "commentary," which does not reveal any particular slant, was repeated in later editions—if not on the title page, nearly always in the introduction. In his new presentation, Publius was becoming depoliticized.[12]

Gone as well, in many editions, was the local attribution. In newspapers, where the essays first appeared, each article had opened with the salutation, "To the People of the State of New York," thereby revealing Publius's main focus, ratification in New York. Whereas some editors have chosen to reprint the essays exactly the way they appeared in the original newspapers, others have not.[13]

The general makeover of Publius gave *The Federalist* a more abstract tone, seemingly devoid of political partisanship and with no restrictive setting or milieu. Clinton Rossiter, in his introduction to the New American Library's *Federalist Papers*, waxed poetic. "With sudden bursts of brilliance," he exclaimed, Publius supplied "an exposition of certain enduring truths that provide an understanding of both the dangers and delights of free government." Because these "enduring truths" spoke specifically to the plan of government proposed by the Federal Convention, they could be viewed as "a uniquely authoritative commentary on the Constitution." *The Federalist*, for Rossiter, served double duty, both as a treatise on government and an indispensable aid to deciphering the Constitution. "A particular interpretation of some clause in that document can be given a special flavor of authenticity by a quotation from Publius," he concluded.[14]

Rossiter, a careful scholar, kept Publius securely rooted in political history, even as the author ascended to that higher plane. "Promises, threats, bargains, and face-to-face debates, not eloquent words" determined the outcomes in key states, he noted. Most casual readers, however, lured by the notion of "enduring truths," have allowed Publius to shed completely his political skin. Thus liberated, Publius has transformed all the framers, by proxy, from thinking politicians into political thinkers. In this popular view, the Constitution is a carefully crafted but ultimately pragmatic set of rules, and accordingly sparse, dry, and mechanical. *The Federalist*, by contrast, is full, rich, and philosophical, a perfectly tuned theoretical engine that powers the Constitution. The two documents are intimately related, or so the claim goes, and because they are, *The Federalist*, like the Constitution itself, is sacrosanct.[15]

Some authors, reading history backwards, take their praise one step further. Because Publius explains the Constitution so well, they say, it must have had a significant effect on events at the time. "*The Federalist* is relevant to modern readers who wish to understand the Constitution" because "it performed a vitally important role in the ratification debates," writes Michael Meyerson in *Liberty's Blueprint: How Madison and Hamilton Wrote the Federalist Papers, Defined the Constitution, and Made Democracy Safe for the World*. For this to be true, Publius's writings must have either influenced voters who elected delegates to the ratification conventions or swayed delegates once they were there. Did they?[16]

We know that both the newspaper articles and the bound volumes circulated widely among Federalist leaders. Among the many rave reviews was that of George Washington, who wrote a celebratory letter to Hamilton shortly after ten states had ratified the Constitution:

> As the perusal of political papers under the signature of Publius has afforded me great satisfaction, I shall certainly consider them as claiming a most distinguished place in my library. I have read every performance which has been printed on one side and the other of the great question lately agitated (so far as I have been able to obtain them) and, without an unmeaning compliment, I will say, that I have seen no other so well calculated (in my judgment) to produce conviction on an unbiased Mind, as the *Production* of your *Triumvirate*. When the transient circumstances & fugitive performances which attended this crisis shall have disappeared, that Work will merit the notice of posterity; because in it are candidly and ably discussed the principles of freedom and the topics of government, which will be always interesting to mankind so long as they shall be connected in Civil Society.[17]

But we also know that the Constitution's opponents mocked "the torrent of misplaced words" that "sprung from the deranged brain of *Publius*," and even some Federalists considered the essays too "elaborate" and not "well calculated for the common people."[18]

When the first essays appeared in the New York City press, Federalist leaders tried to disseminate them, with mixed success. Madison sent Washington the first twenty-two essays and asked him to send them to a Richmond newspaper. Washington obliged, but Richmond's *Virginia Independent Chronicle* reprinted only *The Federalist Nos. 1* and *3*. That was the pattern. Publius's first five essays were reprinted in an average of eight papers outside of New York State, but after that out-of-state publication fell off dramatically. After *The Federalist No. 16*, no essays were printed in more than one paper out of state, and following *The Federalist No. 23*, the remaining sixty-two essays never made it across New York's borders at all, except for an excerpt from *The Federalist No. 38* in the *Freeman's Oracle*, published in Exeter, New Hampshire.[19]

By contrast, James Wilson's speech in support of the Constitution, delivered at the State House Yard in Philadelphia eight days after Congress sent the proposed new plan to the states, was reprinted in its entirety in twelve of the thirteen states, appearing in thirty-four newspapers, and in several pamphlets as well, in twenty-seven different cities or towns from Portsmouth to Augusta. Altogether, some 250 essays and articles appeared in newspapers in six states or more, a broader circulation than for any of Publius's pieces except the first, and at least one hundred of these had a decidedly pro-Constitution or anti-Constitution slant. Reprints were customary at that time, but Publius's last seventy essays stand as anomalies, the *least* likely pieces to have appeared in more than one state.[20]

In the battle for public opinion, Publius's newspaper publications enjoyed no special standing. But what about the bound volumes? *The Federalist*, in its book form, did not have the impact on ratification that Thomas Paine's *Common Sense* did on the declaring of American independence. Compare the print runs: at least twenty-five printings in six colonies for *Common Sense*, yielding tens of thousands of copies, versus a single print run of 500 copies for *The Federalist*, with many of these left unsold. One was read in taverns throughout the land and served as a catalyst for the nation's first grand debate, the other was but a small component of the nation's second grand debate and there is no historical evidence indicating it affected the result.[21]

A timeline is instructive. Six states had already voted for ratification before the first volume of collected essays appeared on March 22, 1788. The nation was only three states shy of the number required to place the Constitution in effect. By May 28, when the second volume appeared, Maryland and South Carolina had already ratified, and only one more state was needed. In the remaining states—New Hampshire, Virginia, New York, and North Carolina (Rhode Island did not hold a convention)—delegates had already been selected. Madison's opinions on federalism and the relationships between the three branches or Hamilton's extensive treatment of the presidency and the federal court system carried little weight as citizens cast ballots.[22]

Might the combined volumes, although appearing late in the game, still change minds *at* the conventions? Hamilton and his allies certainly hoped so, and they worked hard to put copies in the hands of delegates to the four remaining conventions—but other backers and critics of the Constitution circulated their writings to the same end. In the final stage of the "paper war," Publius was but one player among many.

Even in New York, we have no evidence that *The Federalist* was a game changer at the state's 1788 ratification convention in Poughkeepsie. Initially, the convention had a strong tilt against the proposed Constitution. Of the sixty-five delegates, forty-six were "decidedly opposed to the constitution," according to the election returns reported in the *New York Journal*. Whereas we might like to imagine that the last-minute arrival of *The Federalist* converted opponents of the Constitution, news of political events in other states actually turned things around. On June 24, delegates learned that New Hampshire had voted for ratification, providing the needed ninth ratification out of thirteen; this meant that the Constitution would take effect as the new form of government for the United States, no matter what New York did. A week later delegates discovered that Virginia, the largest state in the union, had also ratified the Constitution. If New York failed to ratify, it would be virtually on its own, with only Rhode Island and perhaps North Carolina for company. After that, the critical issue was no longer outright acceptance or rejection of the Constitution, but whether to demand a second constitutional convention to consider amendments that would make the Constitution more palatable to the convention's majority, who still opposed it.[23]

While Publius's first eighty-four essays did not address that matter, a widely circulated nineteen-page pamphlet from the pen of *Federalist* contributor John Jay did. Writing under the pseudonym "A Citizen of New-York," Jay argued persuasively that a second convention, colored by the contentious debates over ratification, would be so highly politicized that it could destroy the nation. Noah Webster, a Federalist editor, wrote that Jay's argument was "altogether unanswerable." Another writer stated that Jay's pamphlet "has had a most astonishing influence in converting Antifoederalists, to a knowledge and belief that the New Constitution was their only political salvation." Alexander Hamilton was also impressed with Jay's pamphlet. In fact, when he finally argued against a second convention in his eighty-fifth and concluding *Federalist* essay, he simply directed readers toward Jay: "The reasons assigned in an excellent little pamphlet lately published in this city, are unanswerable to show the utter improbability of assembling a new convention, under circumstances in any degree so favorable to a happy issue, as those in which the late convention met, deliberated, and concluded. I will not repeat the arguments there used, as I presume the production itself has had an extensive circulation. It is certainly well worthy the perusal of every friend to his country." [24]

By any measure, John Jay's *Address* had a greater impact on the New York convention than did the *The Federalist No. 85*, which appeared in the second volume after the elections for delegates and only days before the convention assembled, and which did not appear in any newspapers until mid-August, weeks after New York had ratified the Constitution. In the final analysis, though, the outcome was more the result of external events and the subsequent maneuverings of the delegates, Hamilton and Jay included. To win votes from delegates opposing the Constitution, Federalists agreed to issue a call for a second convention—but only *after* ratification. It was a strictly political solution and Publius's essays had no hand in it. When modern writers suggest that without Publius "it is possible, perhaps even likely, that New Yorkers would have rejected the Constitution," they engage in after-the-fact musings unsupported by historical evidence. [25]

During the heat of the ratification debates, Americans viewed *The Federalist* for what it declared itself to be, an extensive argument in favor of the Constitution. The Constitution's opponents would have recoiled at the notion that essays springing "from the deranged brain of *Publius*" someday would be deemed "authoritative commentaries" and invoked by Supreme Court justices in determining positions on constitutional law. Could they speak their minds today, and had they known who Publius really was, they would remind us that the lead author, Alexander Hamilton, was known to have taken controversial positions very unlike those he posited as Publius.[26]

Hamilton's ideas were so extreme that other delegates to the Federal Convention refused even to consider them. On June 18, holding the floor for a full day, he had voiced a preference for monarchy and for "extinguishing" the existing state governments and turning them into "subordinate authorities" or "district tribunals" to serve "local purposes." It was a shocking speech, and when the Convention ignored him, and when he was consistently outvoted by New York's other two delegates, he simply left.

Returning later in the summer, Hamilton begrudgingly accepted the Convention's weaker version of a national government and determined to promote ratification. Even so, at the close of the Convention, he entertained some hope that the Constitution would serve as a first step toward greater consolidation. If the Constitution were approved, he conjectured, George Washington would likely serve as the first president, Washington would govern well, and this might set in motion what he viewed as a positive train of events: "A good administration will conciliate the confidence and affection of the people, and perhaps enable the government to acquire more consistency than the proposed constitution seems to promise for so great a country. It may then triumph altogether over the State governments, and reduce them to an entire subordination, dividing the larger States into smaller districts. The organs of the general government may also acquire additional strength." Knowing that the American public at the time feared central government and the concentration of authority, however, Hamilton did not express this view in public. Instead, he co-created Publius, who would heap lavish praise on the proposed federal government, arguing that it posed no threat to state sovereignty.[27]

As any good lawyer would do, Hamilton, when writing as Publius, argued the case he was given, even though it was not the case he would have preferred. In his Convention speech, he had proclaimed that "the British Government was the best in the world, and that he doubted much whether any thing short of it would do in America." In particular, he said the president "ought to be hereditary, and to have so much power, that it will not be his interest to risk much to acquire more." Yet in *The Federalist No. 69*, he boasted there was a "total dissimilitude" between the American president and the "King of Great-Britain, who is an hereditary monarch."

Then, he wanted to give the chief executive an absolute "*negative* upon all laws about to be passed." Now, he boasted proudly that "the qualified negative of the president" in the new Constitution "differs widely from this absolute negative of the British sovereign."

Then, he wanted "the Militia of all the states to be under the sole and exclusive direction" of the United States and its commander in chief, not occasionally, but always. Now, in *The Federalist*, he assured the public that the president "will have only occasional command" of state militias.[28]

And so it went. In his notes for the June 18 Convention speech, he had revealed a deep disregard for republican ideals. "It is said a republican government does not admit a vigorous execution," he jotted down. "It [republican government] is therefore bad; for the goodness of a government consists in a vigorous execution." Yet now he told Americans they need not worry because the Constitution insisted the president must act within a republican framework.[29]

Such reversals were and are common among political figures, part and parcel of the democratic process. Though derided today as "flip-flops," they demonstrate that politicians are responding to public opinion, as Hamilton was doing in *The Federalist*. Although we should not be surprised that key founders, who were engaging in a political process, altered their pronouncements to suit different circumstances, this does present an interpretative problem. Any vacillation discredits the custom of treating everything a founder said, whatever the context, as the final word. We cannot say, "Hamilton believed in republicanism" or "Hamilton believed in limiting the powers of the executive" because he said so in *The Federalist*.

When constructing his arguments for *The Federalist*, Hamilton on occasion engaged in willful misrepresentation. In *The Federalist No. 68* he addressed the matter of presidential selection. The Constitution stipulated that state legislatures "shall appoint" special sets of electors "in such Manner" as they please; they could allow the people to vote on electors if they so desired, but they were under no obligation to do so. Once chosen, these electors would select the president. Hamilton, however, thought the Constitution would be an easier sell if it inserted people directly into the electoral mechanism. Since "it was desirable that *the sense of the people* should operate in the choice of the person to whom so important a trust was to be confided," he wrote, the framers "referred it in the first instance to an *immediate act of the people*," who would select their "agents in the election." The emphases are mine but the repetition his. Over and over Hamilton made populist arguments, setting up a false front: "The executive should be independent for his continuance in office on all but *the people themselves*." From there it was only one small step to factual misrepresentation, and Hamilton did not hesitate to take it: "*The people of each state* shall choose a number of persons as electors," he wrote flatly, although that simply was not so.[30]

This was no incidental error. In *The Federalist No. 60* Hamilton wrote that the president would be selected "by electors chosen for that purpose by the people." In *The Federalist No. 77* he stated again that presidential electors were "immediately chosen by the people," although that was nowhere stated in the Constitution. And in *The Federalist No. 69* he said point-blank, "The President of the United States would be an officer elected by the people for four years," leaving the electors entirely out of the process. This was hardly the intent of the framers. At the convention they had voted repeatedly and overwhelmingly against James Wilson's attempts to select the president by popular vote, and they had instituted the strange new institution we call today the Electoral College specifically to sidestep that democratic process. In *The Federalist*, however, Hamilton pretended otherwise, as if Wilson had prevailed.[31]

The pretense wore thin, for Hamilton was a most unlikely proponent of popular elections. In the notes he prepared for his speech to the Convention on June 18, he had commented on "the unreasonableness of the people" and stated that government should be "capable of resisting the popular current." A prime function of the president was to keep the people in check, he had said back then, but now he was calling the president the people's own. His opponents saw through this sudden turnabout. When Hamilton expressed populist views on the subject of representation in Congress at New York's ratification convention—"in the general course of things," he said there, "the popular views and even prejudices will direct the actions of the rulers"—Charles Tillinghast, an opponent of the Constitution, reported to John Lamb, "You would be surprised . . . what an *amazing Republican* Hamilton wishes to make himself be considered—*But he is known.*" [32]

Some scholars, after noting "errors" in Publius's exposition of the Constitution, pass them off casually. Although Hamilton, Madison, and Jay "wrote quickly," explains Gregory Maggs, professor of law at George Washington University, "we now forgive the errors because they worked in haste." Such missteps, Maggs contends, do not affect reliability: "While they may have made errors or produced incomplete analyses, the *Federalist Papers* still generally may show the original meaning of the Constitution." It's a strange argument. The lowest hurdle an "authoritative" source must clear is accuracy. Working too quickly makes a better argument against reliability than for it. [33]

Although some of Publius's errors—misstating the quorum requirements for the Senate in *The Federalist No. 59*, miscounting the members of the first Congress in *The Federalist No. 84*, and falsely describing the runoff election of the vice president in *The Federalist No. 68*—might have been unintentional, stating that election of the president was "an immediate act of the people" and that "the people of each state" were authorized to choose presidential electors, when the Constitution did not say these things, was either extremely sloppy or purposive. The issue of presidential selection spoke to the heart of the relationship between the people and their rulers, not a matter to be taken lightly and one that Hamilton addressed on many occasions. This was no casual mistake. [34]

In Hamilton's defense, one so-called error in *The Federalist* has been falsely categorized. The Constitution states clearly that presidential appointments for key offices must be accompanied by "the Advice and Consent" of the Senate, but it says nothing about Senate approval in case of a *dismissal* from office. Hamilton, writing as Publius in *The Federalist No. 77*, gave his rendering of the document's intent: "The consent of that body [the Senate] would be necessary to displace as well as to appoint. A change of the Chief Magistrate, therefore, would not occasion so violent or so general a revolution in the officers of the government as might be expected, if he were the sole disposer of offices."

According to Clinton Rossiter and other commentators, Hamilton was mistaken "in assigning the Senate a share of the power of removal." Rossiter forgives him for this, however; although Publius was "understandably wrong in his interpretation of some details in the Constitution," these details can be overlooked because he was "remarkably right about many more." From our vantage point today, Hamilton does appear to be off base, but because the Constitution provided no direction, his interpretation was neither correct nor incorrect in the technical sense. It only became "wrong" the following year when Congress, after an extensive debate that lasted several days, declared that the president could remove an official on his own authority.[35]

Why did Hamilton bother to raise the issue at all, since the Constitution did not? And why would this known proponent of unitary executive authority argue that the president needed to seek approval from the Senate before removing an official? These questions have long troubled some commentators, who have even given the problem its own name: "The Puzzle of Hamilton's Federalist No. 77." [36]

This puzzle is easy to solve. Only if we insist that Hamilton's views, expressed on various occasions to different audiences, must remain logically consistent do we face a problem at all. As soon as we treat *The Federalist No. 77* in its political context the apparent contradictions disappear.

Here is the backstory.

At the Federal Convention, the Committee of Detail's working draft of the Constitution granted the Senate, not the president, authority to appoint ambassadors, Supreme Court justices, and other key officials. On September 4, less than two weeks before adjournment, the Committee of Eleven transferred appointive powers to the president, with the Senate's assent. Eager to be done after meeting for more than three months, delegates agreed to the committee's proposal, but in their haste they did not think to indicate whether dismissal required Senate approval.

When Hamilton penned *The Federalist No. 77* more than half a year later, he had had plenty of time to ponder the document, its weaknesses as well as its strengths. It would have been unlikely at that point for him *not* to notice that the question of removal was subject to competing interpretations: the president could dismiss officials on his own authority, as was eventually the case, or he would need approval from the Senate, as he argued in *The*

Federalist No. 77. To defend the first of these would be a political liability, feeding fears that the president was a thinly disguised monarch who could control lesser officials through intimidation. To alleviate suspicions, therefore, Hamilton proclaimed that the Senate would have to be involved in any dismissals. This safeguard against presidential abuse would make the Constitution appear more acceptable.[37]

The following year, when members of the first House of Representatives tried to create a Department of Foreign Affairs, they found themselves face-to-face with the Constitution's silence. Should the secretary of that department be "removable from office by the President of the United States"? Some argued that if the president could not remove his inferior officers, they would in fact become more powerful than he was; others feared presidential overreach and insisted on Senate participation. During this debate, William Loughton Smith, to support the view that the Senate must be involved, quoted Publius's words from *The Federalist*, which he called "a publication of no inconsiderable eminence, in the class of political writings on the constitution." This created something of a problem for Hamilton, who was not present at the time but who heard that his words were being used to curb presidential authority, contrary to his actual beliefs. Immediately he tried to limit the damage. He sent word to his friends in Congress that since penning *The Federalist No. 77*, "upon more mature reflection he had changed his opinion & was now convinced that the President alone should have the power of removal at pleasure." Had he really changed his opinion, or was he just adjusting his stance due to political contingencies? That does not matter. What counts is that he pushed for executive power during the Convention, then he retreated during the ratification debates to paint the Constitution in its least threatening light, and finally, when he was about to assume an office in Washington's administration, he favored granting the president the exclusive authority of removal. The story makes perfect political sense, no puzzle about it.[38]

A story featuring *The Federalist No. 83* follows a similar pattern. In that essay, Hamilton tried to alleviate fears that the Constitution would eliminate jury trials in civil cases. Not so, he said. True, it "established the trial by jury in criminal cases" while remaining "silent in respect to civil," but that did not mean there was an "implied prohibition" against jury trials in civil cases.

In fact, he argued, the Constitution allowed no such thing as implied prohibitions or implied powers. What the document said, it said; where it was silent, nothing could be inferred or assumed. To support this view, he argued that by giving an "affirmative grant" of specified powers to Congress in Section 1, Article 8, the Constitution actually limited Congress's authority to those enumerated cases. Logically, the listing of special powers "would be absurd as well as useless if a general authority was intended." If a power was not listed, Congress simply didn't have it.[39]

Whereas this argument might appear legalistic to us, it was important at the time. Many people worried that the Constitution, if construed loosely, could give the government unbounded power, so both Hamilton and Madison offered assurance that it would not do so. The "jurisdiction" of the federal government was "limited to certain enumerated objects," Madison said in *The Federalist No. 14*. He repeated this thought in *The Federalist No. 39*, and in *The Federalist No. 45* he calmed his readers once again by stating, "The powers delegated by the proposed Constitution to the federal government are few and defined" (see chapter 5). Hamilton, in *The Federalist No. 83*, was reinforcing this critical theme. The Constitution must be interpreted strictly, both authors proclaimed. They had to say this, for if people believed the Constitution permitted an indefinite expansion of governmental powers, they never would ratify it.

Once the Constitution was ratified, though, Hamilton shifted his tone. In December 1790, as Washington's secretary of the treasury, he proposed a national bank, funded and directed primarily by private investors but receiving up to 20 percent of its capitalization from the federal government. But where, exactly, did the United States Constitution authorize such an arrangement? The first clause of Article I, Section 8, empowered Congress to levy taxes and pay debts, and the second clause of that section permitted Congress to borrow money, yet there was no mention of chartering banks, which had been a province of the states, and the Constitution certainly did not stipulate that one group of private investors could acquire special standing in federal law (see chapter 4).

Hamilton argued that the lack of a specific grant of power to charter banks did not preclude such an action. Congress was authorized to borrow money and pay debts, and in a broader sense it was charged with keeping the nation financially afloat. If a bank could help perform these functions, it was constitutional. Congress therefore had an implied power to charter a bank, and "implied powers are to be considered as delegated equally with express ones"—quite the opposite of what he had argued in *The Federalist No. 83*.[40]

Technically, Hamilton could claim there was no contradiction; instead of adding a new power, chartering a bank was merely a means of executing a stipulated one. (This was in keeping with a position he had taken in *The Federalist No. 33* when supporting the "necessary and proper" clause: "What is the ability to do a thing but the power of employing the *means* necessary to its execution?") In tone and spirit, though, the two views worked at cross-purposes. In *The Federalist No. 83*, he argued for a strict interpretation that would limit governmental authority; in the bank debate, he argued for a broad interpretation that would allow the federal government to engage in any activity that Congress, on its own authority, claimed would further a stipulated end. Imagine if Hamilton had declared in *The Federalist* that "implied powers are to be considered as delegated equally with express ones." That open-ended interpretation would have put people off, so he dared not present it until the Constitution had been ratified.[41]

Whereas Hamilton's primary task in *The Federalist* was to demonstrate the need for a strong and unified government, his secondary task was to assure readers that the new government would not be *too* strong. The president bore no resemblance to a king. The people would elect him and could thereby control him. He would not possess the power to dismiss officeholders without senatorial approval. Congress, meanwhile, would be strictly restrained from venturing beyond the limits of its mandate, as specified in precise terms within Article I, Section 8. In every instance, the authority of the central government and the man chosen by the people to lead it would be narrowly circumscribed. Such safeguards prevented abuses of power.

It was in this vein that Hamilton argued in *The Federalist No. 75* that the president did not have exclusive authority in foreign relations. "Foreign negotiations" were neither executive nor legislative in nature, he said, so they must be shared. It was "utterly unsafe and improper . . . to commit interests of so delicate and momentous a kind, as those which concern its intercourse with the rest of the world, to the sole disposal of a magistrate created and circumstanced as would be a President of the United States."

Five years later, however, in 1793, Hamilton argued differently. Revolutionary France and Great Britain were at war, and President Washington issued an executive proclamation pledging that the United States would "pursue a conduct friendly and impartial toward the belligerent powers." Further, he prohibited American citizens from engaging in any "acts and proceedings whatsoever, which may in any manner tend to contravene such disposition," and he promised to prosecute anyone who aided or abetted the hostile actions of either power. People who had hoped to send aid to France protested that the president had no constitutional authority to take such actions, but Hamilton maintained he did. Adopting the pen name "Pacificus," he wrote a series of essays published by the proadministration *Gazette of the United States*. The executive department was "the *organ* of intercourse between the Nation and foreign Nations" and "the interpreter of the National Treaties," he declared, and the opening of the Constitution's Article II— "The executive power shall be vested in the President"—made it clear that executive authority, when not specifically delegated elsewhere, resided in the presidency. If the president decided to pursue a policy of neutrality, he had every right to issue a proclamation to that effect and require Americans to live up to it.[42]

Which is the "real" Alexander Hamilton? If we wish to quote this particular founder's views on the powers of the executive, do we say that he favored presidential control over "foreign negotiations" or that he felt it was "utterly unsafe and improper" to give "the president alone" the authority to engage in "intercourse with the rest of the world"? James Madison noted the contradiction. Writing as "Helvidius," Madison rebutted Pacificus by quoting Hamilton's very own words from *The Federalist No. 75*: "Tho' several writers on the subject of government place that power (of *making treaties*) in the class of *Executive authorities*, yet this is *evidently* an *arbitrary disposition*." So said Hamilton, writing as Publius, in 1788; but by 1793, as Pacificus, he had become one of those authorities making this "arbitrary disposition."[43]

Given Hamilton's inconsistencies, which reflect in great measure the turbulent and fast-changing conditions of constitutional politics in the early republic, we cannot treat his writings as Publius as *the* authoritative source on the precise meaning of the Constitution without saying that the *other* Alexander Hamilton, the one who helped write the Constitution in the summer of 1787 and who took the lead within Washington's first cabinet in the early 1790s, was at best mistaken in several of his interpretations.

On January 24, 2011, Supreme Court Justice Antonin Scalia told a seminar organized by the Congressional Tea Party Caucus that each attendee should "get a copy of *The Federalist Papers*, read it, underline it and dog-ear it." Scalia has not been Publius's only fan on the High Court. In a dissenting opinion in *Printz v. the United States* (1997), Justice David Souter, a frequent opponent of Scalia, wrote, "In deciding these cases, which I have found closer than I had anticipated, it is *The Federalist* that finally determines my position. I believe that the most straightforward reading of No. 27 is authority for the Government's position here, and that this reading is both supported by No. 44 and consistent with Nos. 36 and 45." Not to be outdone by Souter, Justice Scalia cited *The Federalist Nos. 15, 20, 27, 28, 33, 36, 39, 44, 45, 51*, and *70*.[44]

The competing aims of Publius—presenting the case for a truly national government with extensive powers while simultaneously alleviating people's fears by emphasizing constitutional limitations on federal power—secured *The Federalist* an enduring role in American jurisprudence and political culture. Starting in the 1790s, Americans debating the Constitution referred to Publius to add heft to their arguments. From the disputes over the National Bank and Jay's Treaty to the struggles over control of the judiciary in the early nineteenth century to the state-sovereignty issues that defined the politics of slavery up to the Civil War, advocates on opposing sides in great national debates invoked passages in *The Federalist* that supported their views.[45]

The intimate relationship between Supreme Court justices and *The Federalist* started back in 1798 when Justice Samuel Chase compared Publius favorably to Sir William Blackstone and Richard Wooddeson, leading jurists of eighteenth-century Britain. He praised "the author of *the Federalist*, who I esteem superior to both, for his extensive and accurate knowledge of the *true principles of Government*." Lawyers and jurists citing *The Federalist* included the plaintiff's attorney in the landmark case of *Marbury v. Madison* (1803), Justice William Johnson in his dissent in *Fletcher v. Peck* (1810), and Chief Justice John Marshall in his majority opinion in *McCulloch v. Maryland* (1819). In *Cohens v. Virginia* (1821), Marshall gave *The Federalist* a glowing review: "It is a complete commentary on our constitution; and is appealed to by all parties in the questions to which that instrument has given birth. Its intrinsic merit entitles it to this high rank, and the part two of its authors performed in framing the constitution, put it very much in their power to explain the views with which it was framed."

Supreme Court references to Publius or *The Federalist* continued through the nineteenth century and accelerated in the twentieth. From the 1930s to the end of the century, citations of *The Federalist* (and in later years, *The Federalist Papers*) doubled every twenty to thirty years. Legal scholars, following the High Court's lead, have dissected Publius's views in more than 9,700 articles. Meanwhile, his words have become part of the political vernacular. During the Supreme Court nomination proceedings for Chief Justice John Roberts and Associate Justice Samuel Alito, the nominees and examining senators cited *The Federalist* eleven times.[46]

Judges, attorneys, political figures, and even bloggers will continue to cite *The Federalist* as long as the practice produces any rhetorical leverage. On the Supreme Court, as justices struggle to establish legitimacy by alleging historical authenticity, if one justice cites Publius, others who disagree with his or her opinion feel compelled to countercite. According to a survey of recent Supreme Court cases, "The relative odds of citing a Federalist Paper in majority opinion are sixteen and twenty-fold higher if a dissenting or concurring opinion also cited the Federalist Papers." Given that unilateral disarmament does not appear to be an option, all it takes is a single fan of Publius on the Court to continue the war for *The Federalist*.[47]

Whereas Publius has reigned supreme as the nation's authoritative commenter on the Constitution, historians and legal scholars in recent years have paid more attention to the political purpose of his essays. The "overriding imperative" of authors on both sides of the ratification debates was "to determine whether the Constitution would be adopted, not to formulate definitive interpretations of its individual clauses," wrote Jack Rakove in 1996. Naturally, these scholars began to ask: by what authority can *The Federalist*, an avowedly biased tract, lay claim to the privileged status it has enjoyed for two centuries?[48]

Several justifications have been posited.

Some say its iconic status is reason enough. It is so celebrated, so revered, that we find it "simply unthinkable" that courts could ignore it. But this reasoning is clearly circular: *The Federalist* is authoritative because we have claimed it to be so.[49]

Some say it provides insights into the "legislative history" of the Constitution because its two leading authors figured prominently at the Convention. But Madison and Hamilton were only two of fifty-five framers, and they both defended views in *The Federalist* that differed markedly from those they had expressed at the Federal Convention. (For Madison's contradictory positions, see chapter 5.) Further, if we really wish to know about the Convention, Madison's extensive transcriptions of the debates constitute a far better source.

Some say *The Federalist* provides insights into the legislative history of the ratification conventions, which made the actual decisions to adopt the Constitution, but we have no historical evidence suggesting that the essays influenced outcomes in any convention.

Some, including Justice Scalia, say that Publius helps us understand how words and arguments were construed at the time, thereby revealing "how the text of the Constitution was originally understood." This may be true, but why pay such attention to a single document and so little to all the other writings of the time, penned by the Constitution's opponents as well as its supporters, that could similarly disclose how contemporaries used words and understood the constitutional text? Scalia demonstrates that *The Federalist* can be historically useful, but he stops far short of proving it is authoritative.[50]

Perhaps the most common argument, made implicitly more frequently than explicitly, is that the authors were wise and brilliant men who took the time to think more deeply about the Constitution than anybody else. But if Hamilton was indeed wise and brilliant, when exactly was that so? When he penned his essays as Publius or when he was touting a stronger, more centralized government both before and after that time? And when was Madison so brilliant? While advocating a sweeping national veto of state laws at the Federal Convention, while stating that federal powers were "few and de-fined" in *The Federalist*, or while claiming a state's right to "interpose" and declare federal law "no further valid" a decade later? (See chapter 5.) Both Hamilton and Madison displayed brilliance in their various political incarna-tions, but brilliance and authoritativeness are not synonymous. The former can be fickle, the latter not.[51]

Where, then, does that leave us? Although the purposive intent of *The Federalist*—securing ratification—skews the text and undermines its reli-ability as an authoritative source for interpreting the Constitution, this po-litical function augments rather than diminishes its historical significance. Precisely because the essays were geared to persuade a broad public, they tell us much more than a merely abstract treatise on government possibly could. The authors confronted strong opposition, and we have much to gain by observing the ways they tried to win it over.[52]

The Federalist is instructive on another level. Even though it does not "explicate" the Constitution, it reflects competing strains within that docu-ment. It is no accident that in the hotly contested constitutional debates of the early republic, advocates of opposing positions—strict versus loose con-struction of the "necessary and proper" clause, national supremacy versus state sovereignty—found support from Publius. Until the 1840 publication of Madison's *Notes of Debates in the Federal Convention of 1787*, which shed light on the framers' arguments and decisions, Americans had direct access only to limited and fragmentary accounts of the Convention's proceedings and settled for Publius instead. Historically, we see in the many citations of *The Federalist* how Americans have *always* posited rival interpretations of the Constitution. We learn questions, not answers.

The Federalist reveals much, but it is not conclusive. It does not tell us what the framers of the Constitution really meant in any given passage or what those who ratified the Constitution thought that passage meant. To dis-cover the intent of the framers, if indeed that is ever possible (see chapter 8), we would do better to examine Madison's *Notes of Debates in the Federal Convention*. To discover what the Constitution meant to those who actually voted on ratification, we should look directly at the proceedings of the state conventions, where the document was debated item by item. Those pro-ceedings enjoy a level of authority that *The Federalist* cannot possibly claim.

In Madison's words, delegates to the state conventions, elected by the people and responsible to them, gave the Constitution "all the authority which it possesses."[53]

In a like manner, both the Declaration of Independence and the Constitution, often compared to *The Federalist*, were produced by full bodies of delegates, chosen by other public bodies that in turn were elected by the people. *The Federalist*, by contrast, is the work of three men acting on their own, sanctioned by no one, and without official standing.[54]

Accepting *The Federalist* as a definitive guide to the Constitution fosters three ancillary mythologies. First, it assumes that the various provisions within the Constitution fit together seamlessly, and Publius can tell us exactly how. Second, it masks the real-life drama of the nation's founding. The Constitution was forged through horse trading. Hamilton, Madison, and Jay could not fully acknowledge this blunt truth, particularly with respect to issues surrounding slavery.[55]

Finally, it mimics biblical exegesis. Citing *The Federalist* can be "the secular equivalent to citing the Bible," writes constitutional scholar Melvyn R. Durchslag. Appealing "to a higher and more revered authority" establishes both "an ethos of objectivity" and "the perception of infallibility." In fact, there is *no* objective and infallible authority on the Constitution, and the very act of pretending there is limits inquiry and distorts results. Veneration encourages a cheap form of reasoning: take a preconceived stance, then find quotations from a supreme authority that appear to support it. Anybody from a Supreme Court justice to a partisan blogger can mine the approximately 200,000 words of *The Federalist* for what seem like supporting quotations and let the matter rest there.[56]

People do this. By studying over three hundred Supreme Court cases in which justices cited *The Federalist* in their decisions, Professor Durchslag has shown that "it is hard to come up with more than a small handful of cases where *The Federalist* even arguably played a decisive role in the Court's decision." From this research Durchslag concludes that "it is difficult to assert that the apparent influence of *The Federalist Papers* has matched their rhetorical use." Publius did not change minds but reinforced opinions that were already formed.[57]

This process is replicated outside the judicial system, although not always with the finesse displayed by Supreme Court justices and their talented clerks. The pregnant prose and extensive reasoning in *The Federalist* provide fertile ground for those who wish to enlist the founders in the service of a political agenda but who find the nation's actual founding documents lacking. One partisan website, to justify its various positions, cites *The Federalist Papers* thirty-one times but the Constitution not once.[58]

In 2010 Joshua Charles, a college senior, "translated" *The Federalist* to make it more accessible to the modern reader. Charles presented his project to radio and TV host Glenn Beck, who added some commentary, and the two teamed up to create a runaway bestseller, *The Original Argument: The Federalists' Case for the Constitution, Adapted for the 21st Century*. The "Original Quote" these translators selected for *The Federalist No. 1* says: "The subject speaks its own importance; comprehending in its consequences nothing less than the existence of the UNION, the safety and welfare of the parts of which it is composed, the fate of an empire in many respects the most interesting in the world." The takeaway "message" from this passage, according to Beck and Charles, is: "America is special because our rights come from God, but those rights must be protected by a central government that serves the people." In fact, God made no appearance in *The Federalist No. 1*, and in the same essay Hamilton actually warned against taking the issue of "rights" too far. "The specious mask of zeal for the rights of the people," he wrote, was "dangerous" and "a much more certain road to the introduction of despotism" than a "zeal for the firmness and efficiency in government." What counts for Beck and Charles is not what Publius actually said but the mere fact that they cite him.[59]

Proponents of strict construction and states' rights commonly cite passages from *The Federalist* that were intended to alleviate fears of federal power, and these account in no small measure for Publius's political popularity today. On "Publius-Huldah's Blog: Understanding the Constitution," in a section titled "Why States Must Nullify Unconstitutional Acts of Congress: Instructions from Hamilton, Madison, and Jefferson," the blogger turns to citations from Publius. If "the States have the Right and the Duty to nullify unconstitutional acts of Congress," they can nullify President Obama's Affordable Care Act. "Since the Federalist Papers are the most authoritative commentary on the true meaning of the Constitution," writes the blogger, "let us see what those Papers say about the extent of Congress' legislative powers." Then come the phrases so often repeated from Madison's *The Federalist Nos. 39 and 45* and Hamilton's *The Federalist No. 83*: "national . . . jurisdiction extends to certain enumerated objects only"; "the powers delegated by the proposed Constitution to the federal government are few and defined"; "an affirmative grant of special powers would be absurd as well as useless if a general authority was intended." Not mentioned are Madison's sponsorship of sweeping federal powers or Hamilton's radically nationalist position at the Federal Convention, nor Hamilton's endorsement of a loose construction of the Constitution through the 1790s, a philosophy now labeled "Hamiltonian."[60]

When we play "*The Federalist Papers*" game—extracting the essays from their historical context, mining short passages and treating them as gospel—we inadvertently echo Publius. Like him, we do not explore in a disinterested fashion the textual subtleties of the United States Constitution; rather, we argue a case, as he did, and as we do, we compound his politicization of our founding document.

Instead of adopting a deferential posture that only masks self-interest, perhaps we should follow the lead of Chief Justice Marshall, certainly a great admirer of Publius, as noted above. His majority opinion in *McCulloch v. Maryland* sported fine praise, but it was tempered by an essential caveat:

> In the course of the argument, the Federalist has been quoted; and the opinions expressed by the authors of that work have been justly supposed to be entitled to great respect in expounding the constitution. No tribute can be paid to them which exceeds their merit; but in applying their opinions to the cases which may arise in the progress of our government, a right to judge of their correctness must be retained.[61]

7

"BILL OF RIGHTS"

Myth: The Founding Fathers gave us the Bill of Rights.

"God gave us the Bill of Rights"—2 votes
"The founding fathers gave us the Bill of Rights"—59 votes
—Internet poll from sodahead.com[1]

"Who was the author of the Bill of Rights?"
"Answer: James Madison was the author of the Bill of Rights."
—WikiAnswers[2]

The Bill of Rights . . . comes as close to a libertarian founding legal charter as any in the world. . . . In an America with a full respect for the Bill of Rights, there would be . . . no Food and Drug Administration harassment of pharmaceutical and wine producers . . . no laws disarming Americans, prohibiting airlines from allowing pilots or passengers to carry guns on planes, or limiting how much ammo or what kind of firearms people can buy and own . . . no federal programs not authorized by the Constitution . . . no Departments of Energy or Education, no Medicare or Social Security.
—Anthony Gregory, writing for LewRockwell.com[3]

Kernel of Truth

Revolutionary-era Americans were proud inheritors of a British legal tradition that guarded against governmental abuse. In 1689, almost a century before the Federal Convention, the English Bill of Rights, "vindicating and asserting their ancient rights and liberties," placed precise limits on monarchical power. The Crown, it declared, could not suspend laws, tax the people, or "raise and keep a standing army within the kingdom in times of peace" without the consent of representatives in Parliament. Further, it affirmed English subjects' rights to free elections, to petition, and to jury trials, while it prohibited "excessive bail" and "cruel and unusual punishment."[4]

In the 1760s and '70s, British colonists on the North American mainland believed that not just the Crown but Parliament threatened some of these rights. In 1776, invoking the "social contract" theory of government developed by such philosophers of the European Enlightenment as John Locke, they dissolved the bond between themselves and Great Britain. Because men form governments to secure their "unalienable rights," the Declaration of Independence stated, the people had a right "to alter or abolish" their government when it became "destructive of these ends."

Americans expected their new state constitutions, which supplanted their old colonial charters, to secure the people's rights. Seven of the eleven states that drafted new constitutions prefaced them with detailed declarations of rights, and the remaining four embedded various rights within the bodies of their governing rules. Americans of that era cherished their rights dearly and protected them closely, as we do today.[5]

But . . .

The Constitution of the United States, drafted in 1787 and ratified in 1788, did not follow the precedent set by these state constitutions. Despite spending almost four months drafting their new plan, the framers did not include within it a thoughtful listing of rights but only a scattering of guarantees. On September 12, just five days before the end of the Convention, George Mason finally suggested that delegates add a "Bill of Rights" similar to the state declarations of rights, but his motion failed to garner the support of a single state delegation.

Although state conventions ratified the Constitution, several included a caveat: the new plan should be amended as soon as possible. In fact, they proposed scores of amendments, some resembling provisions of what we now know as the Bill of Rights, but many others altering or even deleting structural features of the Constitution. New York's convention coupled its list of proposed amendments with a demand for a second federal convention to consider these various proposals. The profusion of proposed

amendments, plus the prospect of a second convention, frightened supporters of the Constitution, who feared that a new convention, if it met, would
revise the fledgling Constitution before it could be put into effect and gut
some of its major provisions.

Most leading Federalists hunkered down. In arguing against a second
federal convention, they insisted that a bill of rights was not necessary and
could even jeopardize rights that were not included. The job of the Constitution, they said, was to state what government *could* do, not what it *couldn't*
do. Rights already were secured because the government possessed no power
that allowed it to impinge upon them. In fact, any catalog of specified rights
would imply that rights were limited to those in the catalog, and not others.

James Madison and George Washington agreed with this argument, but
they also took an accurate measure of people's displeasure. It was strong
and it was widespread. Rather than fight a rearguard action against the wave
of discontent, they preferred to channel and control it. Article V of the Constitution stipulated that either Congress or state conventions might propose
amendments. If Congress acted first, Madison and Washington reasoned, it
could take charge of the issue and protect the substantive features of the
new plan—congressional taxation, for instance—while giving ground elsewhere. Madison, meanwhile, pledged to his Virginia constituents that he
would work to add a bill of rights if they elected him to represent them in
Congress.

Once elected, in the First Federal Congress, Madison whittled down the
large list of amendments suggested by the states' ratifying conventions.
With President Washington's blessing, he proposed nineteen that did not
endanger key constitutional components. After considerable debate and
some revision, Congress pared Madison's list down to twelve amendments,
which it sent to the states for approval. Ten of these, which we call today the
Bill of Rights, were ratified by three-quarters of the states, as required by
the new Constitution. The genesis of the Bill of Rights, like the origins of
the Constitution, was political as well as theoretical.

The short-term effect of the framing and ratification of the Bill of Rights
was to put a Federalist stamp on the amendments and to doom the attempts
by the Constitution's opponents to modify the substantive or structural
features of the new plan. The long-term effect was to reinforce America's

culture of rights and to infuse specific rights into American jurisprudence. After more than two centuries, the Bill of Rights, which had been so casually dismissed by the framers, figures so prominently in our minds that it often eclipses the Constitution itself. In an era when the word "government" has a bad name, the ten amendments that circumscribe the federal government's authority over individuals are often viewed more favorably than the Constitution the framers created in 1787.

The Full Story

Anglo Americans have always embraced a culture of rights. The first colonial charter, granted to the founders of Virginia in 1606, promised that people who immigrated to America would "have and enjoy all liberties, franchises, and immunities . . . as if they had been abiding and born, within this our realm of England." In several other colonies, either the Crown or the colonial proprietors specified liberties that the government was duty bound to respect. In Maryland, Massachusetts, and New York, the people, acting through their representatives in the legislatures, passed laws foreshadowing the Bill of Rights.[6]

In 1641, in the Massachusetts Body of Liberties, the people of that colony listed ninety-eight specific rights they were entitled to enjoy. Number 45, for example, stated: "No man shall be forced by Torture to confesse any Crime against himselfe nor any other unlesse it be in some Capitall case where he is first fullie convicted by cleare and suffitient evidence to be guilty." Other protections were afforded to those accused of crimes, including bail, legal representation, presentation of evidence, a speedy trial by jury, appeal to a higher court, security against double jeopardy, and a prohibition against "bodilie punishments" that are "inhumane Barbarous or cruel." (This limitation meant no more than forty lashes, "unles his crime be very shamefull.")

The guarantees did not end there. Foreigners escaping persecution were to be welcomed. Monopolies were prohibited. No man could be pressed into fighting an offensive war without his consent. A man could not beat his wife, except in his own defense. Parents could not "wilfullie and unreasonably deny any childe timely or convenient mariage." Servants could flee from cruel masters, and if a master "smite out" an eye or a tooth, the servant could go free. Witches, on the other hand, were to be put to death, as were blasphemers, adulterers, and homosexuals. The secured rights are all the more striking because they were protected by a Puritanical society we remember more for its witch hunts than for its attention to individual liberties.[7]

After independence, new constitutions adopted in eleven states guaranteed trial by jury in criminal cases and protected the freedom of worship. All but two guaranteed a free press. Most states prohibited excessive fines or bail, forced self-incrimination, and general search warrants; some included freedom of assembly, the right to legal counsel, and trial by jury in civil cases; a few banned ex post facto laws, bills of attainder, and double jeopardy. Not all of these were constitutional commands protecting individual liberties enforceable in courts of law, as we think of rights today; many were phrased as codifications of right principles that would guide government and politics. Most Revolutionary-era declarations of rights were written in "ought not" language rather than "shall not" language.[8]

Such was the constitutional heritage of the fifty-five men who drew up a new plan of government in 1787. Realizing that the government they were creating had a broader and deeper reach than the old Confederation did, the framers might naturally be expected to go to some lengths to guarantee that the government authorized by the Constitution would not trample on people's time-honored rights.

Except they did not.

The first draft of what would become the Constitution, the Virginia Plan, merely laid out the outlines for a new federal government. Understandably, at this embryonic stage, the draft did not consider protections against governmental abuse, nor did its chief alternative, the New Jersey Plan. During the first two months of debates, delegates did address the fundamental right of representation and the right not to be taxed without that representation, but they did not concern themselves with the kinds of protections against governmental abuse we see in the Bill of Rights.

Not until the August 6 Committee of Detail report, issued in the third month of the Convention's proceedings, did other safeguards appear. "The trial of all criminal offences (except in cases of impeachments) shall be in the State where they shall be committed; and shall be by Jury," the committee stated. But beyond that there was nothing.

Two weeks later, on August 20, Charles Pinckney recommended the protection of writs of habeas corpus and liberty of the press, as well as prohibitions against religious oaths for public office and forced quartering of soldiers. His suggestions were sent to committee but never reported out.

Two days after that, Elbridge Gerry and James McHenry moved to prohibit bills of attainder (legislations imposing penalties on specified individuals or groups) and ex post facto (retrospective) laws. Their motion passed, although some delegates thought that ex post facto laws were so scorned that judges would treat them as "void of themselves" even without a specific prohibition. On August 28, Gouverneur Morris formally moved to protect writs of habeas corpus except in cases of rebellion. The Convention assented without debate. The new government would not be allowed to hold prisoners secretly or without showing cause, a protection guaranteed by British law for over a century. Two days later, Charles Pinckney brought to the floor one of his earlier suggestions, moving to outlaw the use of any religious test as a qualification for holding public office. This proposal also passed without serious dissent. Slowly, piece by piece, protections of individual rights were mounting.

On September 12, Hugh Williamson moved that the right to a jury trial, already in the working draft for criminal cases, should be extended to civil cases as well. George Mason was not entirely convinced, but the expanding list of protected rights led him to a new idea: why not preface the Constitution with a full "Bill of Rights," as many of the states had done with their constitutions? "It would give great quiet to the people; and with the aid of the State declarations, a bill might be prepared in a few hours," he said. Elbridge Gerry, agreeing with Mason, moved that the preparation of a Bill of Rights be assigned to committee.[9]

Roger Sherman, the only other delegate to address the motion, spoke tersely against it. "The State Declarations of Rights are not repealed by this Constitution; and being in force are sufficient," he said—but then he returned quickly to jury trials in civil cases, the item on the floor when Gerry and Mason had interrupted with their motion. That ended the discussion. When the question was called on Gerry's motion, not a single state voted "ay." The idea of a bill of rights might have found a warmer reception if offered earlier, but the Committee of Style had just presented its almost-final draft, and delegates thought their work was done. Perhaps it was weariness, not logic, that doomed a bill of rights at the Federal Convention.

The framers' neglect was a colossal political blunder. Mason had offered a strong argument for a bill of rights—"It would give great quiet to the people"—and the implication was clear: its omission would cause great displeasure. That argument alone should have sufficed. The framers had spent over three months conjuring their plan, purposely shielded from the external input of people "out-of-doors." They failed to realize that some express mitigation of governmental power would make their plan more palatable to Revolutionary-era Americans who had come to expect such assurances.[10]

Rebuffed on a bill of rights in the final week of the convention, Mason took his fight to the people. He prepared a list of objections to the proposed Constitution, and its first item charged: "There is no Declaration of Rights, and the laws of the general government being paramount to the laws and constitution of the several States, the Declarations of Rights in the separate States are no security." From that moment, the absence of constitutional provisions securing treasured rights served as a rallying call for opponents of ratification.[11]

Seemingly taken by surprise at the spirited response, the Constitution's supporters conjured a dizzying array of defensive arguments. James Wilson, in his much-publicized speech outside the Pennsylvania State House on October 6 (see chapter 6), opened by drawing a philosophical distinction. When creating state governments, he said, the people had "invested their representatives with every right and authority which they did not in explicit terms reserve," and that was why they had needed to define the rights they were *not* giving to their new governments. "In delegating federal powers," on the other hand, they had made a "positive grant" of specific powers, while reserving all other authority to themselves. Since they had never granted Congress any power over the press, for instance, it would have been "superfluous and absurd" to protect against a power Congress did not have. Indeed, to declare liberty of the press would falsely imply that Congress *did* have power over the press, a dangerous prospect.[12]

Federalists loved Wilson's tidy reasoning and repeated it often, but it failed to address people's concerns. The new federal government did possess the power to raise a standing army, and unless otherwise prohibited, it might force citizens to quarter that army as the British had only two decades earlier. It did have the power to levy and collect imposts, and unless prohibited, federal agents, without a warrant or warning, could march into a person's house at any time of night or day in search of smuggled goods, an injustice that had aroused a colonial people in 1761. The federal judiciary did have the power to punish crimes, yet there were no precautions against torture to force confessions, indefinite detention through prohibitive bail, or cruel or unusual punishments. No sophisms about reserved powers versus granted powers spoke to these real-life possiblilites.

Alexander Hamilton, in *The Federalist No. 84* (Publius's next-to-last essay), did his best at damage control. He repeated Wilson's basic message—"Why declare that things shall not be done, which there is no power to do?"—but to this he added other curious arguments. He listed the rights that the Constitution *did* protect—writs of habeas corpus, jury trials in criminal cases, prohibitions against ex post facto laws and bills of attainder, the requirement for two witnesses in treason trials—and then padded that list with obscure "rights" that were politically meaningful but seemed of little direct use to ordinary citizens: federal officeholders, if convicted of impeachment, could not be punished without subsequent legal proceedings, and Congress could not grant titles of nobility. Because these "certain immunities" specified "the political privileges" of its citizens, Hamilton concluded, "The Constitution is itself, in every rational sense, and to every useful purpose, A BILL OF RIGHTS." He did not acknowledge that his meager list fell far short of people's expectations.

Taking the opposite tack, but again revealing more disdain than respect for individual rights, Hamilton proclaimed that specified protections, such as those listed in the state declarations of rights, were mere "aphorisms . . . which would sound much better in a treatise of ethics than in a constitution of government." Although he did have a point—those declarations of rights were not judicially enforceable constitutional commands—his dismissive tone probably won few converts. Understandably, *The Federalist No. 84* is rarely quoted today by those who praise the founders for their advocacy of rights.[13]

Similarly, James Madison believed the state declarations of rights were mere "parchment barriers" and of little use. He argued repeatedly that overzealous state legislatures—including the legislature of his own Virginia—had ignored these declarations and enacted intrusive legislation. A national bill of rights would not do much good either, he felt, except perhaps from a political standpoint. Unlike Hamilton and Wilson, though, he was not adamantly opposed to a bill of rights. "I never thought the omission a material defect, nor been anxious to supply it by subsequent amendments, for any other reason than that it is anxiously desired by others," Madison wrote to Jefferson in the fall of 1788, after Jefferson voiced his support for a bill of rights. "I have not viewed it in an important light," he stated flatly.[14]

Except for Jefferson, who was in Paris at the time and did not help write the Constitution, the men most commonly referred to as founders greeted the clamor for a bill of rights with hostility or, at best, indifference. The Constitution took no one's rights away, they believed. Besides, they had included measures that protected the states in their new plan, and those states, by jealously guarding their own authority, would provide sufficient checks on federal power. The division of powers among the separate branches of the federal government would also protect against abuses, and, ultimately, officials of the new government would be directly or indirectly responsible to the people or to their state legislatures. Wasn't that enough?

No, it wasn't. People out-of-doors wanted more, as the Federalists would learn soon enough.

At the close of the Federal Convention, George Mason had issued a sweeping indictment: "It was improper to say to the people, take this or nothing." The people had no say in writing the proposed Constitution, and the ratification process required a simple up-or-down vote. There was no in-between.[15]

This stark choice bothered many of the Constitution's opponents, many of whom acknowledged the defects of the Articles of Confederation and the need to revise or even perhaps to replace them. These critics made various counterproposals: a state could refuse to ratify unless the document were revised by previous amendments; a state would ratify under the condition that certain amendments be adopted; a state could refer the Constitution, together with lists of either previous amendments or conditional amendments, to a second federal convention. The Constitution's supporters indignantly rejected these proposals, some invoking the authority and patriotism of the framers, others pointing out the impossibility or undesirability of a second convention, still others questioning the motives of the critics. They insisted the choice must be all or nothing.

A simple up-or-down vote bothered many citizens of Massachusetts, the sixth state to vote on ratification. The Southborough town meeting, when electing its representatives to the state ratification convention, issued these instructions: "It is our opinion that the Federal Constitution, as it now stands ought not to be ratifyed, but under certain limitations and amendments it may be a salutary form of government." Massachusetts Speaker of the House James Warren, writing as "A Republican Federalist," objected to the idea that states were supposed to "take this or have none," without any chance to add, subtract, or alter it. "This may be language adopted to slaves, but not to freemen," he wrote.[16]

At the Massachusetts convention, Federalists found themselves just shy of the number of votes required for ratification. After weeks of debate, moderate Federalists approached moderate delegates on the other side with an innovative and ultimately game-changing proposal. They suggested the convention ratify the Constitution but "recommend" nine amendments for future consideration, and in exchange they pledged to work for those amendments' ratification. This deal procured the votes needed to secure ratification by Massachusetts.

Those nine amendments, it is commonly reported today, were an embryonic "Bill of Rights." According to one popular website: "The impasse was finally overcome by what is known as the Massachusetts Compromise. The Massachusetts ratifying convention finally got enough Anti-Federalists on board by recommending a number of amendments be adopted by the First Congress under the new constitution. So the Anti-Federalists voted yes, on the promise that a Bill of Rights would be added."[17]

These nine amendments, however, were in no way a cohesive "Bill of Rights." A varied assortment, they resulted from in-house, last-minute scrambling as delegates weighed this complaint or that. One required juries for civil cases, another required grand juries for major criminal cases, and a third reserved to the states powers "not expressly delegated" to the federal government, a stronger version of what would become the Tenth Amendment (see chapter 4). The rest, though, bore no resemblance to protections that would later be enshrined in the Bill of Rights. Some chipped away at the powers of the national government, most critically Congress's authority to levy direct taxes without first requisitioning the states (see chapter 2). One said "that Congress erect no company with exclusive advantages of commerce." Another stated that no federal officeholder could accept a "title of nobility . . . from any king, prince, or foreign state." [18]

The Massachusetts example transformed the ratification controversy. Five of the six remaining ratifying conventions to vote in 1788 recommended amendments. (Maryland, the exception, failed to do so only because committee members could not agree on which amendments to recommend.) Each of these states, like Massachusetts, wanted to regulate federal taxation, assign nondelegated powers to the states, and affirm state control over elections. The lists included several other amendments that shifted the balance of power back toward the states. Virginia proposed twenty amendments as well as a detailed "declaration or bill of rights" containing twenty additional items. North Carolina copied Virginia's lists and then added six additional amendments. New York proposed thirty-two amendments plus twenty-four "principles," essentially its own declaration of rights that it included in its official ratification, what we might call today a "signing statement." [19]

What was to be done with all these amendments and declarations of rights?

In Virginia, Federalists secured ratification with no more than a promise to forward the amendments to Congress and a pledge to support them, but in two other states the Constitution's opponents were less easily led. The New York convention ratified the Constitution but simultaneously managed to get the convention to send a circular letter to the other states, proposing a second national convention to consider all amendments that had been suggested, including its own. The North Carolina convention declared flatly it would not ratify the Constitution until a national convention was called and had actually met. [20]

The growing prospect of a second federal convention horrified Federalists. After the Virginia convention, Madison fretted to Washington and Hamilton, "A variety of amendments have been recommended; several of them highly objectionable." The most worrisome of the lot was the prohibition against direct federal taxation unless states failed to meet their requisitions. This popular amendment, he warned, placed the essence of the Constitution in jeopardy, even after ratification. New York's official call for a second federal convention sent Madison into a near panic. "Those who opposed the Constitution," he wrote to Jefferson, would try to load such a convention with "men who will essentially mutilate the system, particularly in the article of taxation, without which in my opinion the system cannot answer the purposes for which it was intended." He also alerted Washington: "If an early general convention cannot be parried, it is seriously to be feared that the system which has resisted so many direct attacks may be successfully undermined by its enemies." [21]

Washington agreed. New York's circular letter "will be attended with pernicious consequences," he wrote back to Madison. [22]

How, then, might friends of the new Constitution prevent a second federal convention?

Madison saw a way. The best defense was a good offense, he reasoned. If *Congress* seized the initiative and proposed amendments to the Constitution, leaders of the opposition could not "blow the trumpet for a second convention." Congress could then pick and choose amendments that did not threaten the basic integrity of the Constitution—a bill of rights, yes; a weakening of congressional taxation, no. Despite his previous opposition to a constitutional enumeration of rights, Madison entertained and then embraced this simple political calculus. [23]

Madison's scheme meshed well with his own political needs. In the winter following ratification, he faced a tough election battle for a seat in the First Federal Congress. To gain the critical support of persecuted Baptists in his district, who had long supported him because of his battles for separation of church and state, he promised that if elected, he would work to protect "the rights of Conscience in the fullest latitude." Madison, with Jefferson, was a firm believer in religious liberty—in fact, he had engineered the passage of Virginia's unique Statute for Religious Freedom in 1786—so he had no difficulty in making this promise. He did need to adjust his dismissive attitude toward a bill of rights, however. To a constituent he wrote, "[I]t is my sincere opinion that the Constitution ought to be revised. . . . [A]mendments, if pursued with a proper moderation and in a proper mode, will be not only safe, but may serve the double purpose of satisfying the minds of well meaning opponents, and of providing additional guards in favour of their liberty." Madison won the election, prevailing over one of the popular opponents of the Constitution, a man who would later succeed him as president: James Monroe.[24]

Washington, who faced no opposition in the first presidential election, gave Madison's plan his blessing. In his inaugural address to Congress on April 30, 1789, which Madison helped him to draft, he addressed the lingering "inquietude" of the Constitution's opponents and the amendments they had put forward. Swaying from Federalist orthodoxy, he suggested in a most delicate manner that Congress consider proposing some amendments. "It will remain within your judgment," he said, to decide what amendments to propose, but he did suggest general guidelines: "I assure myself that whilst you carefully avoid every alteration which might endanger the benefits of an united and effective government, or which ought to await the future lessons of experience, a reverence for the characteristic rights of freemen and a regard for the public harmony will sufficiently influence your deliberations on the question how far the former can be impregnably fortified or the latter be safely and advantageously promoted." [25]

In private communication, Washington ardently opposed only one amendment: "There are scarcely any of the amendments which have been suggested, to which I have *much* objection, except that which goes to the prevention of direct taxation." He did not need to say that publicly. He could rest assured that the new Federalist-dominated Congress would not weaken its own power to tax.[26]

Madison, ostensibly executing the president's will, set to work and combed through the numerous amendments suggested at state ratifying conventions. In line with Washington's instructions, he separated those that could be "safely and advantageously promoted" from those that might "endanger the benefits of an united and effective government." He condensed those he favored and then sent his preliminary draft to Washington for his input. On May 31 Washington responded: "As far as a momentary consideration has enabled me to judge, I see nothing exceptionable in the proposed amendments. Some of them, in my opinion, are importantly necessary; others, though in themselves (in my conception) not very essential, are necessary to quiet the fears of some respectable characters and well meaning men.

Upon the whole, therefore, not foreseeing any evil consequences that can result from their adoption, they have my wishes for a favourable reception in both houses." [27]

All seemed in place, and on June 8, 1789, Madison took the floor in the House of Representatives and offered nineteen additions to the Constitution, which he grouped into nine amendments (see appendix F). In his presentation, he focused more on placating opponents than on the actual need to protect rights. "It will be a desirable thing to extinguish from the bosom of every member of the community any apprehensions, that there are those among his countrymen who wish to deprive them of the liberty for which they valiantly fought and honorably bled," he noted. "On principles of amity and moderation," Congress should "conform to [the] wishes" of "a great number of our constituents" and "expressly declare the great rights of mankind secured under this constitution." He then revealed his political reasoning:

There have been objections of various kinds made against the constitution. Some were levelled against its structure . . . because it grants more power than is supposed to be necessary for every good purpose, and controls the ordinary powers of the State Governments. I know some respectable characters who opposed this Government on these grounds; but I believe that the great mass of the people who opposed it, disliked it because it did not contain effectual provisions against the encroachments on particular rights, and those safeguards which they have been long accustomed to have interposed between them and the magistrate who exercises the sovereign power. . . . It is a fortunate thing that the objection to the Government has been made on the ground I stated; because it will be practicable, on that ground, to obviate the objection, so far as to satisfy the public mind that their liberties will be perpetual, and this without endangering any part of the constitution.

Almost begrudgingly, he paid lip service to the inherent value of amendments that enumerated rights. "It is possible the abuse of the powers of the general government may be guarded against in a more secure manner than is now done, while no one advantage, arising from the exercise of that power, shall be damaged or endangered by it," he said. "We have in this way something to gain, and, if we proceed with caution, nothing to lose."[28]

Madison's lukewarm endorsement of a listing of rights did not convince many of his Federalist colleagues in Congress, who saw the amendment issue as a nuisance, interrupting urgent business. Congress had yet to settle on impost duties to pay its bills, a matter of top priority. It hadn't begun to establish federal courts, nor had it established how representatives and senators would be paid. "The executive part of the Government wants organization; the business of the revenue is incomplete, to say nothing of the judiciary business," said Roger Sherman. "Now, will gentlemen give up these points to go into a discussion of amendments, when no advantage can arise from them?"[29]

Nor did Madison win the hearts of colleagues favoring amendments, who did not appreciate being upstaged by a Federalist. Why should Madison's list, prepared by one individual, take precedence over those suggested by full bodies of elected representatives of their respective states? Why his and not the extensive lists of amendments approved by the Virginia and New York ratification conventions?

At first, the House tabled Madison's list of amendments, but despite the indifference of Federalists and the resentment of their adversaries, Madison pressed the issue. Six weeks after his initial presentation, he "begged the House to indulge him in the further consideration of amendments." This time the House formed a committee and assigned Madison's list to them; that committee made a few small changes; and finally, on August 13, in the middle of a midsummer New York heat wave, and with "the political thermometer high each day," the House of Representatives debated the amendments on the floor.[30]

Before addressing the substance of each amendment, representatives discussed their placement. Following Madison's lead, the committee had woven the amendments into the text of the Constitution, indicating precisely where each change would be placed, but Roger Sherman took issue with this approach. Interweaving the amendments would be "destructive of the whole fabric," he contended. "We might as well endeavor to mix brass, iron, and clay, as to incorporate such heterogeneous articles." Madison countered, "There is a neatness and propriety in incorporating the amendments into the constitution itself." Had Madison prevailed, we would not have a distinct "Bill of Rights," but Madison lost and the amendments were placed at the end of the original Constitution.[31]

Substantively, the list proposed by Madison and revised by the House committee contained protections that would evolve into what we call the Bill of Rights. It included a few additional items that were later rejected, but none of these addressed the major structural revisions that the Constitution's opponents had called for at the state ratifying conventions. This glaring omission infuriated Aedanus Burke of South Carolina, who said the proposals were "not those solid and substantial amendments which the people expect; they are little better than whip syllabub, frothy and full of wind, formed only to please the palate. . . . All the important amendments were omitted."[32]

At various times during more than a week of vigorous debates, representatives who had opposed the Constitution in 1787–1788, and who still had their doubts in 1789, tried to place more "important amendments" on the table. On August 18 Elbridge Gerry moved that *all* the amendments "proposed by the several states" be discussed, but his motion was defeated by a margin exceeding two-to-one. Thomas Tudor Tucker of South Carolina then presented a list of seventeen structural amendments, but the House dismissed them without debate. Those demanding substantive amendments also staged more pointed attacks. They tried to guarantee the right of people to instruct their representatives, and although this move stirred extensive debate, it failed by a four-to-one margin. Following the lead of several state ratifying conventions, they tried to insert the word "expressly" before "delegated" in the amendment that stated, "The powers not delegated by the Constitution, nor prohibited by it to the States, are reserved to the States respectively." This revision would have forced a strict interpretation of the Constitution and would have prohibited the expansion of federal powers, but it too went down to defeat (see chapter 4). When they moved to require a two-thirds vote of Congress to form a standing army in time of peace, that proposal lost by thirteen votes. They tried to limit federal control of congressional elections, and although that motion failed by only five votes, this was far short of the two-thirds supermajority required for constitutional amendments.[33]

And finally, the amendment most dear to the hearts of the Constitution's critics and deemed most dangerous by its supporters: circumscribing Congress's powers of taxation (see chapter 2). On Saturday, August 22, South Carolina's Tucker moved to prohibit Congress from levying direct taxes unless the states had failed to meet their requisitions. This amendment was "of more importance than any yet obtained," argued Samuel Livermore of New Hampshire, and if Congress failed to include it, "he knew his constituents would be dissatisfied." They would value all the others—the eventual Bill of Rights—as no more "than a pinch of snuff." Although Tucker and Livermore might have spoken for the majority of Americans, within Congress they were a distinct minority. Their motion to check federal taxation failed by an overwhelming vote of nine to thirty-nine. In one vote after another, the House preserved the federal government's stipulated powers, most particularly the power of taxation.[34]

On August 24 the House approved Madison's revised amendments and sent them on to the Federalist-dominated Senate, where once again they received a cool reception. South Carolina senator Pierce Butler commented: "A few *milk-and-water* amendments have been proposed by Mr. M., such as liberty of conscience, a free press, and one or two other things already well secured. I suppose it was done to keep his promise with his constituents, to move for alteration; but, if I am not greatly mistaken, he is not hearty in the cause of amendments." Likewise, Pennsylvania senator Robert Morris treated the amendments dismissively: "Poor Madison got so cursedly frightened in Virginia, that I believe he has dreamed of amendments ever since." Morris was perhaps the strongest senatorial opponent—he called the amendments "nonsense" and a "waste of precious time"—but even he admitted they would result in "neither good or harm being perfectly innocent." The handful of senators who had opposed the Constitution introduced less "innocent" amendments akin to those offered by the state ratifying conventions, but these were immediately rejected. Deeming the amendments sent from the House inconsequential, Federalists in the Senate acted with dispatch, making some adjustments but then granting their approval.[35]

In the midst of the House debates, frustrated by the resistance he encountered from both sides, Madison referred privately to his diversionary scheme as "the nauseous project of amendments," but however distasteful the "project" worked. He had hoped to "kill the opposition every where" and end "the disaffection to the Govt."—and he did just that. Even before final approval of the amendments, debates in the House of Representatives were reprinted in the press, and the mere fact that Congress was *considering* amendments helped defuse dissent.

Although many former critics were warming to the new Constitution, diehard opponents realized Madison had outflanked them. Senator Richard Henry Lee of Virginia complained that "the English language has been carefully culled to find words feeble in their nature or doubtful in their meaning," and the amendments that emerged were "much mutilated and enfeebled. . . . The great points of free election, . . . the unlimited right of taxation, and standing armies in peace, remain as they were." Patrick Henry, who had led the Constitution's foes in the Virginia ratifying convention the previous year, regretted the defeat of the amendment limiting direct taxation, which he said was worth more than all Congress's weak amendments put together. William Grayson, Virginia's other senator, said the amendments were "so mutilated & gutted that in fact they are good for nothing, & I believe as many others do that they will do more harm than benefit." [36]

The politics surrounding a bill of rights had come full circle. Those who had originally supported a bill of rights as their strongest case against the Constitution had become opponents, whereas Federalists, who originally had opposed a bill of rights, now were the ones working out the details and ushering the amendments through Congress.

Revolutionary-era Americans were fond of celebrating their nation's remarkable transformations. Back in 1776, following the congressional vote for independence, Americans did so by reading in public Congress's declaration, by tearing down statues of King George III and destroying other signs of royalty, and by drinking through the night, offering toast after toast to American heroes and America's destiny. On the night of July 3, 1776, John Adams wrote enthusiastically to his wife, Abigail: "The second day of July, 1776 [the day Congress voted for independence], will be the most memorable epocha in the history of America. I am apt to believe that it will be celebrated by succeeding generations as the great anniversary festival. It ought to be commemorated as the day of deliverance, by solemn acts of devotion to God Almighty. It ought to be solemnized with pomp and parade, with shows, games, sports, guns, bells, bonfires, and illumination, from one end of this continent to the other, from this time forward forevermore." [37]

On July 4, 1788, just days after New Hampshire and Virginia ratified the Constitution, ensuring that it would take effect, the people of Philadelphia staged a parade, called "The Federal Procession," the like of which had never been seen and has rarely been equaled since. Some 5,000 participants strung out for a mile and a half along the three-mile route, with forty-four different groups of tradesmen—cordwainers, bricklayers, coopers, brewers, engravers, whip manufacturers, and so on—outdoing each other with creative, gargantuan floats. Butchers marched two oxen side by side down the street, one labeled ANARCHY and the other CONFUSION. The banner strung between their horns read, "The Death of ANARCHY and CONFUSION Shall Feed the Poor and Hungry," and at the conclusion of the parade, the men who led the oxen made good on their word by practicing their trade. On another float, blacksmiths heated swords in a working forge and then pounded them into plowshares. The featured display was the "Grand Federal Edifice," a large dome supported by thirteen Corinthian columns (one per state, of course) and adorned with a frieze showing thirteen stars. Constructed on a carriage and drawn by ten horses, the edifice rose to a height of thirty-six feet above street level. The previous evening, workers had climbed and limbed trees along the course to accommodate the magnificent structure.[38]

So what happened when news spread that ten amendments to the Constitution had just been ratified?

Nothing. We have no record of a single public celebration and barely any mention in the press. There was one official notice, a letter by Secretary of State Thomas Jefferson to the state governors, on March 1, 1792—almost five years after the opening of the Federal Convention in Philadelphia:

I have the honor to send you herein enclosed, two copies duly authenticated, of an Act concerning certain fisheries of the United States, and for the regulation and government of the fisherman employed therein; also of an Act to establish the post office and post roads within the United States; also the ratification by three fourths of the Legislatures

149

of the Several States, of certain articles in addition and amendment of the Constitution of the United States, proposed by Congress to the said Legislatures, and being with sentiments of the most perfect respect, your Excellency's &c.[39]

Fisheries, post roads, and "certain articles"—it was not a ceremonial inauguration. Jefferson, one of the few national leaders who had advocated a bill of rights from the outset, did not even call these amendments the "Bill of Rights." Placed at the end of the Constitution, they seemed like an afterthought. They contained no sweeping, memorable statements as appeared in the Declaration of Independence and several state declarations of rights, no talk of *inherent rights* or the *pursuit of happiness*. Rhetorically, they had little appeal. In many minds, too, they fell far short of demands made at the ratifying conventions. "Enfeebled," Anti-Federalists complained. Mere "milk-and-water," Federalists boasted.[40]

From these inglorious beginnings, the Bill of Rights eventually emerged as a founding document in its own right that serves multiple ideological purposes. On one end of the political spectrum, the First and the Fourth through Ninth Amendments provide support for Americans who advocate free speech, resist state-sponsored religion, and wish to protect privacy and the rights of the accused. On the other end, citizens who oppose gun control, support states' rights, or want to limit the role of government base their arguments on the Second and Tenth Amendments. Each group benefits not only from the specific enumeration of rights but also from branding the overall package the "Bill of Rights" and treating it as the constitutional equivalent of scripture.

On a grand scale, the naming and ascension of the Bill of Rights supports an even larger, overarching narrative: the founding fathers created the Bill of Rights to promote liberty over government. There must always be a tradeoff, people say, and the founders wanted to ensure that liberty came first.

While many Americans of the time certainly felt that way, the men who wrote the Constitution did not. Too much focus on liberty, this group believed, could lead to anarchy and a state of nature, a fearful war of all against all that endangered life and property. A well-constituted state or nation, on the other hand, was liberty's ally, not its enemy. Whether valid or not, this was their argument. Consider Hamilton's forthright statement in the first *Federalist* essay: "An over-scrupulous jealousy of danger to the rights of the people . . . will be represented as mere pretense and artifice, the stale bait for popularity at the expense of the public good. It will be forgotten, on the one hand, . . . that the noble enthusiasm of liberty is apt to be infected with a spirit of narrow and illiberal distrust. On the other hand, it will be equally forgotten that the vigor of government is essential to the security of liberty; that, in the contemplation of a sound and well-informed judgment, their interest can never be separated."

By enshrining the Bill of Rights and even placing that appendage ahead of the Constitution itself, we turn the framers' argument on its head. Ask Americans today what they value most about their Constitution, and they will likely say the freedoms it guarantees, not the "vigor" of the central government it created, which was the framers' major goal. If you then ask which freedoms those are, you might hear a list gleaned from amendments that most framers' originally opposed. Few will tell you that with the exception of Jefferson, who supported a bill of rights all along, the men we most venerate as the founding fathers—including almost all of the framers of the Constitution—backed into the protection of rights grudgingly, or, worse yet, that the political function of the first ten amendments, the reason Madison bothered to propose them and other Federalists belatedly supported them, was to prevent *other* amendments from weakening the federal government.

8

ORIGINALISM

Myth: By discovering what the framers intended or how the founding generation understood the text, we can determine how each provision of the Constitution must be applied.

Unless interpretive methodologies are tied to the original intent of the framers, they have no more basis in the Constitution than the latest football scores.

—Supreme Court Justice Clarence Thomas[1]

The originalist at least knows what he is looking for: the original meaning of the text. Often—indeed, I dare say usually—that is easy to discern and simple to apply.

—Supreme Court Justice Antonin Scalia[2]

Kernel of Truth

Unlike the British Constitution, which evolved over the centuries and blends written and unwritten components, the United States Constitution is contained in a single document that was adopted at a specific point in time, though later amended. Whereas it does not give us our laws, it does set guidelines for what types of laws are permitted and how they are to be enacted and enforced. The framers deliberately set the ground rules for governance in clear, simple writing, and we should listen to what they were saying. Casting aside overlays from later history that only confuse the matter, we can try to understand what they had in mind, the framers' "original intent."

The Constitution was a contract fashioned by "We the People." It could not take effect without the assent of the citizens, represented by their delegates to state ratifying conventions, who were parties to the contract. The delegates who gave their approval did so with a particular understanding of its contents, so it is appropriate to ask what a "reasonable ratifier" thought he was voting for, and even more to the point, from a legal point of view, what he *was* voting for. What did the contract actually say, in the language of those times? That was the "original meaning" of their agreement.

These variations of originalism—explicating the Constitution by calling upon the framers, the ratifiers, or the original meaning of the text—are part and parcel of our culture today. We all ascribe to originalism on some level. Even those who disavow these methods of interpretation often make use of them, marshaling quotations from the framers and their contemporaries to buttress their arguments.

But . . .

"Original intent" presupposes a unitary body with a clear, common intent, but what was the "original intent" of a compromise engineered to satisfy competing interests or philosophies? Even the intention of a specific framer remains elusive. We might know that he favored this provision or that, but we cannot glean his full understanding of any issue from a speech he made to garner votes. Persuasion and explication are not the same.[3]

Further, when we think of the Constitution as a contract, the issue is not what those who wrote it wanted it to say or what interested parties hoped it might say, but what it *did* say. To understand a contract, we should look at how the words were understood at the particular time it was signed. So it is with our Constitution. We want to know what the words and phrases signified when it was written and ratified.

Yet how, precisely, is *that* to be determined? We do have an abundance of primary sources to consult, but more often than not, these sources are affected by partisan leanings. When we search for clear meanings in political pamphlets, newspaper essays, and the records of the contentious state ratifying conventions, we find words and phrases twisted in ways geared to promote or denigrate the Constitution.[4]

All these issues point to an overarching quandary. We want to know what the Constitution *really* says, as if that document were a simple list of rules passed down from above on a tablet, the work of a single mastermind. Many

Americans imagine it was and treat it that way. This is the phantom Constitution they wave in the air, exclaiming, "Just read this and you will see!" Yet answers to such interpretative questions are rarely as absolute as we might hope. The meaning of the Constitution was disputed from the moment Congress submitted it to the states on September 28, 1787. It's a sobering truth.[5]

Constitutional disputes have three causes. First, not all provisions within the Constitution are designed to cover narrowly defined sets of circumstances, as routine statutes do. Many, like the length of terms for officeholders, are cut and dried; but others, like grants of powers to Congress or the president, are not. Precisely because these clauses are phrased in broad, sweeping terms, their applications will be subject to interpretation. The framers claimed only to be setting outlines, and by including words like "necessary and proper" in the grants of power to Congress (see chapter 4), they ensured that the exact borders would never be determined in a manner acceptable to all.

Second, circumstances change with time, and meanings change as well. In 1787, when nations went to war, they "declared war," yet for two-thirds of a century we have ignored this convention, as have other nations. Wars are still waged, yet the Constitution, stuck forever in its old ways, does not comment on prolonged, undeclared military conflicts. How we deal with changes in the waging of war, and the accompanying breakdown of traditional nomenclature, presents a puzzle we have not yet solved.

Altered circumstances and meanings challenge originalism in any form. The founders lived in their world, we live in ours, and the two are very different. The founders were very smart, but soothsayers they were not. The future was a closed book to them, as it is to us. Lacking knowledge of today's world, and with no appropriate experience to guide them, they are not the best authorities on regulating the Internet or securing airports from terrorists, matters wholly unknown to their experience. We can look to them for general principles, but principles must be applied, and the devil is in the details. More than we wish to admit, we are on our own.

Finally, the Constitution did not provide a methodology for resolving interpretative differences, nor did it even state clearly who should resolve them. In the absence of such instruction, originalism can never be a panacea.

Since the framers, as a body, said nothing on the one matter upon which all else depends, we cannot rely exclusively on their guidance.

That said, originalism as an *attitude* is here to stay. The pervasive sense that the Constitution is fixed, not malleable, fosters continuity. For over two centuries, with one major exception, the nation has changed leaders without altering governmental structures, and the mystique of the Constitution—a set of allegedly clear ground rules that all must obey—is no small part of that success story. We debate current meanings by debating historical meanings, affirming allegiance to our founding document as we do so. We always have and we always will.

The Full Story

The First Federal Congress was not yet three months old when members discovered a hole in the new Constitution. While creating the job description for a secretary of foreign affairs, congressmen understood that the president would make the appointment "by and with the Advice and Consent of the Senate," as stated in Article II, Section 2, of the Constitution. But who could *remove* that officer? The president alone, or did he need the advice and consent of the Senate? Since the founding document was silent on that matter, congressmen took sides and went at it tooth and nail. Georgia's James Jackson argued that if the Senate were to have a say in an official's appointment, it must of course have a say in his removal. No single individual should be entrusted with such power: "The liberties of my country may be suspended on the decision of this question," Jackson warned. But Virginia's Richard Bland Lee, who believed that removal was clearly the province of the president, was even more apocalyptical: "The day on which this question shall be decided will be a memorable day, not only in the history of our own times, but in the history of mankind," he proclaimed. "On a proper or improper decision, will be involved the future happiness or misery of the people of America."[6]

Interpretative problems continued. The Constitution stipulated that the president also needed the "Advice and Consent" of the Senate in making treaties. The standard for consent was clearly stated—two-thirds of the members present—but what did the framers mean by advice? Should the president consult the Senate before international negotiations? During negotiations? In either case, how was he to approach the Senate? President Washington, while working on an Indian treaty in 1789, spent two disappointing days in the Senate chamber, never to return. To this day, the constitutional role of the Senate in offering advice on treaties remains unclear.[7]

Congress was empowered to levy taxes, borrow money, pay debts, regulate commerce, and coin and regulate the value of money—but could it charter a national bank, allegedly in service to its stipulated constitutional powers? In 1791 Hamilton and Madison offered opposing answers (see chapters 4 and 6).

In 1793 President Washington proclaimed that American citizens were not to offer material support to either Britain or France, then at war with each other. Did he, or did he not, possess the constitutional authority to do so? Again, Hamilton responded one way, Madison the other (see chapter 6).[8]

Two years later, President Washington dispatched Chief Justice John Jay to Britain to negotiate a treaty. When Jay returned, treaty in hand, several representatives argued that because the treaty dealt with commercial matters constitutionally under the jurisdiction of the House, the treaty could not take effect unless the House approved it. Yet the Constitution stated clearly that the Senate ratifies treaties, making no mention of the House. Who was right—or were they both right? Had the Constitution given mixed messages here? And what was the head of the judicial branch of government doing on a clearly executive mission? The Constitution neither authorized nor prohibited such a move.[9]

In 1798, when the Alien and Sedition Acts banned certain forms of dissent and authorized the president to deport enemy aliens, did those statutes violate the Constitution? If so, did states possess the right to declare such federal laws "void and of no force" or to "interpose" between that law and the citizens (see chapter 5)?

And so it went. Even though the Constitution was indelibly set in print, its meaning was still in doubt.

Worse yet, the framers failed to stipulate who was to settle interpretative disputes. In *Hylton v. United States* (1796) the United States Supreme Court determined that a federal carriage tax was constitutional, and in *Marbury v. Madison* (1803) it determined that a provision of the Federal Judiciary Act of 1789 was unconstitutional, but in neither case could justices point to a specific provision in the Constitution granting the High Court the authority to be the final arbiter on issues of constitutionality. Though judicial review had its advocates, the notion that judges alone could settle constitutional disputes was not widely accepted in the founding era. Each of the early presidents thought *he* had the right of interpretation, at least in matters pertaining to the executive branch of government. Congress thought *it* was empowered to determine the constitutionality of the laws it passed. Meanwhile, "We the People," as actual parties to the agreement that enshrined the Constitution as the law of the land, thought *they* had the ultimate say.

But which people? In the 1790s opposing political camps laid claim to their own interpretations of the Constitution. In several communities on the Fourth of July, each side staged its own patriotic parade. Effigies were burned and declarations made: we are the *real* Americans, the others not. The men who had written the Constitution were themselves divided, although more sided with Hamilton and Washington than with Madison.[10]

The Constitution did not address these underlying methodological questions, nor did it embed any practical suggestions within its structure. In 1796, eight years after the document's ratification, Madison hinted at a method of constitutional interpretation, but his choice was not what we might suspect. Today, people seeking to discover the original intent of the Constitution turn first and foremost to the authority of its presumed "father," but Madison himself scorned appeals to the framers. Arguing that Jay's Treaty required the sanction of the House as well as the Senate, he stated,

[W]hatever veneration might be entertained for the body of men who formed our constitution, the sense of that body could never be regarded as the oracular guide in expounding the constitution. As the instrument came from them, it was nothing more than the draft of a plan, nothing but a dead letter, until life and validity were breathed into it, by the voice of the people, speaking through the several state conventions. If we were to look therefore, for the meaning of the instrument, beyond the face of the instrument, we must look for it, not in the general convention, which proposed, but in the state conventions, which accepted and ratified the constitution.[11]

Legally, Madison's argument seemed sound. Since the Constitution, like any contract, was a "dead letter" until signed, or in this case ratified, the proceedings leading to ratification took precedence over the "General Convention," which had only *proposed* it. Yet Madison also had a personal reason for insisting that people look beyond the framers to determine the Constitution's meaning. His own notes of the debates at the Federal Convention would be an invaluable reference if people turned to the Convention's proceedings as the final authority, yet he felt committed to keep that work secret "till the Constitution should be well settled in practice, & till a knowledge of the controversial part of the proceedings of its framers could be turned to no improper account." Disclosing the repugnant details of the debates at the Convention would embarrass the framers, undermine respect for the Constitution, increase partisan divisions in the new republic, and violate the framers' pledge of secrecy. Honesty and good sense kept Madison from publishing his notes, but this stricture also prevented him from endorsing any investigation into the framers' intent.[12]

Elbridge Gerry agreed with Madison that it would be "improper" to cite any of the framers in defense of a particular position. "The opinions of the individual members, who debated, are not to be considered as the opinions of the convention," Gerry said. But unlike Madison, he placed no stock in the presumed authority of ratification conventions either. "The Union at that time divided into two great parties," Gerry said, referring to the Constitution's proponents and opponents. "The object on either side was so important as perhaps to induce the parties to depart from candor, and to call in the aid of art, flattery, professions of friendship, promises of office, and even good cheer. . . . Under such circumstances, the opinions of great men ought not to be considered as authorities, and in many instances could not be recognized by themselves." Partisan debates were no place to look for definitive meanings.[13]

With no prescribed method for settling interpretive differences, disputants argued however they might. During the 1791 national bank debates, Fisher Ames, a Massachusetts representative, noted that for the previous two years, since the new Congress first met, "we have scarcely made a law, in which we have not exercised our discretion, with respect to the true intent of the constitution." They picked through the text, revealed inconsistencies in opposing positions, appealed to so-called first principles, and sprinkled their arguments with quotations from the ratification conventions and suppositions about the framers' intentions at the Federal Convention. With no published record of the framers' debates, however, senators and representatives who had been there could only say, "as I recall," while those who had not been delegates were left to speculate.[14]

Even Madison could not resist appealing to the framers on occasion. When opposing Hamilton's national bank in 1791, he "well recollected that a power to grant charters of incorporation had been proposed in the General Convention but rejected." Unlike other framers, who relied only on their memories, Madison could consult his own notes, although he did not publicly admit this—and his notes for August 18 and September 14 indicated that *he* had been the one to make that proposal (see chapter 5). No matter that he had reversed positions; the defeat of his own motion seemed to demonstrate that the Convention had opposed granting powers of incorporation. Despite claiming that the framers made poor "oracular guides," Madison called upon them when he needed to score a crucial point.[15]

Nor did others hesitate to seek the framers' support, if such authority could bolster their arguments. Appealing to the framers was grounded not on solid theory, as Madison and Gerry pointed out, but on pragmatic wisdom. It produced results. In the 1790s, with no published records at their disposal, Americans allowed themselves to believe that the framers acted with great equanimity, unaffected by partisanship, and since they were the ones who wrote the Constitution, they were the ultimate authorities on what it meant. Only a few years after the Federal Convention, the mystique of original intent was setting down roots.[16]

For the better part of two centuries, Americans of various persuasions appealed to what we now call original intent. In 1857, Chief Justice Roger B. Taney, delivering the opinion of the Court in the famous Dred Scott case, upheld the exclusive right of slaveholders over their so-called property. "The duty of the court is, to interpret the instrument they have framed, with the best lights we can obtain on the subject, and to administer it as we find it, according to its true intent and meaning when it was adopted," Taney wrote. He then outlined a history of slavery in America, up to and including the writing of the Constitution, to demonstrate that blacks, for the founders, were not to be included in "all men are created equal." [17]

In *Reynolds v. United States* (1878), Chief Justice Morrison Waite cited Jefferson's now famous claim that the First Amendment built "a wall of separation between church and State." Even though Jefferson made this pronouncement in 1802, he had prepared the first draft of what would become Virginia's 1786 Statute for Religious Freedom, a precursor to the First Amendment, and that qualified him as an authority on the true meaning of the First Amendment. Chief Justice Waite wrote, "Coming as this does from an acknowledged leader of the advocates of the measure, it may be accepted almost as an authoritative declaration of the scope and effect of the amendment thus secured." Through the doctrine of original intent, the "wall of separation" was inaugurated into First Amendment jurisprudence.[18]

Social transformations in the late nineteenth and early twentieth centuries favored a rival interpretative approach. The Constitution, drafted in and for a different time, would need to adapt, many held. "Government is not a machine, but a living thing," President Woodrow Wilson said in 1913. "It falls, not under the theory of the universe, but under the theory of organic life. It is accountable to Darwin, not to Newton." The Constitution, then, should be interpreted "according to the Darwinian Principle." Although this "organic" view came to shape many Supreme Court decisions, some justices stuck closely to the historical founders. In *Griswold v. Connecticut* (1965), when the Court determined that the Fourteenth Amendment implied a "right to marital privacy," Justice Hugo Black dissented:

> I realize that many good and able men have eloquently spoken and written, sometimes in rhapsodical strains, about the duty of this Court to keep the Constitution in tune with the times. The idea is that the Constitution must be changed from time to time, and that this Court is charged with a duty to make those changes. For myself, I must, with all deference, reject that philosophy. The Constitution makers knew the need for change, and provided for it. Amendments suggested by the people's elected representatives can be submitted to the people or their

selected agents for ratification. That method of change was good for our Fathers, and, being somewhat old-fashioned, I must add it is good enough for me.[19]

In the last quarter of the twentieth century, originalism coalesced into a self-conscious school of constitutional interpretation, boasting a popular name and a frequently articulated rationale. The Supreme Court had been tilting leftward since the 1950s, supporting the rights of alleged criminals, enforcing strict separation of church and state, challenging the death penalty, striking down antiabortion laws, favoring federal authority over the states, and so on. This rash of decisions amounted to "judicial activism," conservatives cried, and they saw a way to reverse it: justices should anchor their decisions on the views of the founders, not base them on personal preferences or societal values. "The truth is that the judge who looks outside the Constitution always looks inside himself and nowhere else," wrote Robert Bork, a former United States solicitor general.[20]

In 1985 President Reagan's attorney general, Edwin Meese III, presented the basic case for originalism in a speech to the American Bar Association at its annual convention: "Those who framed the Constitution chose their words carefully; they debated at great length the minutest points. The language they chose meant something. It is incumbent upon the Court to determine what that meaning was." In professional journals he argued that judges would free the courts of bias by focusing on the original language of the founders. "A jurisprudence seriously aimed at the explication of original intention would produce defensible principles of government that would not be tainted by ideological predilection." This, he said, would "prevent passing fads and passions in the body politic from overriding fundamental values and principles."[21]

Since Antonin Scalia and Clarence Thomas joined the Supreme Court in 1986 and 1991, respectively, originalism has been a formidable presence in American constitutional jurisprudence. Justice Thomas wants to ground all decisions on originalist methodology; precedent alone will not suffice. While concurring with Chief Justice William H. Rehnquist's carefully reasoned opinion for the Court in *United States v. Lopez*, Thomas did not approve of his method, which was based only on previous Court decisions. "Although

I join the majority, I write separately to observe that our case law has drifted far from the original understanding of the Commerce Clause," he wrote. "We ought to temper our Commerce Clause jurisprudence in a manner that both makes sense of our more recent case law and is more faithful to the original understanding of that Clause." In case after case, whether concurring or dissenting, Thomas has offered his own originalist arguments.[22]

Justice Thomas does not always distinguish which variant of originalism he embraces. "In *United States v. Lopez* (1991), he based his argument on the original meaning of the term "commerce," citing dictionaries published in 1773, 1789, and 1796. In *U.S. Term Limits, Inc. v. Thornton* (1995) and *United States v. International Business Machines Corp.* (1996), he used records from the Federal Convention to surmise the original intent of the framers. In *Missouri v. Jenkins* (1995) and *Gonzales v. Raich* (2005), he analyzed proceedings of the state ratifying conventions to infer how the ratifiers understood provisions in the Constitution. "This Court has believed itself bound by the text of the Constitution and by the intent of those who drafted and ratified it," he wrote in *McIntyre v. Ohio Elections Commission* (1995), lumping three criteria into one.[23]

Whichever version of originalism he uses in a given case, Justice Thomas's overriding concern is to fix the Constitution at the founding moment. By highlighting "the practices and beliefs held by the Founders," he contends, he can clarify any and all issues. His concurring opinion for *McIntyre* reasoned that because anonymous political writings were common in the founding era, we have no business regulating them now. In *Baze v. Rees* (2008), to defend the death penalty, he offered a catalogue of horrors from the eighteenth century: "burning at the stake," " 'gibbeting,' or hanging the condemned in an iron cage so that his body would decompose in public view," "embowelling alive, beheading, and quartering," and so on. It was these punishments, not ordinary hanging, that the founders prohibited by framing and adopting the Eighth Amendment, he maintained. Dissenting in *Brown v. Entertainment Merchants Association* (2011), he argued that the founders would not think a ban on the sale of violent video games to children "an abridgment of 'the freedom of speech.' " Deciding the case required "a complete understanding of the founding generation's views on children and the parent-child relationship," and that generation, he concluded, "believed parents had absolute authority over their minor children and expected parents to use that authority to direct the proper development of their children."[24]

Despite his commitment to originalism, Justice Thomas is selective in applying it. He opposes any limits on political advertising, but he does not demonstrate that the founders considered money a form of speech deserving of First Amendment protection. He follows precedent by affording corporations the rights of people, but he has not defended that position by appealing to the founding generation or to the original intent or original meaning of the Fourteenth Amendment, which was passed in the wake of the Civil War to protect former slaves, not corporations.[25]

The lapses are not accidental. In *Citizens United v. Federal Election Commission* (2010), a strong originalist argument can be made, but it would not lead to the results Justice Thomas preferred. The solicitor general cited Supreme Court precedents to show that "corporate political speech can be banned in order to prevent corruption or its appearance." This argument would have appealed to the founders because corporations at that time were not seen as possessing the rights that people enjoyed and government held unquestioned regulatory authority over them.

More critically, they would think that political influence over elected representatives undermined the essence of republican government. Public officials were to make up their own minds, and the notion that a representative, senator, or president might owe his election and therefore his allegiance to a particular group that had financed his campaign would appear to them an invitation to corruption. Article IV, Section 4 of the Constitution *demanded* republicanism—"The United States shall guarantee to every State in this Union a Republican Form of Government"—and republicanism, in the original meaning of that term, required disinterested leadership. The influence of wealth over government frightened the framers, who themselves were quite well-to-do. At the Federal Convention, Gouverneur Morris, whose father was the Lord of Morrisania (New York's present-day Bronx), worried that "the rich will strive to establish their dominion and enslave the rest." Like other framers, Morris feared too much democracy because he thought the people could be too easily misled, particularly by men as wealthy as he was: "The rich will take advantage of their passions and make these the instruments for oppressing them."[26]

John Adams also viewed the threat of influence over voters as anathema to republican government. Like Morris, he predicted that democracy might revert to aristocracy because some men would learn to command the votes of others. "By an aristocrat," he wrote, "I mean any man who can command or influence *two votes, one besides his own*" (his emphases). Aristocracy, rule by the elite few, did not have to be marked by "artificial titles, tinsel decorations of stars, garters, ribbons, golden eagles and golden fleeces, crosses and roses and lilies, exclusive privileges, hereditary descents, established by kings or by positive laws of society." Instead, his "aristocrat" might command or influence votes "by his virtues, his talents, his reserve, his face, figure, eloquence, grace, air, attitude, movements, wealth, birth, art, address, intrigue, good fellowship, drunkenness, debauchery, fraud, perjury, violence, treachery, pyrrhonism [skepticism], deism, or atheism; for by every one of these instruments have votes been obtained and will be obtained." [27]

Today, these various means of influence, more often devious than virtuous, are embodied in the political vernacular of campaign advertisements. Morris and Adams and a host of other founders would be horrified at the transformative reach of concentrated wealth accelerated by the power of mass media. Yet in *Citizens United*, Justice Thomas opted to ignore their salient concerns.

Nor did Justice Thomas offer an originalist argument in *Bush v. Gore* (2000). According to both the original intent and the original meaning of the Constitution, a dispute over hanging chads was in the hands of the state administering the election, so any adjudication should be performed by Florida's courts. The legislature could have chosen presidential electors on its own if it preferred to do so (see chapters 3, 4, and 6), and had the system operated as the framers intended, each elector would not be obligated to vote for *any* particular candidate, whether Bush or Gore. In claiming that citizens had a "fundamental" right to vote for a presidential candidate, the Court's majority overlooked an originalist fact: the framers had specifically and overwhelmingly rejected popular election of the president three times at the Federal Convention, on June 1, July 17, and August 24. Sometimes, if the legislature allowed them to do so, citizens could vote for electors, but since they were never allowed to vote directly for the president, voting for

Bush or Gore could hardly be declared a "fundamental right." George W. Bush, a presidential candidate, had no legal grievance.[28]

Perhaps Justice Thomas showed good sense in not presenting this straightforward but archaic argument in *Bush v. Gore*, for the original understanding of presidential selection quickly broke down. Ever since 1800, electors have not exercised independent judgment, and with the ascension of democracy in the early nineteenth century, state legislatures ceded the choice of electors to the people. But for Justice Thomas, the pure originalist, this would be an insufficient excuse for not treating the case as the founders would have treated it.

"Originalism has the advantage of being legitimate and, I might add, impartial," Justice Thomas declares, but his discretionary use of originalist arguments—highlighting only those appearing to support a preferred conclusion—undermines that claim. Originalism does not in some mystical way immunize against bias.[29]

Justice Thomas trusts his own assessment of the founders' intent or meaning more than he trusts precedent. In *McIntyre*, he professed that he was "loath to overturn a century of practice," but in the same sentence he asserted boldly that "historical evidence from the framing outweighs recent tradition." In legal terminology, he prefers originalism to *stare decisis*, or respecting precedent, the standard that was developed in Roman times and has always anchored English and American jurisprudence. To an admiring audience at Stetson University College of Law in Gulfport, Florida, which presented him with an honorary doctorate, Justice Thomas said, "If it's wrong, it's wrong, and we are obligated to revisit it."[30]

Justice Antonin Scalia, the Supreme Court's other professed originalist, assumes a somewhat milder stance. "If a constitutional line of authority is wrong, he [Thomas] would say let's get it right," Justice Scalia said informally in 2004. "I wouldn't do that. He does not believe in *stare decisis* period."[31]

Justice Scalia's theoretical defense of originalism is more discriminating, explicitly disavowing original intent in favor of original meaning: "I will consult the writings of some men who happened to be delegates to the Constitutional Convention—Hamilton's and Madison's writings in *The*

Federalist, for example. I do so, however, not because they were Framers and therefore their intent is authoritative and must be the law; but rather because their writings, like those of other intelligent and informed people of the time, display how the text of the Constitution was originally understood." [32]

Original intent, which Justice Scalia rejects, at least focuses on discrete and clearly identifiable sources, whereas original meaning opens the floodgates. Sources to examine include the papers of Washington, Adams, Jefferson, Madison, Franklin, and Hamilton (the most updated collections currently total 216 volumes, but they do not yet include a combined 108 years of their lives); smaller collections for many other founders; records of numerous local committees before and during the Revolutionary War; journals of the Continental and Confederation Congresses, the first few federal congresses under the Constitution, and state legislatures, as well as published letters of delegates to those bodies; twenty-two volumes of the *Documentary History of the Ratification of the Constitution* (with additional material not yet published); countless unpublished letters housed in local archives; extant newspapers for the latter third of the eighteenth century, with their flamboyant and often partisan writings; and of course dictionaries. Reasonably large samples of these materials must be explored if we wish to know precisely what "general welfare," "freedom of speech," "well regulated Militia," "excessive bail," "unreasonable searches and seizures," "necessary and proper," "regulate Commerce," "Republican Form of Government," or other such terms meant to the people of that time, or, in Justice Scalia's words, "the original meaning of the text." For a controversial passage, we need to discern how the disputed words or phrases are used in various contexts and then compare those contexts to the context within the Constitution. Rarely will we find a direct match, so even at its best, the results of our inquiry will be tentative. [33]

By substituting the generic "intelligent and informed people of the time" for the identifiable "framers" or "ratifiers," Justice Scalia removes us from actual historical events with real protagonists, and this provides great license for conjecture and personal discretion. Diffuse materials are more readily mined for evidence in support of preconceived conclusions. The pursuit of original meaning does not always involve passive *discovery*, where the answer simply awaits us in the texts; more often, it is a determined act of *construction*, building an argument on behalf of a preferred interpretation. The greater the number and variety of sources to choose from, the easier it is to find material to fashion an argument.[34]

Unwittingly, Justice Scalia illustrates the hazards of selective application. In *Printz v. United States* (1997), he argued against Justice David Souter's reference to Alexander Hamilton as an appropriate authority on the meaning of the Constitution. Hamilton held "the most expansive view of federal authority ever expressed," he maintained. "To choose Hamilton's view, as Justice Souter would, is to turn a blind eye to the fact that it was Madison's—not Hamilton's—that prevailed, not only at the Constitutional Convention and in popular sentiment, but in the subsequent struggle to fix the meaning of the Constitution by early congressional practice." From his distant vantage point, Justice Scalia makes a sweeping assessment of "popular sentiment," ignores Madison's extreme nationalism at the Constitutional Convention, and turns the history of the 1790s upside down. Madison did not "prevail" over Hamilton. He lost to Hamilton in constitutional disputes over a national bank in 1791, over Washington's neutrality proclamation in 1793, and over the ratification of Jay's Treaty in 1796 (see chapters 5 and 6). Even if we look beyond such dubious historical assessments, the nature of Justice Scalia's pronouncement is problematic. If some framers are right but others are wrong, there can be no single, correct doctrine of original intent or original meaning. It comes down to a game, with one justice selecting a winner whom another deems a loser.[35]

Like Attorney General Meese and Justice Thomas, Justice Scalia presents originalism as an antidote to judicial bias. "The main danger in judicial interpretation," he says, is that "judges will mistake their own predilections for the law." Originalism promises to combat that danger by establishing "a historical criterion that is conceptually quite separate from the preferences of the judge himself." Anchored by the founders, Justice Scalia insists, the Constitution cannot be swept this way or that by changing currents.[36]

In reality, originalism allows justices to overturn precedents with less restraint than they would otherwise display, altering the Court's direction at a moment's notice by a simple appeal to the founders. The doctrine does not enforce *tradition*, which in legal terms means abiding by precedent, but instead facilitates *change*. Originalism's capacity to catalyze change in constitutional law makes the Court, which has the final say in constitutional interpretation, more volatile and *less* stable—exactly the reverse of what originalism's advocates have promised.

Politically, originalism has provided both a justification and a strategy for reversing the trend toward centralization and regulation that started with the Progressives in the early twentieth century, gained full force with the New Deal, and culminated in the Great Society, enforced social equality, and environmental regulation in the 1960s and 1970s. The vast array of legal precedents that buttressed changes in American society over those years can be annulled in an instant by a comparatively simple change in jurisprudence. If the founders would not have liked one of those decisions, it must go, originalists say. In this manner, the liberalization of American society can be reversed through the judicial system, conveniently bypassing the cumbersome legislative process. To some, this reversal is an extreme application of "judicial activism"—a pejorative term high on the litany of conservative complaints—but its proponents view it differently. Using originalism to overturn unwarranted precedents simply rights previous wrongs, they claim.[37]

"Let me put it this way," Justice Thomas said in a 2008 talk. "There are really only two ways to interpret the Constitution—try to discern as best we can what the framers intended or make it up." "Make it up" refers to originalism's rival, the so-called Living Constitution, which Justice Scalia characterizes as "a body of law that grows and changes from age to age, in order to meet the needs of a changing society." It is the originalists' bête noire. "The Constitution that I interpret and apply is not living but dead," Justice Scalia scoffs.[38]

"I certainly do not regard the Constitution as something that 'grows and changes' by some mystical kind of organic, morphing process of the sort Justice Scalia mocks," protests Justice Scalia's longtime antagonist Laurence Tribe, a professor of constitutional law at Harvard Law School who has argued dozens of cases before the Supreme Court. "It seems to me quite impossible to sustain the proposition that understanding or meanings frozen circa 1791 can possibly serve as the definitive limits to those freedoms as enforced today," he writes. Instead, the Constitution in 1788 and the Bill of

Rights in 1791 were "launched upon a historic voyage of interpretation in which succeeding generations . . . would elaborate what the text means in ways all but certain not to remain static." [39]

Justice Stephen Breyer, who has served with Scalia on the Supreme Court since 1994, has outlined a methodology to justify this evolutionary approach. Judges must first take the wide view of the Constitution and then interpret its various components in ways that further its overall purpose. The initial step in constitutional interpretation, he says, is to identify the critical values underlying the various clauses; next, judges should evaluate the "likely consequences" of their decisions in terms of those values. The overriding value, he says, is "active liberty" or "a sharing of a nation's sovereign authority among its people." This is "the Constitution's democratic objective." [40]

These methodologies are far too general, originalists counter. Justice Scalia, playing on Professor Tribe's provocative metaphor, states: "When the question arises, as it must in any reader's mind, *which* provisions embark 'upon a historic voyage of interpretation' and which stay home—and the further question, what determines the direction of those that wander— Professor Tribe . . . acknowledges that he does not know the answer to either of these questions." Taking the image one step further, Justice Scalia refers to Tribe's "vagrant Constitution" and complains that such a conjured text is "indistinguishable from poetry." [41]

Justice Scalia boasts that "the originalist at least knows what he is looking for: the original meaning of the text." Yet, though the Constitution is real— it is written on parchment and we all vow to live by it—its so-called original meaning is quite literally a fiction, conjured by trying to reconstruct how anonymous citizens in 1788 or 1791 might have understood the Constitution and the Bill of Rights. If the Living Constitution is poetry, originalism is fictive prose. Neither methodology adequately reflects how people today actually use the Constitution. In practice, we are all originalists, basing arguments when we can on what the founders said and did; we are nonoriginalists as well, adapting words from the founding era so they make sense to us today; and we are all textualists too, claiming the same starting point: the text itself. Yet precise applications, and the theories that justify them, differ markedly. [42]

Developing a consistent method for interpreting the Constitution—and then sticking to it—is no easy matter. One method, for starters, is to distinguish two sorts of provisions within the document, those that establish "concrete or dated rules" and those that lay out "abstract principles." The Constitution's Preamble and provisions in the Bill of Rights, for example, express abstract goals and values; subject to interpretation, their precise application will evolve over time. Most provisions in the body of the Constitution, however, are more precise. They stipulate how old a president must be, how he will be selected, how long he will serve, and who could try his impeachment, if it comes to that. Because the Constitution and the Bill of Rights lack "stylistic homogeneity," writes legal philosopher Ronald Dworkin of New York University Law School, rules and principles may be treated differently. Whereas rules are frozen in time, "majestic" principles should be revisited "generation by generation." [43]

By contrast, Justice Scalia insists that even abstract principles cannot be subjected to evolutionary interpretations. The meaning of each principle is "rooted in the moral perceptions *of the time*" (his emphasis). Imagine, though, if the nine justices on the Supreme Court in 1954 had used this standard in *Brown v. Board of Education*, which questioned whether "separate but equal" schools violated the "equal protection" clause of the Fourteenth Amendment. The case would turn on whether the congressional authors and sponsors of the amendment in 1866, and/or state legislators who ratified the amendment over the course of the next two years, thought that the principle of equality was compatible with racial segregation. That is an interesting if somewhat esoteric historical question with evidence to support both sides, and any answer would be tentative at best. It is at least plausible that moderates in state legislatures from 1866 to 1868 would not have voted to ratify the amendment had they thought it required the schools their children attended to be integrated, but we can never be certain. Nevertheless, to determine whether "equality" in 1954 necessitated the integration of public schools, justices not necessarily steeped in the history of Reconstruction would need to interpret evidence from almost a century earlier, in a country just rocked by the Civil War and still replete with racial and sectional tensions, and make a final pronouncement on the "moral perceptions" of that time. [44]

Even the doctrine of coverture (a married woman has no legal existence beyond her husband, so she can possess no property of her own) could receive constitutional protection by a strict adherence to Scalia's "moral perceptions of the time." Whereas the Nineteenth Amendment gave women the right to vote, it did not address property rights or coverture, which embraced a moral perception of the founding generation, what we now call a family value: the man of the family owns the property and calls the shots. That "moral perception of the time," embodied in eighteenth-century state statutes, was left unaltered by the Nineteenth Amendment; a woman could vote even if she owned no property. All subsequent laws that ran counter to it, including those that terminated coverture, should be considered unconstitutional under a consistent application of Justice Scalia's standard.[45]

There is clearly something amiss here, and constitutional scholar Jack Balkin of Yale Law School, among others, analyzes the fallacy. Originalists like Justice Scalia confuse "original meaning"—what people at the time thought a provision *meant*—with "original expected application"—how people at the time thought a provision would be *applied* in *specific* situations. There is a significant difference.[46]

Consider Justice Scalia's stance on capital punishment and his particular attention to a clause within the Fifth Amendment: "No person shall be . . . deprived of life, liberty, or property, without due process of law." This indicates that a person *can* be deprived of life *with* due process of law. The framers of the Bill of Rights no doubt considered dismemberment a cruel and unusual method of executing a heinous criminal, but certainly not hanging, a common practice for the era. That was how people at the time expected the principle to be applied.[47]

Yet when the Eighth Amendment was written and ratified, public lashing and branding of a hand were common punishments for minor offenses. Because the expected application of the "cruel and unusual" standard would not have prohibited such practices, an originalist judge today, faced with a prisoner's complaint that he was whipped and branded for shoplifting, should declare those punishments well within the limits of the Constitution. In practice, though, it would be difficult to find a modern judge of any persuasion willing to do so, and this shows that we are not willing to accept the founding era's expected applications of "cruel and unusual." To his credit, Justice Scalia has grappled with this case and admits that "any espousal of originalism as a practical theory of exegesis must somehow come to terms with that reality." Originalism is only "The Lesser Evil"—his own title for an article—and might not be applicable in every instance. This weakened version, however, would qualify as a comprehensive methodology only if it offered guidelines for when to apply originalism and when not to.[48]

Consider also mixed race marriages. In *Loving v. Virginia* (1967), the United States Supreme Court overturned a Virginia antimiscegenation law, claiming that it violated the "equal protection" and "due process of law" clauses of the Fourteenth Amendment. Yet in 1868, had people thought antimiscegenation laws would be declared unconstitutional because of the Fourteenth Amendment, moderates in Congress would probably have voted against that amendment and state legislatures would probably not have ratified it. Although the original expected application of the Fourteenth Amendment did not include legalization of interracial marriages, no mainstream judge today would uphold an antimiscegenation law on that basis. Using the founders' moral code to determine our moral code would transform the Constitution's broad principles into mere rules—and worse yet, into rules that we no longer wish to follow.[49]

This problem stems from a misconception of what a constitution, at its best, is all about. The "whole purpose" of a constitution, Scalia writes, "is to prevent change—to embed certain rights in such a manner that future generations cannot readily take them away."[50]

Not so, Professor Balkin responds. Constitutions "are designed to create political institutions and to set up the basic elements of future political decision making. Their basic job is not to prevent future decision making but to enable it." Our Constitution, Balkin says, "channels" and "disciplines" us; it does not order us. Yes, we must stay within its bounds, but *we* are the ones to determine what those bounds will be, and that determination has changed, and must change, with time.[51]

Whether or not preventing change is the whole purpose of some constitutions, it certainly was not the whole purpose of ours. From a historical point of view, if there was a single purpose to the Federal Convention, it was to create a vigorous and energetic government that would enable American citizens to enjoy the benefits of republican self-rule. With the exception of George Mason and Elbridge Gerry, delegates to the Convention did not even think to "embed" the protections that we now enshrine as the Bill of Rights within the text of the proposed Constitution. It was not their overriding concern. The framers did not proclaim, "Our purpose is to prevent change at all costs. We must make future generations act as we do." That would have been a very un-republican approach.

On the final day of the Convention, Benjamin Franklin delivered a different message. He is often quoted and praised for his humility ("the older I grow, the more apt I am to doubt my own judgment, and to pay more respect to the judgment of others"), his optimism (the sun painted on the president's chair must be rising, not setting), and his belief in the proposed Constitution ("thus I consent, Sir, to this Constitution because I expect no better, and because I am not sure, that it is not the best"). Less celebrated is the reason he supported the Constitution, what he considered its primary purpose: "I agree to this Constitution with all its faults, if they are such; because I think a general Government necessary for us, and there is no form of Government but what may be a blessing to the people if well administered." Although Franklin was as wary of concentrated power as was any other framer, his Constitution was about possibility, not limitation. Government was a necessary and vital step toward the solution; it was not the problem. That is why the framers established a stronger and more viable government.[52]

The Constitution that created and buttressed our government has lasted for more than two centuries, but nobody knew at the start whether it would work at all. Even Franklin's optimism was as much hope as expectation. Just after the Convention's close, a woman from Philadelphia was said to have asked him, "Well, Doctor, what have we got, a republic or a monarchy?"

"A republic, if you can keep it," he is said to have responded.[53]

People read this story differently. Conservative commentator Patrick J. Buchanan, who concludes an article with this anecdote, adds a moral: "Let us restore that republic." For Buchanan and many others, the story calls for a return to the golden age of the founders; we, the errant sinners who have gone astray, need only rediscover their truths, heed what they said, and agree to live by the rules they set down and the values they upheld.[54]

A different reading puts a wink in Franklin's eye. Whereas Buchanan focused on the word "keep," with its passive connotation, we can honor Franklin's wisdom, wit, and ironic sensitivities by placing the emphasis on the conjectural "if," which in his teasing way invites a more active commitment from future generations. We have set a direction, he said for the framers, but now it's up to you. Do what you can to make the experiment work.[55]

DOCUMENT A:
ARTICLES OF CONFEDERATION

Submitted to the states on November 15, 1777,
and ratified on March 1, 1781

Articles of Confederation and perpetual Union between the states of New Hampshire, Massachusetts-bay Rhode Island and Providence Plantations, Connecticut, New York, New Jersey, Pennsylvania, Delaware, Maryland, Virginia, North Carolina, South Carolina and Georgia.

I. The Stile of this Confederacy shall be "The United States of America."

II. Each state retains its sovereignty, freedom, and independence, and every power, jurisdiction, and right, which is not by this Confederation expressly delegated to the United States, in Congress assembled.

III. The said States hereby severally enter into a firm league of friendship with each other, for their common defense, the security of their liberties, and their mutual and general welfare, binding themselves to assist each other, against

Source: Yale Law School, Avalon Project.

all force offered to, or attacks made upon them, or any of them, on account of religion, sovereignty, trade, or any other pretense whatever.

IV. The better to secure and perpetuate mutual friendship and intercourse among the people of the different States in this Union, the free inhabitants of each of these States, paupers, vagabonds, and fugitives from justice excepted, shall be entitled to all privileges and immunities of free citizens in the several States; and the people of each State shall free ingress and regress to and from any other State, and shall enjoy therein all the privileges of trade and commerce, subject to the same duties, impositions, and restrictions as the inhabitants thereof respectively, provided that such restrictions shall not extend so far as to prevent the removal of property imported into any State, to any other State, of which the owner is an inhabitant; provided also that no imposition, duties or restriction shall be laid by any State, on the property of the United States, or either of them.

If any person guilty of, or charged with, treason, felony, or other high misdemeanor in any State, shall flee from justice, and be found in any of the United States, he shall, upon demand of the Governor or executive power of the State from which he fled, be delivered up and removed to the State having jurisdiction of his offense.

Full faith and credit shall be given in each of these States to the records, acts, and judicial proceedings of the courts and magistrates of every other State.

V. For the most convenient management of the general interests of the United States, delegates shall be annually appointed in such manner as the legislatures of each State shall direct, to meet in Congress on the first Monday in November, in every year, with a power reserved to each State to recall its delegates, or any of them, at any time within the year, and to send others in their stead for the remainder of the year.

No State shall be represented in Congress by less than two, nor more than seven members; and no person shall be capable of being a delegate for more than three years in any term of six years; nor shall any person, being a delegate, be capable of holding any office under the United States, for which he, or another for his benefit, receives any salary, fees or emolument of any kind.

Each State shall maintain its own delegates in a meeting of the States, and while they act as members of the committee of the States.

In determining questions in the United States in Congress assembled, each State shall have one vote.

Freedom of speech and debate in Congress shall not be impeached or questioned in any court or place out of Congress, and the members of Congress shall be protected in their persons from arrests or imprisonments, during the time of their going to and from, and attendence on Congress, except for treason, felony, or breach of the peace.

VI. No State, without the consent of the United States in Congress assembled, shall send any embassy to, or receive any embassy from, or enter into any conference, agreement, alliance or treaty with any King, Prince or State; nor shall any person holding any office of profit or trust under the United States, or any of them, accept any present, emolument, office or title of any kind whatever from any King, Prince or foreign State; nor shall the United States in Congress assembled, or any of them, grant any title of nobility.

No two or more States shall enter into any treaty, confederation or alliance whatever between them, without the consent of the United States in Congress assembled, specifying accurately the purposes for which the same is to be entered into, and how long it shall continue.

No State shall lay any imposts or duties, which may interfere with any stipulations in treaties, entered into by the United States in Congress assembled, with any King, Prince or State, in pursuance of any treaties already proposed by Congress, to the courts of France and Spain.

No vessel of war shall be kept up in time of peace by any State, except such number only, as shall be deemed necessary by the United States in Congress assembled, for the defense of such State, or its trade; nor shall any body of forces be kept up by any State in time of peace, except such number only, as in the judgement of the United States in Congress assembled, shall be deemed requisite to garrison the forts necessary for the defense of such State; but every State shall always keep up a well-regulated and disciplined militia, sufficiently armed and accoutered, and shall provide and constantly have ready for use, in public stores, a due number of filed pieces and tents, and a proper quantity of arms, ammunition and camp equipage.

No State shall engage in any war without the consent of the United States in Congress assembled, unless such State be actually invaded by enemies, or shall have received certain advice of a resolution being formed by some nation of Indians to invade such State, and the danger is so imminent as not to admit of a delay till the United States in Congress assembled can be consulted; nor shall any State grant commissions to any ships or vessels of war, nor letters of marque or reprisal, except it be after a declaration of war by the United States in Congress assembled, and then only against the Kingdom or State and the subjects thereof, against which war has been so declared, and under such regulations as shall be established by the United States in Congress assembled, unless such State be infested by pirates, in which case vessels of war may be fitted out for that occasion, and kept so long as the danger shall continue, or until the United States in Congress assembled shall determine otherwise.

VII. When land forces are raised by any State for the common defense, all officers of or under the rank of colonel, shall be appointed by the legislature of each State respectively, by whom such forces shall be raised, or in such manner as such State shall direct, and all vacancies shall be filled up by the State which first made the appointment.

VIII. All charges of war, and all other expenses that shall be incurred for the common defense or general welfare, and allowed by the United States in Congress assembled, shall be defrayed out of a common treasury, which shall be supplied by the several States in proportion to the value of all land within each State, granted or surveyed for any person, as such land and the buildings and improvements thereon shall be estimated according to such mode as the United States in Congress assembled, shall from time to time direct and appoint.

The taxes for paying that proportion shall be laid and levied by the authority and direction of the legislatures of the several States within the time agreed upon by the United States in Congress assembled.

IX. The United States in Congress assembled, shall have the sole and exclusive right and power of determining on peace and war, except in the cases mentioned in the sixth article—of sending and receiving ambassadors—entering into treaties and alliances, provided that no treaty of commerce shall be made whereby the legislative power of the respective States shall be restrained from imposing such imposts and duties on foreigners, as their own people are subjected to, or from prohibiting the exportation or importation of any species of goods or commodities whatsoever—of establishing rules for deciding in all cases, what captures on land or water shall be legal, and in what manner prizes taken by land or naval forces in the service of the United States shall be divided or appropriated—of granting letters of marque and reprisal in times of peace—appointing courts for the trial of piracies and felonies commited on the high seas and establishing courts for receiving and determining finally appeals in all cases of captures, provided that no member of Congress shall be appointed a judge of any of the said courts.

The United States in Congress assembled shall also be the last resort on appeal in all disputes and differences now subsisting or that hereafter may arise between two or more States concerning boundary, jurisdiction or any other causes whatever; which authority shall always be exercised in the manner following. Whenever the legislative or executive authority or lawful agent of any State in controversy with another shall present a petition to Congress stating the matter in question and praying for a hearing, notice thereof shall be given by order of Congress to the legislative or executive authority of the other State in controversy, and a day assigned for the appearance of the parties by their lawful agents, who shall then be directed to appoint by joint consent, commissioners or judges to constitute a court for hearing and determining the matter in question: but if they cannot agree, Congress shall name three persons out of each of the United States, and from the list of such persons each party shall alternately strike out one, the petitioners beginning, until the number shall be reduced to thirteen; and from that number not less than seven, nor more than nine names as Congress shall direct, shall in the presence of Congress be drawn out by lot, and the persons whose names shall be so drawn or any five of them, shall be commissioners or judges, to hear and finally determine the controversy, so always as a major part of the judges who shall hear the cause shall agree in the determination: and if either party shall neglect to attend at the day appointed, without showing reasons, which Congress shall judge sufficient, or being present shall refuse to strike, the Congress shall proceed to nominate three persons out of each State, and the secretary of Congress shall strike in behalf of such party absent or refusing; and the judgement and sentence of the court to be appointed, in the manner before prescribed, shall be final and conclusive; and if any of the parties shall refuse to submit to the authority of such court, or to appear or defend their claim or cause, the court shall nevertheless proceed to pronounce sentence, or judgement, which shall in like manner be final and decisive, the judgement or sentence and other proceedings being in either case transmitted to Congress, and lodged among the acts of Congress for the security of the parties concerned: provided that every commissioner, before he sits in judgement, shall take an oath to be administered by one of the judges of the supreme or superior court of the State, where the cause shall be tried, 'well and truly to hear and determine the matter in question, according to the best of his judgement, without favor, affection or hope of reward': provided also, that no State shall be deprived of territory for the benefit of the United States.

All controversies concerning the private right of soil claimed under different grants of two or more States, whose jurisdictions as they may respect such lands, and the States which passed such grants are adjusted, the said grants or either of them being at the same time claimed to have originated antecedent to such settlement of jurisdiction, shall on the petition of either party to the Congress of the United States, be finally determined as near as may be in the same manner as is before presecribed for deciding disputes respecting territorial jurisdiction between different States.

The United States in Congress assembled shall also have the sole and exclusive right and power of regulating the alloy and value of coin struck by their own authority, or by that of the respective States—fixing the standards of weights and measures throughout the United States—regulating the trade and managing all affairs with the Indians, not members of any of the States, provided that the legislative right of any State within its own limits be not infringed or violated—establishing or regulating post offices from one State to another, throughout all the United States, and exacting such postage on the papers passing through the same as may be requisite to defray the expenses of the said office—appointing all officers of the land forces, in the service of the United States, excepting regimental officers—appointing all the officers of the naval forces, and commissioning all officers whatever in the service of the United States—making rules for the government and regulation of the said land and naval forces, and directing their operations.

The United States in Congress assembled shall have authority to appoint a committee, to sit in the recess of Congress, to be denominated 'A Committee of the States', and to consist of one delegate from each State; and to appoint such other committees and civil officers as may be necessary for managing the

general affairs of the United States under their direction—to appoint one of
their members to preside, provided that no person be allowed to serve in the
office of president more than one year in any term of three years; to ascertain the
necessary sums of money to be raised for the service of the United States, and
to appropriate and apply the same for defraying the public expenses—to borrow
money, or emit bills on the credit of the United States, transmitting every half-
year to the respective States an account of the sums of money so borrowed or
emitted—to build and equip a navy—to agree upon the number of land forces,
and to make requisitions from each State for its quota, in proportion to the
number of white inhabitants in such State; which requisition shall be binding, and
thereupon the legislature of each State shall appoint the regimental officers, raise
the men and cloath, arm and equip them in a solid-like manner, at the expense
of the United States; and the officers and men so cloathed, armed and equipped
shall march to the place appointed, and within the time agreed on by the United
States in Congress assembled. But if the United States in Congress assembled
shall, on consideration of circumstances judge proper that any State should not
raise men, or should raise a smaller number of men than the quota thereof, such
extra number shall be raised, officered, cloathed, armed and equipped in the same
manner as the quota of each State, unless the legislature of such State shall judge
that such extra number cannot be safely spread out in the same, in which case
they shall raise, officer, cloath, arm and equip as many of such extra number as
they judeg can be safely spared. And the officers and men so cloathed, armed, and
equipped, shall march to the place appointed, and within the time agreed on by the
United States in Congress assembled.

The United States in Congress assembled shall never engage in a war, nor
grant letters of marque or reprisal in time of peace, nor enter into any treaties or
alliances, nor coin money, nor regulate the value thereof, nor ascertain the sums
and expenses necessary for the defense and welfare of the United States, or any
of them, nor emit bills, nor borrow money on the credit of the United States,
nor appropriate money, nor agree upon the number of vessels of war, to be built
or purchased, or the number of land or sea forces to be raised, nor appoint a
commander in chief of the army or navy, unless nine States assent to the same:
nor shall a question on any other point, except for adjourning from day to day be
determined, unless by the votes of the majority of the United States in Congress
assembled.

The Congress of the United States shall have power to adjourn to any time within the year, and to any place within the United States, so that no period of adjournment be for a longer duration than the space of six months, and shall publish the journal of their proceedings monthly, except such parts thereof relating to treaties, alliances or military operations, as in their judgement require secrecy; and the yeas and nays of the delegates of each State on any question shall be entered on the journal, when it is desired by any delegates of a State, or any of them, at his or their request shall be furnished with a transcript of the said journal, except such parts as are above excepted, to lay before the legislatures of the several States.

X. The Committee of the States, or any nine of them, shall be authorized to execute, in the recess of Congress, such of the powers of Congress as the United States in Congress assembled, by the consent of the nine States, shall from time to time think expedient to vest them with; provided that no power be delegated to the said Committee, for the exercise of which, by the Articles of Confederation, the voice of nine States in the Congress of the United States assembled be requisite.

XI. Canada acceding to this confederation, and adjoining in the measures of the United States, shall be admitted into, and entitled to all the advantages of this Union; but no other colony shall be admitted into the same, unless such admission be agreed to by nine States.

XII. All bills of credit emitted, monies borrowed, and debts contracted by, or under the authority of Congress, before the assembling of the United States, in pursuance of the present confederation, shall be deemed and considered as a charge against the United States, for payment and satisfaction whereof the said United States, and the public faith are hereby solemnly pleged.

XIII. Every State shall abide by the determination of the United States in Congress assembled, on all questions which by this confederation are submitted to them. And the Articles of this Confederation shall be inviolably observed by every State, and the Union shall be perpetual; nor shall any alteration at any time hereafter be made in any of them; unless such alteration be agreed to in a Congress of the United States, and be afterwards confirmed by the legislatures of every State.

And Whereas it hath pleased the Great Governor of the World to incline the hearts of the legislatures we respectively represent in Congress, to approve of, and to authorize us to ratify the said Articles of Confederation and perpetual Union. Know Ye that we the undersigned delegates, by virtue of the power and authority to us given for that purpose, do by these presents, in the name and in behalf of our respective constituents, fully and entirely ratify and confirm each and every of the said Articles of Confederation and perpetual Union, and all and singular the matters and things therein contained: And we do further solemnly plight and engage the faith of our respective constituents, that they shall abide by the determinations of the United States in Congress assembled, on all questions, which by the said Confederation are submitted to them. And that the Articles thereof shall be inviolably observed by the States we respectively represent, and that the Union shall be perpetual.

DOCUMENT B:
WASHINGTON'S "LEGACY" LETTER
TO THE STATES

Head Quarters, Newburgh, June 8, 1783

Sir: The great object for which I had the honor to hold an appointment in the
Service of my Country, being accomplished, I am now preparing to resign it
into the hands of Congress, and to return to that domestic retirement, which, it
is well known, I left with the greatest reluctance, a Retirement, for which I have
never ceased to sigh through a long and painful absence, and in which (remote
from the noise and trouble of the World) I meditate to pass the remainder of life
in a state of undisturbed repose; But before I carry this resolution into effect, I
think it a duty incumbent on me, to make this my last official communication,
to congratulate you on the glorious events which Heaven has been pleased to
produce in our favor, to offer my sentiments respecting some important subjects,
which appear to me, to be intimately connected with the tranquility of the United
States, to take my leave of your Excellency as a public Character, and to give
my final blessing to that Country, in whose service I have spent the prime of my

Source: John C. Fitzpatrick, ed., *The Writings of George Washington from the Original
Manuscript Sources,* 1745–1789 (Washington, D.C.: U.S. Government Printing Office,
1931–44), 26:483–96.

life, for whose sake I have consumed so many anxious days and watchfull nights, and whose happiness being extremely dear to me, will always constitute no inconsiderable part of my own.

Impressed with the liveliest sensibility on this pleasing occasion, I will claim the indulgence of dilating the more copiously on the subjects of our mutual felicitation. When we consider the magnitude of the prize we contended for, the doubtful nature of the contest, and the favorable manner in which it has terminated, we shall find the greatest possible reason for gratitude and rejoicing; this is a theme that will afford infinite delight to every benevolent and liberal mind, whether the event in contemplation, be considered as the source of present enjoyment or the parent of future happiness; and we shall have equal occasion to felicitate ourselves on the lot which Providence has assigned us, whether we view it in a natural, a political or moral point of light.

The Citizens of America, placed in the most enviable condition, as the sole Lords and Proprietors of a vast Tract of Continent, comprehending all the various soils and climates of the World, and abounding with all the necessaries and conveniencies of life, are now by the late satisfactory pacification, acknowledged to be possessed of absolute freedom and Independency; They are, from this period, to be considered as the Actors on a most conspicuous Theatre, which seems to be peculiarly designated by Providence for the display of human greatness and felicity; Here, they are not only surrounded with every thing which can contribute to the completion of private and domestic enjoyment, but Heaven has crowned all its other blessings, by giving a fairer oppertunity for political happiness, than any other Nation has ever been favored with. Nothing can illustrate these observations more forcibly, than a recollection of the happy conjuncture of times and circumstances, under which our Republic assumed its rank among the Nations; The foundation of our Empire was not laid in the gloomy age of Ignorance and Superstition, but at an Epocha when the rights of mankind were better understood and more clearly defined, than at any former period, the researches of the human mind, after social happiness, have been carried to a great extent, the Treasures of knowledge, acquired by the labours of Philosophers, Sages and Legislatures, through a long succession of years, are laid open for our use, and their collected wisdom may be happily applied in the Establishment of our forms of Government; the free cultivation of Letters, the unbounded extension of Commerce, the progressive refinement of Manners, the growing liberality of sentiment, and above all, the pure and benign light of Revelation, have had ameliorating influence on mankind and increased the blessings of Society. At this auspicious period, the United States came into existence as a Nation, and if their Citizens should not be completely free and happy, the fault will be intirely their own.

Such is our situation, and such are our prospects: but notwithstanding the cup of blessing is thus reached out to us, notwithstanding happiness is ours, if we have a disposition to seize the occasion and make it our own; yet, it appears to me there is an option still left to the United States of America, that it is in their choice, and depends upon their conduct, whether they will be respectable and prosperous, or contemptible and miserable as a Nation; This is the time of their political probation, this is the moment when the eyes of the whole World are turned upon them, this is the moment to establish or ruin their national Character forever, this is the favorable moment to give such a tone to our Federal Government, as will enable it to answer the ends of its institution, or this may be the ill-fated moment for relaxing the powers of the Union, annihilating the cement of the Confederation, and exposing us to become the sport of European politics, which may play one State against another to prevent their growing importance, and to serve their own interested purposes. For, according to the system of Policy the States shall adopt at this moment, they will stand or fall, and by their confirmation or lapse, it is yet to be decided, whether the Revolution must ultimately be considered as a blessing or a curse: a blessing or a curse, not to the present age alone, for with our fate will the destiny of unborn Millions be involved.

With this conviction of the importance of the present Crisis, silence in me would be a crime; I will therefore speak to your Excellency, the language of freedom and of sincerity, without disguise; I am aware, however, that those who differ from me in political sentiment, may perhaps remark, I am stepping out of the proper line of my duty, and they may possibly ascribe to arrogance or ostentation, what I know is alone the result of the purest intention, but the rectitude of my own heart, which disdains such unworthy motives, the part I have hitherto acted in life, the determination I have formed, of not taking any share in public business hereafter, the ardent desire I feel, and shall continue to manifest, of quietly enjoying in private life, after all the toils of War, the benefits of a wise and liberal Government, will, I flatter myself, sooner or later convince my Countrymen, that I could have no sinister views in delivering with so little reserve, the opinions contained in this Address.

There are four things, which I humbly conceive, are essential to the well being, I may even venture to say, to the existence of the United States as an Independent Power:

1st. An indissoluble Union of the States under one Federal Head.

2dly. A Sacred regard to Public Justice.

3dly. The adoption of a proper Peace Establishment, and

4thly. The prevalence of that pacific and friendly Disposition, among the People of the United States, which will induce them to forget their local prejudices and policies, to make those mutual concessions which are requisite to the general prosperity, and in some instances, to sacrifice their individual advantages to the interest of the Community.

These are the pillars on which the glorious Fabrick of our Independency and National Character must be supported; Liberty is the Basis, and whoever would dare to sap the foundation, or overturn the Structure, under whatever specious pretexts he may attempt it, will merit the bitterest execration, and the severest punishment which can be inflicted by his injured Country.

On the three first Articles I will make a few observations, leaving the last to the good sense and serious consideration of those immediately concerned.

Under the first head, altho' it may not be necessary or proper for me in this place to enter into a particular disquisition of the principles of the Union, and to take up the great question which has been frequently agitated, whether it be expedient and requisite for the States to delegate a larger proportion of Power to Congress, or not, Yet it will be a part of my duty, and that of every true Patriot, to assert without reserve, and to insist upon the following positions, That unless the States will suffer Congress to exercise those prerogatives, they are undoubtedly invested with by the Constitution, every thing must very rapidly tend to Anarchy and confusion, That it is indispensable to the happiness of the individual States, that there should be lodged somewhere, a Supreme Power to regulate and govern the general concerns of the Confederated Republic, without which the Union cannot be of long duration. That there must be a faithfull and pointed compliance on the part of every State, with the late proposals and demands of Congress, or the most fatal consequences will ensue, That whatever measures have a tendency to dissolve the Union, or contribute to violate or lessen the Sovereign Authority, ought to be considered as hostile to the Liberty and Independency of America, and the Authors of them treated accordingly, and lastly, that unless we can be enabled by the concurrence of the States, to participate of the fruits of the Revolution, and enjoy the essential benefits of Civil Society, under a form of Government so free and uncorrupted, so happily guarded against the danger of oppression, as has been devised and adopted by the Articles of Confederation, it will be a subject of regret, that so much blood and treasure have been lavished for no purpose, that so many sufferings have been encountered without a compensation, and that so many sacrifices have been made in vain. Many other considerations might here be adduced to prove, that without an entire conformity to the Spirit of the Union, we cannot exist as an Independent Power; it will be sufficient for my purpose to mention but one or two which seem to me of the greatest importance. It is only in our united Character as an Empire, that our Independence is acknowledged, that our power can be regarded, or our Credit supported among Foreign Nations. The Treaties of the European Powers with the United States of America, will have no validity on a dissolution of the Union. We shall be left nearly in a state of Nature, or we may find by our own unhappy experience, that there is a natural and necessary progression, from the extreme of anarchy to the extreme of Tyranny; and that arbitrary power is most easily established on the ruins of Liberty abused to licentiousness.

As to file second Article, which respects the performance of Public Justice, Congress have, in their late Address to the United States, almost exhausted the subject, they have explained their Ideas so fully, and have enforced the obligations the States are under, to render compleat justice to all the Public Creditors, with so much dignity and energy, that in my opinion, no real friend to the honor and Independency of America, can hesitate a single moment respecting the propriety of complying with the just and honorable measures proposed; if their Arguments do not produce conviction, I know of nothing that will have greater influence; especially when we recollect that the System referred to, being the result of the collected Wisdom of the Continent, must be esteemed, if not perfect, certainly the least objectionable of any that could be devised; and that if it shall not be carried into immediate execution, a National Bankruptcy, with all its deplorable consequences will take place, before any different Plan can possibly be proposed and adopted; So pressing are the present circumstances I and such is the alternative now offered to the States!

The ability of the Country to discharge the debts which have been incurred in its defence, is not to be doubted, an inclination, I flatter myself, will not be wanting, the path of our duty is plain before us, honesty will be found on every experiment, to be the best and only true policy, let us then as a Nation be just, let us fulfil the public Contracts, which Congress had undoubtedly a right to make for the purpose of carrying on the War, with the same good faith we suppose ourselves bound to perform our private engagements; in the mean time, let an attention to the chearfull performance of their proper business, as Individuals, and as members of Society, be earnestly inculcated on the Citizens of America, that will they strengthen the hands of Government, and be happy under its protection: every one will reap the fruit of his labours, every one will enjoy his own acquisitions without molestation and without danger.

In this state of absolute freedom and perfect security, who will grudge to yield a very little of his property to support the common interest of Society, and insure the protection of Government? Who does not remember, the frequent declarations, at the commencement of the War, that we should be compleatly satisfied, if at the expence of one half, we could defend the remainder of our possessions? Where is the Man to be found, who wishes to remain indebted, for the defence of his own person and property, to the exertions, the bravery, and the blood of others, without making one generous effort to repay the debt of honor and of gratitude? In what part of the Continent shall we find any Man, or body of Men, who would not blush to stand up and propose measures, purposely calculated to rob the Soldier of his Stipend, and the Public Creditor of his due? and were it possible that such a flagrant instance of Injustice could ever happen, would it not excite the general indignation, and tend to bring down, upon the Authors of such measures, the aggravated vengeance of Heaven? If after all, a spirit of dis-union or a temper of obstinacy and perverseness, should manifest itself in any of the States, if such an ungracious disposition should attempt to frustrate all the happy effects that might be expected to flow from the Union, if there should be a refusal to comply with the requisitions for Funds to discharge the annual interest of the public debts, and if that refusal should revive again all those jealousies and produce all those evils, which are now happily removed, Congress, who have in all their Transaction shewn a great degree of magnanimity and justice, will stand justified in the sight of God and Man, and the State alone which puts itself in opposition to the aggregate Wisdom of the Continent, and follows such mistaken and pernicious Councils, will be responsible for all the consequences.

For my own part, conscious of having acted while a Servant of the Public, in the manner I conceived best suited to promote the real interests of my Country; having in consequence of my fixed belief in some measure pledged myself to the Army, that their Country would finally do them compleat and ample Justice, and not wishing to conceal any instance of my official conduct from the eyes of the World, I have thought proper to transmit to your Excellency the inclosed collection of Papers, *31* relative to the half pay and commutation granted by Congress to the Officers of the Army; From these communications, my decided sentiment will be clearly comprehended, together with the conclusive reasons which induced me, at an early period, to recommend the adoption of the measure, in the most earnest and serious manner. As the proceedings of Congress, the Army, and myself are open to all, and contain in my opinion, sufficient information to remove the prejudices and errors which may have been entertained by any; I think it unnecessary to say any thing more, than just to observe, that the Resolutions of Congress, now alluded to, are undoubtedly as absolutely binding upon the United States, as the most solemn Acts of Confederation or Legislation. As to the Idea, which I am informed has in some instances prevailed, that the half pay and commutation are to be regarded merely in the odious light of a Pension, it ought to be exploded forever; that Provision, should be viewed as it really was, a reasonable compensation offered by Congress, at a time when they had nothing else to give, to the Officers of the Army, for services then to be performed. It was the only means to prevent a total dereliction of the Service, It was a part of their hire, I may be allowed to say, it was the price of their blood and of your Independency, it is therefore more than a common debt, it is a debt of honour, it can never be considered as a Pension or gratuity, nor be cancelled until it is fairly discharged.

With regard to a distinction between Officers and Soldiers, it is sufficient that the uniform experience of every Nation of the World, combined with our own, proves the utility and propriety of the discrimination. Rewards in proportion to the aids the public derives from them, are unquestionably due to all its Servants; In some Lines, the Soldiers have perhaps generally had as ample a compensation for their Services, by the large Bounties which have been paid to them, as their

Officers will receive in the proposed Commutation, in others, if besides the donation of Lands, the payment of Arrearages of Cloathing and Wages (in which Articles all the component parts of the Army must be put upon the same footing) we take into the estimate, the Bounties many of the Soldiers have received and the gratuity of one Year's full pay, which is promised to all, possibly their situation (every circumstance being duly considered) will not be deemed less eligible than that of the Officers. Should a farther reward, however, be judged equitable, I will venture to assert, no one will enjoy greater satisfaction than myself, on seeing an exemption from Taxes for a limited time, (which has been petitioned for in some instances) or any other adequate immunity or compensation, granted to the brave defenders of their Country's Cause; but neither the adoption or rejection of this proposition will in any manner affect, much less militate against, the Act of Congress, by which they have offered five years full pay, in lieu of the half pay for life, which had been before promised to the Officers of the Army.

Before I conclude the subject of public justice, I cannot omit to mention the obligations this Country is under, to that meritorious Class of veteran Non-commissioned Officers and Privates, who have been discharged for inability, in consequence of the Resolution of Congress of the 23d of April 1782, on an annual pension for life, their peculiar sufferings, their singular merits and claims to that provision need only be known, to interest all the feelings of humanity in their behalf: nothing but a punctual payment of their annual allowance can rescue them from the most complicated misery, and nothing could be a more melancholy and distressing sight, than to behold those who have shed their blood or lost their limbs in the service of their Country, without a shelter, without a friend, and without the means of obtaining any of the necessaries or comforts of Life; compelled to beg their daily bread from door to door! suffer me to recommend those of this discription, belonging to your State, to the warmest patronage of your Excellency and your Legislature.

It is necessary to say but a few words on the third topic which was proposed, and which regards particularly the defence of the Republic, As there can be little doubt but Congress will recommend a proper Peace Establishment for the United States, in which a due attention will be paid to the importance of placing the Militia of the Union upon a regular and respectable footing; If this should be the case, I would beg leave to urge the great advantage of it in the strongest terms. The Militia of this Country must be considered as the Palladium of our security, and the first effectual resort in case of hostility; It is essential therefore, that the same system should pervade the whole; that the formation and discipline of the Militia of the Continent should be absolutely uniform, and that the same species of Arms, Accoutrements and Military Apparatus, should be introduced in every part of the United States; No one, (who has not learned it from experience, can conceive the difficulty, expence, and confusion which result from a contrary system, or the vague Arrangements which have hitherto prevailed.

If in treating of political points, a greater latitude than usual has been taken in the course of this Address, the importance of the Crisis, and the magnitude of the objects in discussion, must be my apology: It is, however, neither my wish or expectation, that the preceding observations should claim any regard, except so far as they shall appear to be dictated by a good intention, consonant to the immutable rules of Justice; calculated to produce a liberal system of policy, and founded on whatever experience may have been acquired by a long and close attention to public business. Here I might speak with the more confidence from my actual observations, and, if it would not swell this Letter (already too prolix) beyond the bounds I had prescribed myself: I could demonstrate to every mind open to conviction, that in less time and with much less expence than has been incurred, the War might have been brought to the same happy conclusion, if the resourses of the Continent could have been properly drawn forth, that the distresses and disappointments which have very often occurred, have in too many instances, resulted more from a want of energy, in the Continental Government, than a deficiency of means in the particular States. That the inefficiency of measures, arising from the want of an adequate authority in the Supreme Power, from a partial compliance with the Requisitions of Congress in some of the States, and from a failure of punctuality in others, while it tended to damp the zeal of those which were more willing to exert themselves; served also to accumulate the expences of the War, and to frustrate the best concerted Plans, and that the discouragement occasioned by the complicated difficulties and embarrassments, in which our affairs were, by this means involved, would have long ago produced the dissolution of any Army, less patient, less virtuous and less persevering, than that which I have had the honor to command. But while I mention these things, which are notorious facts, as the defects of our Federal Constitution, particularly in the prosecution of a War, I beg it may be understood, that as I have ever taken a pleasure in gratefully acknowledging the assistance and support I have derived from every Class of Citizens, so shall I always be happy to do justice to the unparalleled exertion of the individual States, on many interesting occasions.

I have thus freely disclosed what I wished to make known, before I surrendered up my Public trust to those who committed it to me, the task is now accomplished, I now bid adieu to your Excellency as the Chief Magistrate of your State, at the same time I bid a last farewell to the cares of Office, and all the imployments of public life.

It remains then to be my final and only request, that your Excellency will communicate these sentiments to your Legislature at their next meeting, and that they may be considered as the Legacy of One, who has ardently wished, on all occasions, to be useful to his Country, and who, even in the shade of Retirement, will not fail to implore the divine benediction upon it.

I now make it my earnest prayer, that God would have you, and the State over which you preside, in his holy protection, that he would incline the hearts of the Citizens to cultivate a spirit of subordination and obedience to Government, to entertain a brotherly affection and love for one another, for their fellow Citizens of the United States at large, and particularly for their brethren who have served in the Field, and finally, that he would most graciously be pleased to dispose us all, to do Justice, to love mercy, and to demean ourselves with that Charity, humility and pacific temper of mind, which were the Characteristicks of the Divine Author of our blessed Religion, and without an humble imitation of whose example in these things, we can never hope to be a happy Nation.

DOCUMENT C: VIRGINIA PLAN

May 29, 1787

1. Resolved that the articles of Confederation ought to be so corrected & enlarged as to accomplish the objects proposed by their institution; namely. "common defence, security of liberty and general welfare."

2. Resd. therefore that the rights of suffrage in the National Legislature ought to be proportioned to the Quotas of contribution, or to the number of free inhabitants, as the one or the other rule may seem best in different cases.

3. Resd. that the National Legislature ought to consist of two branches.

4. Resd. that the members of the first branch of the National Legislature ought to be elected by the people of the several States every _____ for the term of _____; to be of the age of _____ years at least, to receive liberal stipends by which they may be compensated for the devotion of their time to public service; to be ineligible to any office established by a particular State, or under the authority of the United States, except those beculiarly belonging to the functions of the first

Source: Max Farrand, ed., *Records of the Federal Convention*, 1:20–22.

branch, during the term of service, and for the space of NA after its expiration; to be incapable of re-election for the space of _____ after the expiration of their term of service, and to be subject to recall.

5. Resold. that the members of the second branch of the National Legislature ought to be elected by those of the first, out of a proper number of persons nominated by the individual Legislatures, to be of the age of _____ years at least; to hold their offices for a term sufficient to ensure their independency, to receive liberal stipends, by which they may be compensated for the devotion of their time to public service; and to be ineligible to any office established by a particular State, or under the authority of the United States, except those peculiarly belonging to the functions of the second branch, during the term of service, and for the space of _____ after the expiration thereof.

6. Resolved that each branch ought to possess the right of originating Acts; that the National Legislature ought to be impowered to enjoy the Legislative Rights vested in Congress by the Confederation & moreover to legislate in all cases to which the separate States are incompetent, or in which the harmony of the United States may be interrupted by the exercise of individual Legislation; to negative all laws passed by the several States, contravening in the opinion of the National Legislature the articles of Union; and to call forth the force of the Union agst. any member of the Union failing to fulfill its duty under the articles thereof.

7. Resd. that a National Executive be instituted; to be chosen by the National Legislature for the term of _____ years, to receive punctually at stated times, a fixed compensation for the services rendered, in which no increase or diminution shall be made so as to affect the Magistracy, existing at the time of increase or diminution, and to be ineligible a second time; and that besides a general authority to execute the National laws, it ought to enjoy the Executive rights vested in Congress by the Confederation.

8. Resd. that the Executive and a convenient number of the National Judiciary, ought to compose a council of revision with authority to examine every act of the National Legislature before it shall operate, & every act of a particular Legislature

before a Negative thereon shall be final; and that the dissent of the said Council shall amount to a rejection, unless the Act of the National Legislature be again passed, or that of a particular Legislature be again negatived by _____ of the members of each branch.

9. Resd. that a National Judiciary be established to consist of one or more supreme tribunals, and of inferior tribunals to be chosen by the National Legislature, to hold their offices during good behaviour; and to receive punctually at stated times fixed compensation for their services, in which no increase or diminution shall be made so as to affect the persons actually in office at the time of such increase or diminution. that the jurisdiction of the inferior tribunals shall be to hear & determine in the first instance, and of the supreme tribunal to hear and determine in the dernier resort, all piracies & felonies on the high seas, captures from an enemy; cases in which foreigners or citizens of other States applying to such jurisdictions may be interested, or which respect the collection of the National revenue; impeachments of any National officers, and questions which may involve the national peace and harmony.

10. Resolvd. that provision ought to be made for the admission of States lawfully arising within the limits of the United States, whether from a voluntary junction of Government & Territory or otherwise, with the consent of a number of voices in the National legislature less than the whole.

11. Resd. that a Republican Government & the territory of each State, except in the instance of a voluntary junction of Government & territory, ought to be guaranteed by the United States to each State.

12. Resd. that provision ought to be made for the continuance of Congress and their authorities and privileges, until a given day after the reform of the articles of Union shall be adopted, and for the completion of all their engagements.

13. Resd. that provision ought to be made for the amendment of the Articles of Union whensoever it shall seem necessary, and that the assent of the National Legislature ought not to be required thereto.

14. Resd. that the Legislative Executive & Judiciary powers within the several States ought to be bound by oath to support the articles of Union.

15. Resd. that the amendments which shall be offered to the Confederation, by the Convention ought at a proper time, or times, after the approbation of Congress to be submitted to an assembly or assemblies of Representatives, recommended by the several Legislatures to be expressly chosen by the people, to consider & decide thereon.

DOCUMENT D: COMMITTEE OF DETAIL DRAFT

August 6, 1787

We the people of the States of New Hampshire, Massachussetts, Rhode-Island and Providence Plantations, Connecticut, New-York, New-Jersey, Pennsylvania, Delaware, Maryland, Virginia, North-Carolina, South-Carolina, and Georgia, do ordain, declare, and establish the following Constitution for the Government of Ourselves and our Posterity.

I. The stile of the Government shall be, "The United States of America."

II. The Government shall consist of supreme legislative, executive; and judicial powers.

III. The legislative power shall be vested in a Congress, to consist of two separate and distinct bodies of men, a House of Representatives and a Senate; each of which shall in all cases have a negative on the other. The Legislature shall meet on the first Monday in December every year.

Source: James Madison, *Notes of Debates in the Federal Convention of 1787*, ed. Adrienne Koch (New York: W. W. Norton, 1987), 385–96.

IV. *Sect. 1.* The members of the House of Representatives shall be chosen every second year, by the people of the several States comprehended within this Union. The qualifications of the electors shall be the same, from time to time, as those of the electors in the several States, of the most numerous branch of their own legislatures.

Sect. 2. Every member of the House of Representatives shall be of the age of twenty five years at least; shall have been a citizen in the United States for at least three years before his election; and shall be, at the time of his election, a resident of the State in which he shall be chosen.

Sect. 3. The House of Representatives shall, at its first formation, and until the number of citizens and inhabitants shall be taken in the manner herein after described, consist of sixty five Members, of whom three shall be chosen in New-Hampshire, eight in Massachusetts, one in Rhode-Island and Providence Plantations, five in Connecticut, six in New-York, four in New-Jersey, eight in Pennsylvania, one in Delaware, six in Maryland, ten in Virginia, five in North-Carolina, five in South-Carolina, and three in Georgia.

Sect. 4. As the proportions of numbers in different States will alter from time to time; as some of the States may hereafter be divided; as others may be enlarged by addition of territory; as two or more States may be united; as new States will be erected within the limits of the United States, the Legislature shall, in each of these cases, regulate the number of representatives by the number of inhabitants, according to the provisions herein after made, at the rate of one for every forty thousand.

Sect. 5. All bills for raising or appropriating money, and for fixing the salaries of the officers of Government, shall originate in the House of Representatives, and shall not be altered or amended by the Senate. No money shall be drawn from the Public Treasury, but in pursuance of appropriations that shall originate in the House of Representatives.

Sect. 6. The House of Representatives shall have the sole power of impeachment. It shall choose its Speaker and other officers.

Sect. 7. Vacancies in the House of Representatives shall be supplied by writs of election from the executive authority of the State in the representation from which it shall happen.

V. *Sect. 1.* The Senate of the United States shall be chosen by the Legislatures of the several States. Each Legislature shall chuse two members. Vacancies may be supplied by the Executive until the next meeting of the Legislature. Each member shall have one vote.

Sect. 2. The Senators shall be chosen for six years; but immediately after the first election they shall be divided, by lot, into three classes, as nearly as may be, numbered one, two and three. The seats of the members of the first class shall be vacated at the expiration of the second year, of the second class at the expiration of the fourth year, of the third class at the expiration of the sixth year, so that a third part of the members may be chosen every second year.

Sect. 3. Every member of the Senate shall be of the age of thirty years at least; shall have been a citizen in the United States for at least four years before his election; and shall be, at the time of his election, a resident of the State for which he shall be chosen.

Sect. 4. The Senate shall chuse its own President and other officers.

VI. *Sect. 1.* The times and places and manner of holding the elections of the members of each House shall be prescribed by the Legislature of each State; but their provisions concerning them may, at any time be altered by the Legislature of the United States.

Sect. 2. The Legislature of the United States shall have authority to establish such uniform qualifications of the members of each House, with regard to property, as to the said Legislature shall seem expedient.

Sect. 3. In each House a majority of the members shall constitute a quorum to do business; but a smaller number may adjourn from day to day.

Sect. 4. Each House shall be the judge of the elections, returns and qualifications of its own members.

Sect. 5. Freedom of speech and debate in the Legislature shall not be impeached or questioned in any Court or place out of the Legislature; and the members of each House shall, in all cases, except treason felony and breach of the peace, be privileged from arrest during their attendance at Congress, and in going to and returning from it.

Sect. 6. Each House may determine the rules of its proceedings; may punish its members for disorderly behaviour; and may expel a member.

Sect. 7. The House of Representatives, and the Senate, when it shall be acting in a legislative capacity, shall keep a journal of their proceedings, and shall, from time to time, publish them: and the yeas and nays of the members of each House, on any question, shall at the desire of one-fifth part of the members present, be entered on the journal.

Sect. 8. Neither House, without the consent of the other, shall adjourn for more than three days, nor to any other place than that at which the two Houses are sitting. But this regulation shall not extend to the Senate, when it shall exercise the powers mentioned in the ____ article.

Sect. 9. The members of each House shall be ineligible to, and incapable of holding any office under the authority of the United States, during the time for which they shall respectively be elected: and the members of the Senate shall be ineligible to, and incapable of holding any such office for one year afterwards.

Sect. 10. The members of each House shall receive a compensation for their services, to be ascertained and paid by the State, in which they shall be chosen.

Sect. 11. The enacting stile of the laws of the United States shall be. "Be it enacted by the Senate and Representatives in Congress assembled."

Sect. 12. Each House shall possess the right of originating bills, except in the cases beforementioned.

Sect. 13. Every bill, which shall have passed the House of Representatives and the Senate, shall, before it become a law, be presented to the President of the United States for his revision: if, upon such revision, he approve of it, he shall signify his approbation by signing it: But if, upon such revision, it shall appear to him improper for being passed into a law, he shall return it, together with his objections against it, to that House in which it shall have originated, who shall enter the objections at large on their journal and proceed to reconsider the bill. But if after such reconsideration, two thirds of that House shall, notwithstanding the objections of the President, agree to pass it, it shall together with his objections, be sent to the other House, by which it shall likewise be reconsidered, and if approved by two thirds of the other House also, it shall become a law. But in all such cases, the votes of both Houses shall be determined by yeas and nays; and the names of the persons voting for or against the bill shall be entered on the journal of each House respectively. If any bill shall not be returned by the President within seven days after it shall have been presented to him, it shall be a law, unless the legislature, by their adjournment, prevent its return; in which case it shall not be a law.

VII. *Sect. 1.* The Legislature of the United States shall have the power to lay and collect taxes, duties, imposts and excises;
To regulate commerce with foreign nations, and among the several States;
To establish an uniform rule of naturalization throughout the United States;
To coin money;
To regulate the value of foreign coin;
To fix the standard of weights and measures;
To establish Post-offices;
To borrow money, and emit bills on the credit of the United States;
To appoint a Treasurer by ballot;
To constitute tribunals inferior to the Supreme Court;
To make rules concerning captures on land and water;
To declare the law and punishment of piracies and felonies committed on the high

seas, and the punishment of counterfeiting the coin of the United States, and of offenses against the law of nations;

To subdue a rebellion in any State, on the application of its legislature;

To make war;

To raise armies;

To build and equip fleets;

To call forth the aid of the militia, in order to execute the laws of the Union, enforce treaties, suppress insurrections, and repel invasions;

And to make all laws that shall be necessary and proper for carrying into execution the foregoing powers, and all other powers vested, by this Constitution, in the government of the United States, or in any department or officer thereof;

Sect. 2. Treason against the United States shall consist only in levying war against the United States, or any of them; and in adhering to the enemies of the United States, or any of them. The Legislature of the United States shall have power to declare the punishment of treason. No person shall be convicted of treason, unless on the testimony of two witnesses. No attainder of treason shall work corruption of blood, nor forfeiture, except during the life of the person attainted.

Sect. 3. The proportions of direct taxation shall be regulated by the whole number of white and other free citizens and inhabitants of every age, sex and condition, including those bound to servitude for a term of years, and three fifths of all other persons not comprehended in the foregoing description, (except Indians not paying taxes) which number shall, within six years after the first meeting of the Legislature, and within the term of every ten years afterwards, be taken in such manner as the said Legislature shall direct.

Sect. 4. No tax or duty shall be laid by the Legislature on articles exported from any State; nor on the migration or importation of such persons as the several States shall think proper to admit; nor shall such migration or importation be prohibited.

Sect. 5. No capitation tax shall be laid, unless in proportion to the Census hereinbefore directed to be taken.

Sect. 6. No navigation act shall be passed without the assent of two thirds of the members present in the each House.

Sect. 7. The United States shall not grant any title of Nobility.

VIII. The Acts of the Legislature of the United States made in pursuance of this Constitution, and all treaties made under the authority of the United States shall be the supreme law of the several States, and of their citizens and inhabitants; and the judges in the several States shall be bound thereby in their decisions; any thing in the Constitutions or laws of the several States to the contrary notwithstanding.

IX. *Sect 1.* The Senate of the United States shall have power to make treaties, and to appoint Ambassadors, and Judges of the Supreme Court.

Sect. 2. In all disputes and controversies now subsisting, or that may hereafter subsist between two or more States, respecting jurisdiction or territory, the Senate shall possess the following powers. Whenever the Legislature, or the Executive authority, or lawful agent of any State, in controversy with another, shall by memorial to the Senate, state the matter in question, and apply for a hearing; notice of such memorial and application shall be given by order of the Senate, to the Legislature or the Executive authority of the other State in Controversy. The Senate shall also assign a day for the appearance of the parties, by their agents, before the House. The Agents shall be directed to appoint, by joint consent, commissioners or judges to constitute a Court for hearing and determining the matter in question. But if the Agents cannot agree, the Senate shall name three persons out of each of the several States; and from the list of such persons each party shall alternately strike out one, until the number shall be reduced to thirteen; and from that number not less than seven nor more than nine names, as the Senate shall direct, shall in their presence, be drawn out by lot; and the persons whose names shall be so drawn, or any five of them shall be commissioners or Judges to hear and finally determine the controversy; provided a majority of the Judges, who shall hear the cause, agree in the determination. If either party shall neglect to attend at the day assigned, without shewing sufficient reasons for not attending, or being present shall refuse to strike, the Senate shall proceed to nominate three persons out of each State, and the Clerk of the Senate shall strike in behalf of the party absent or refusing. If any of the parties shall refuse to submit to the authority of such Court; or shall not appear to prosecute or defend their claim or cause, the Court shall nevertheless proceed to pronounce judgment. The judgment shall be final and conclusive. The proceedings shall be transmitted to the President of the Senate, and shall be lodged among the public records, for the security of the parties concerned. Every Commissioner shall, before he sit in judgment, take an oath, to be administred by one of the Judges of the Supreme or Superior Court of the State where the cause shall be tried, "well and truly to hear and determine the matter in question according to the best of his judgment, without favor, affection, or hope of reward."

Sect. 3. All controversies concerning lands claimed under different grants of two or more States, whose jurisdictions, as they respect such lands shall have been decided or adjusted subsequent to such grants, or any of them, shall, on application to the Senate, be finally determined, as near as may be, in the same manner as is before prescribed for deciding controversies between different States.

X. *Sect. 1.* The Executive Power of the United States shall be vested in a single person. His stile shall be, "The President of the United States of America;" and his title shall be, "His Excellency." He shall be elected by ballot by the Legislature. He shall hold his office during the term of seven years; but shall not be elected a second time.

Sect. 2. He shall, from time to time, give information to the Legislature, of the state of the Union: he may recommend to their consideration such measures as he shall judge necessary, and expedient: he may convene them on extraordinary occasions. In case of disagreement between the two Houses, with regard to the time of adjournment, he may adjourn them to such time as he thinks proper: he shall take care that the laws of the United States be duly and faithfully executed: he shall commission all the officers of the United States; and shall appoint officers in all cases not otherwise provided for by this Constitution. He shall receive Ambassadors, and may correspond with the supreme Executives of the several States. He shall have power to grant reprieves and pardons; but his pardon shall not be pleadable in bar of an impeachment. He shall be commander in chief of the

Army and Navy of the United States, and of the Militia of the several States. He shall, at stated times, receive for his services, a compensation, which shall neither be increased nor diminished during his continuance in office. Before he shall enter on the duties of his department, he shall take the following oath or affirmation, "I—solemnly swear, (or affirm) that that I will faithfully execute the office of President of the United States of America." He shall be removed from his office on impeachment by the House of Representatives, and conviction in the supreme Court, of treason, bribery, or corruption. In case of his removal as aforesaid, death, resignation, or disability to discharge the powers and duties of his office, the President of the Senate shall exercise those powers and duties, until another President of the United States be chosen, or until the disability of the President be removed.

XI. *Sect. 1.* The Judicial Power of the United States shall be vested in one Supreme Court, and in such inferior Courts as shall, when necessary, from time to time, be constituted by the Legislature of the United States.

Sect. 2. The Judges of the Supreme Court, and of the Inferior Courts, shall hold their offices during good behaviour. They shall, at stated times, receive for their services, a compensation, which shall not be diminished during their continuance in office.

Sect. 3. The Jurisdiction of the Supreme Court shall extend to all cases arising under laws passed by the Legislature of the United States; to all cases affecting Ambassadors, other Public Ministers and Consuls; to the trial of impeachments of officers of the United States; to all cases of Admiralty and maritime jurisdiction; to controversies between two or more States, (except such as shall regard Territory or Jurisdiction) between a State and Citizens of another State, between Citizens of different States, and between a State or the Citizens thereof and foreign States, citizens or subjects. In cases of impeachment, cases affecting Ambassadors, other Public Ministers and Consuls, and those in which a State shall be party, this jurisdiction shall be original. In all the other cases beforementioned, it shall be appellate, with such exceptions and under such regulations as the Legislature shall make. The Legislature may assign any part of the jurisdiction abovementioned (except the trial of the President of the United States) in the manner, and under the limitations which it shall think proper, to such Inferior Courts, as it shall constitute from time to time.

Sect. 4. The trial of all criminal offences (except in cases of impeachments) shall be in the State where they shall be committed; and shall be by Jury.

Sect. 5. Judgment, in cases of Impeachment, shall not extend further than to removal from office, and disqualification to hold and enjoy any office of honour, trust or profit, under the United States. But the party convicted shall, nevertheless be liable and subject to indictment, trial, judgment and punishment according to law.

XII. No State shall coin money; nor grant letters of marque and reprisal; nor enter into any Treaty, alliance, or confederation; nor grant any title of Nobility.

XIII. No State, without the consent of the Legislature of the United States, shall emit bills of credit, or make any thing but specie a tender in payment of debts; nor lay imposts or duties on imports; nor keep troops or ships of war in time of peace; nor enter into any agreement or compact with another State, or with any foreign power; nor engage in any war, unless it shall be actually invaded by enemies, or the danger of invasion be so imminent, as not to admit of delay, until the Legislature of the United States can be consulted.

XIV. The Citizens of each State shall be entitled to all privileges and immunities of citizens in the several States.

XV. Any person charged with treason, felony or high misdemeanor in any State, who shall flee from justice, and shall be found in any other State, shall, on demand of the Executive power of the State from which he fled, be delivered up and removed to the State having jurisdiction of the offence.

XVI. Full faith shall be given in each State to the acts of the Legislatures, and to the records and judicial proceedings of the Courts and magistrates of every other State.

XVII. New States lawfully constituted or established within the limits of the United States may be admitted, by the Legislature, into this Government; but to such admission the consent of two thirds of the members present in each House shall be necessary. If a new State shall arise within the limits of any of the present States, the consent of the Legislatures of such States shall be also necessary to its admission. If the admission be consented to, the new States shall be admitted on the same terms with the original States. But the Legislature may make conditions with the new States, concerning the public debt which shall be then subsisting.

XVIII. The United States shall guaranty to each State a Republican form of Government; and shall protect each State against foreign invasions, and, on the application of its Legislature, against domestic violence.

XIX. On the application of the Legislatures of two thirds of the States in the Union, for an amendment of this Constitution, the Legislature of the United States shall call a Convention for that purpose.

XX. The members of the Legislatures, and the Executive and Judicial officers of the United States, and of the several States, shall be bound by oath to support this Constitution.

XXI. The ratifications of the Conventions of _____ States shall be sufficient for organizing this Constitution.

XXII. This Constitution shall be laid before the United States in Congress assembled, for their approbation; and it is the opinion of this Convention, that it should be afterwards submitted to a Convention chosen, under the recommendation of its legislature, in order to receive the ratification of such Convention.

XXIII. To introduce this government, it is the opinion of this Convention, that each assenting Convention should notify its assent and ratification to the United States in Congress assembled; that Congress, after receiving the assent and ratification of the Conventions of _____ States, should appoint and publish a day, as early as may be, and appoint a place for commencing proceedings under this

Constitution; that after such publication, the Legislatures of the several States should elect members of the Senate, and direct the election of members of the House of Representatives; and that the members of the Legislature should meet at the time and place assigned by Congress, and should, as soon as may be, after their meeting, choose the President of the United States, and proceed to execute this Constitution.

DOCUMENT E:
ORIGINAL UNITED STATES
CONSTITUTION

Submitted by the Federal Convention September 17, 1787, and ratified June 21, 1788

*The following text is a transcription of the Constitution in its original form. Items that are **boldfaced** have since been amended or superseded.*

We the People of the United States, in Order to form a more perfect Union, establish Justice, insure domestic Tranquility, provide for the common defence, promote the general Welfare, and secure the Blessings of Liberty to ourselves and our Posterity, do ordain and establish this Constitution for the United States of America.

Article I.

Section. 1. All legislative Powers herein granted shall be vested in a Congress of the United States, which shall consist of a Senate and House of Representatives.

Source: National Archives, Charters of Freedom.

Section 2. The House of Representatives shall be composed of Members chosen every second Year by the People of the several States, and the Electors in each State shall have the Qualifications requisite for Electors of the most numerous Branch of the State Legislature.

No Person shall be a Representative who shall not have attained to the Age of twenty five Years, and been seven Years a Citizen of the United States, and who shall not, when elected, be an Inhabitant of that State in which he shall be chosen.

Representatives and direct Taxes shall be apportioned among the several States which may be included within this Union, according to their respective Numbers, which shall be determined by adding to the whole Number of free Persons, including those bound to Service for a Term of Years, and excluding Indians not taxed, three fifths of all other Persons. The actual Enumeration shall be made within three Years after the first Meeting of the Congress of the United States, and within every subsequent Term of ten Years, in such Manner as they shall by Law direct. The Number of Representatives shall not exceed one for every thirty Thousand, but each State shall have at Least one Representative; and until such enumeration shall be made, the State of New Hampshire shall be entitled to chuse three, Massachusetts eight, Rhode-Island and Providence Plantations one, Connecticut five, New-York six, New Jersey four, Pennsylvania eight, Delaware one, Maryland six, Virginia ten, North Carolina five, South Carolina five, and Georgia three.

When vacancies happen in the Representation from any State, the Executive Authority thereof shall issue Writs of Election to fill such Vacancies.

The House of Representatives shall chuse their Speaker and other Officers; and shall have the sole Power of Impeachment.

Section 3. The Senate of the United States shall be composed of two Senators from each State, **chosen by the Legislature** thereof for six Years; and each Senator shall have one Vote.

Immediately after they shall be assembled in Consequence of the first Election, they shall be divided as equally as may be into three Classes. The Seats of the Senators of the first Class shall be vacated at the Expiration of the second Year, of the second Class at the Expiration of the fourth Year, and of the third Class at the Expiration of the sixth Year, so that one third may be chosen every second

Year; and if Vacancies happen by Resignation, or otherwise, during the Recess of the Legislature of any State, the Executive thereof may make temporary Appointments until the next Meeting of the Legislature, which shall then fill such Vacancies.

No Person shall be a Senator who shall not have attained to the Age of thirty Years, and been nine Years a Citizen of the United States, and who shall not, when elected, be an Inhabitant of that State for which he shall be chosen.

The Vice President of the United States shall be President of the Senate, but shall have no Vote, unless they be equally divided.

The Senate shall chuse their other Officers, and also a President pro tempore, in the Absence of the Vice President, or when he shall exercise the Office of President of the United States.

The Senate shall have the sole Power to try all Impeachments. When sitting for that Purpose, they shall be on Oath or Affirmation. When the President of the United States is tried, the Chief Justice shall preside: And no Person shall be convicted without the Concurrence of two thirds of the Members present.

Judgment in Cases of Impeachment shall not extend further than to removal from Office, and disqualification to hold and enjoy any Office of honor, Trust or Profit under the United States: but the Party convicted shall nevertheless be liable and subject to Indictment, Trial, Judgment and Punishment, according to Law.

Section 4. The Times, Places and Manner of holding Elections for Senators and Representatives, shall be prescribed in each State by the Legislature thereof; but the Congress may at any time by Law make or alter such Regulations, except as to the Places of chusing Senators.

The Congress shall assemble at least once in every Year, and such Meeting shall be on the first Monday in December, unless they shall by Law appoint a different Day.

Section 5. Each House shall be the Judge of the Elections, Returns and Qualifications of its own Members, and a Majority of each shall constitute a Quorum to do Business; but a smaller Number may adjourn from day to day, and may be authorized to compel the Attendance of absent Members, in such Manner, and under such Penalties as each House may provide.

Each House may determine the Rules of its Proceedings, punish its Members for disorderly Behaviour, and, with the Concurrence of two thirds, expel a Member.

Each House shall keep a Journal of its Proceedings, and from time to time publish the same, excepting such Parts as may in their Judgment require Secrecy; and the Yeas and Nays of the Members of either House on any question shall, at the Desire of one fifth of those Present, be entered on the Journal.

Neither House, during the Session of Congress, shall, without the Consent of the other, adjourn for more than three days, nor to any other Place than that in which the two Houses shall be sitting.

Section 6. The Senators and Representatives shall receive a Compensation for their Services, to be ascertained by Law, and paid out of the Treasury of the United States. They shall in all Cases, except Treason, Felony and Breach of the Peace, be privileged from Arrest during their Attendance at the Session of their respective Houses, and in going to and returning from the same; and for any Speech or Debate in either House, they shall not be questioned in any other Place.

No Senator or Representative shall, during the Time for which he was elected, be appointed to any civil Office under the Authority of the United States, which shall have been created, or the Emoluments whereof shall have been encreased during such time; and no Person holding any Office under the United States, shall be a Member of either House during his Continuance in Office.

Section 7. All Bills for raising Revenue shall originate in the House of Representatives; but the Senate may propose or concur with Amendments as on other Bills.

Every Bill which shall have passed the House of Representatives and the Senate, shall, before it become a Law, be presented to the President of the United States: If he approve he shall sign it, but if not he shall return it, with his Objections to that House in which it shall have originated, who shall enter the Objections at large on their Journal, and proceed to reconsider it. If after such Reconsideration two thirds of that House shall agree to pass the Bill, it shall be sent, together with the Objections, to the other House, by which it shall likewise be reconsidered, and if approved by two thirds of that House, it shall become a Law. But in all such Cases the Votes of both Houses shall be determined by yeas and Nays, and the Names of the Persons voting for and against the Bill shall be entered on the Journal of each House respectively. If any Bill shall not be returned by the President within ten Days (Sundays excepted) after it shall have been presented to him, the Same shall be a Law, in like Manner as if he had signed it, unless the Congress by their Adjournment prevent its Return, in which Case it shall not be a Law.

Every Order, Resolution, or Vote to which the Concurrence of the Senate and House of Representatives may be necessary (except on a question of Adjournment) shall be presented to the President of the United States; and before the Same shall take Effect, shall be approved by him, or being disapproved by him, shall be repassed by two thirds of the Senate and House of Representatives, according to the Rules and Limitations prescribed in the Case of a Bill.

Section 8. The Congress shall have Power To lay and collect Taxes, Duties, Imposts and Excises, to pay the Debts and provide for the common Defence and general Welfare of the United States; but all Duties, Imposts and Excises shall be uniform throughout the United States;

To borrow Money on the credit of the United States;

To regulate Commerce with foreign Nations, and among the several States, and with the Indian Tribes;

To establish an uniform Rule of Naturalization, and uniform Laws on the subject of Bankruptcies throughout the United States;

To coin Money, regulate the Value thereof, and of foreign Coin, and fix the Standard of Weights and Measures;

To provide for the Punishment of counterfeiting the Securities and current Coin of the United States;

To establish Post Offices and post Roads;

To promote the Progress of Science and useful Arts, by securing for limited Times to Authors and Inventors the exclusive Right to their respective Writings and Discoveries;

To constitute Tribunals inferior to the supreme Court;

To define and punish Piracies and Felonies committed on the high Seas, and Offences against the Law of Nations;

To declare War, grant Letters of Marque and Reprisal, and make Rules concerning Captures on Land and Water;

To raise and support Armies, but no Appropriation of Money to that Use shall be for a longer Term than two Years;

To provide and maintain a Navy;

To make Rules for the Government and Regulation of the land and naval Forces;

To provide for calling forth the Militia to execute the Laws of the Union, suppress Insurrections and repel Invasions;

To provide for organizing, arming, and disciplining, the Militia, and for governing such Part of them as may be employed in the Service of the United States, reserving to the States respectively, the Appointment of the Officers, and the Authority of training the Militia according to the discipline prescribed by Congress;

To exercise exclusive Legislation in all Cases whatsoever, over such District (not exceeding ten Miles square) as may, by Cession of particular States, and the Acceptance of Congress, become the Seat of the Government of the United States, and to exercise like Authority over all Places purchased by the Consent of the Legislature of the State in which the Same shall be, for the Erection of Forts, Magazines, Arsenals, dock-Yards, and other needful Buildings;—And

To make all Laws which shall be necessary and proper for carrying into Execution the foregoing Powers, and all other Powers vested by this Constitution in the Government of the United States, or in any Department or Officer thereof.

Section 9. The Migration or Importation of such Persons as any of the States now existing shall think proper to admit, shall not be prohibited by the Congress prior to the Year one thousand eight hundred and eight, but a Tax or duty may be imposed on such Importation, not exceeding ten dollars for each Person.

The Privilege of the Writ of Habeas Corpus shall not be suspended, unless when in Cases of Rebellion or Invasion the public Safety may require it.

No Bill of Attainder or ex post facto Law shall be passed.

No Capitation, or other direct, Tax shall be laid, **unless in Proportion to the Census or enumeration herein before directed to be taken.**

No Tax or Duty shall be laid on Articles exported from any State.

No Preference shall be given by any Regulation of Commerce or Revenue to the Ports of one State over those of another; nor shall Vessels bound to, or from, one State, be obliged to enter, clear, or pay Duties in another.

No Money shall be drawn from the Treasury, but in Consequence of Appropriations made by Law; and a regular Statement and Account of the Receipts and Expenditures of all public Money shall be published from time to time.

No Title of Nobility shall be granted by the United States: And no Person holding any Office of Profit or Trust under them, shall, without the Consent of the Congress, accept of any present, Emolument, Office, or Title, of any kind whatever, from any King, Prince, or foreign State.

Section 10. No State shall enter into any Treaty, Alliance, or Confederation; grant Letters of Marque and Reprisal; coin Money; emit Bills of Credit; make any Thing but gold and silver Coin a Tender in Payment of Debts; pass any Bill of Attainder, ex post facto Law, or Law impairing the Obligation of Contracts, or grant any Title of Nobility.

No State shall, without the Consent of the Congress, lay any Imposts or Duties on Imports or Exports, except what may be absolutely necessary for executing it's inspection Laws: and the net Produce of all Duties and Imposts, laid by any State on Imports or Exports, shall be for the Use of the Treasury of the United States; and all such Laws shall be subject to the Revision and Controul of the Congress.

No State shall, without the Consent of Congress, lay any Duty of Tonnage, keep Troops, or Ships of War in time of Peace, enter into any Agreement or Compact with another State, or with a foreign Power, or engage in War, unless actually invaded, or in such imminent Danger as will not admit of delay.

Article II.

Section 1. The executive Power shall be vested in a President of the United States of America. He shall hold his Office during the Term of four Years, and, together with the Vice President, chosen for the same Term, be elected, as follows:

Each State shall appoint, in such Manner as the Legislature thereof may direct, a Number of Electors, equal to the whole Number of Senators and Representatives to which the State may be entitled in the Congress: but no Senator or Representative, or Person holding an Office of Trust or Profit under the United States, shall be appointed an Elector.

The Electors shall meet in their respective States, and vote by Ballot for two Persons, of whom one at least shall not be an Inhabitant of the same State with themselves. And they shall make a List of all the Persons voted for, and of the Number of Votes for each; which List they shall sign and certify, and transmit sealed to the Seat of the Government of the United States, directed to the President of the Senate. The President of the Senate shall, in the Presence of the Senate and House of Representatives, open all the Certificates, and the Votes shall then be counted. The Person having the greatest Number of Votes shall be the President, if such Number be a Majority of the whole Number of Electors appointed; and if there be more than one who have such Majority, and have an equal Number of Votes, then the House of Representatives shall immediately chuse by Ballot one of them for President; and if no Person have a Majority, then from the five highest on the List the said House shall in like Manner chuse the President. But in chusing the President, the Votes shall be taken by States, the Representation from each State having one Vote; A quorum for this purpose shall consist of a Member or Members from two thirds of the States, and a Majority of all the States shall be necessary to a Choice. In every Case, after the Choice of the President, the Person having the greatest Number of Votes of the Electors shall be the Vice President. But if there should remain two or more who have equal Votes, the Senate shall chuse from them by Ballot the Vice President.

The Congress may determine the Time of chusing the Electors, and the Day on which they shall give their Votes; which Day shall be the same throughout the United States.

No Person except a natural born Citizen, or a Citizen of the United States, at the time of the Adoption of this Constitution, shall be eligible to the Office of President; neither shall any Person be eligible to that Office who shall not have attained to the Age of thirty five Years, and been fourteen Years a Resident within the United States.

In Case of the Removal of the President from Office, or of his Death, Resignation, or Inability to discharge the Powers and Duties of the said Office, the Same shall devolve on the Vice President, and the Congress may by Law provide for the Case of Removal, Death, Resignation or Inability, both of the President and Vice President, declaring what Officer shall then act as President, and such Officer shall act accordingly, until the Disability be removed, or a President shall be elected.

The President shall, at stated Times, receive for his Services, a Compensation, which shall neither be increased nor diminished during the Period for which he shall have been elected, and he shall not receive within that Period any other Emolument from the United States, or any of them.

Before he enter on the Execution of his Office, he shall take the following Oath or Affirmation: —"I do solemnly swear (or affirm) that I will faithfully execute the Office of President of the United States, and will to the best of my Ability, preserve, protect and defend the Constitution of the United States."

Section 2. The President shall be Commander in Chief of the Army and Navy of the United States, and of the Militia of the several States, when called into the actual Service of the United States; he may require the Opinion, in writing, of the principal Officer in each of the executive Departments, upon any Subject relating to the Duties of their respective Offices, and he shall have Power to grant Reprieves and Pardons for Offences against the United States, except in Cases of Impeachment.

He shall have Power, by and with the Advice and Consent of the Senate, to make Treaties, provided two thirds of the Senators present concur; and he shall nominate, and by and with the Advice and Consent of the Senate, shall appoint Ambassadors, other public Ministers and Consuls, Judges of the supreme Court, and all other Officers of the United States, whose Appointments are not herein otherwise provided for, and which shall be established by Law: but the Congress may by Law vest the Appointment of such inferior Officers, as they think proper, in the President alone, in the Courts of Law, or in the Heads of Departments.

The President shall have Power to fill up all Vacancies that may happen during the Recess of the Senate, by granting Commissions which shall expire at the End of their next Session.

Section 3. He shall from time to time give to the Congress Information of the State of the Union, and recommend to their Consideration such Measures as he shall judge necessary and expedient; he may, on extraordinary Occasions, convene both Houses, or either of them, and in Case of Disagreement between them, with Respect to the Time of Adjournment, he may adjourn them to such Time as he shall think proper; he shall receive Ambassadors and other public Ministers; he shall take Care that the Laws be faithfully executed, and shall Commission all the Officers of the United States.

Section 4. The President, Vice President and all civil Officers of the United States, shall be removed from Office on Impeachment for, and Conviction of, Treason, Bribery, or other high Crimes and Misdemeanors.

Article III.

Section 1. The judicial Power of the United States shall be vested in one supreme Court, and in such inferior Courts as the Congress may from time to time ordain and establish. The Judges, both of the supreme and inferior Courts, shall hold their Offices during good Behaviour, and shall, at stated Times, receive for their Services a Compensation, which shall not be diminished during their Continuance in Office.

Section 2. The judicial Power shall extend to all Cases, in Law and Equity, arising under this Constitution, the Laws of the United States, and Treaties made, or which shall be made, under their Authority; —to all Cases affecting Ambassadors, other public Ministers and Consuls; —to all Cases of admiralty and maritime Jurisdiction;—to Controversies to which the United States shall be a Party; —to Controversies between two or more States; —**between a State and Citizens of another State,** —between Citizens of different States, —between Citizens of the same State claiming Lands under Grants of different States, and between a State, or the Citizens thereof, and foreign States, Citizens or Subjects.

In all Cases affecting Ambassadors, other public Ministers and Consuls, and those in which a State shall be Party, the supreme Court shall have original Jurisdiction. In all the other Cases before mentioned, the supreme Court shall have appellate Jurisdiction, both as to Law and Fact, with such Exceptions, and under such Regulations as the Congress shall make.

The Trial of all Crimes, except in Cases of Impeachment, shall be by Jury; and such Trial shall be held in the State where the said Crimes shall have been committed; but when not committed within any State, the Trial shall be at such Place or Places as the Congress may by Law have directed.

Section 3. Treason against the United States, shall consist only in levying War against them, or in adhering to their Enemies, giving them Aid and Comfort. No Person shall be convicted of Treason unless on the Testimony of two Witnesses to the same overt Act, or on Confession in open Court.

The Congress shall have Power to declare the Punishment of Treason, but no Attainder of Treason shall work Corruption of Blood, or Forfeiture except during the Life of the Person attainted.

Article IV.

Section 1. Full Faith and Credit shall be given in each State to the public Acts, Records, and judicial Proceedings of every other State. And the Congress may by general Laws prescribe the Manner in which such Acts, Records and Proceedings shall be proved, and the Effect thereof.

Section 2. The Citizens of each State shall be entitled to all Privileges and Immunities of Citizens in the several States.

A Person charged in any State with Treason, Felony, or other Crime, who shall flee from Justice, and be found in another State, shall on Demand of the executive Authority of the State from which he fled, be delivered up, to be removed to the State having Jurisdiction of the Crime.

No Person held to Service or Labour in one State, under the Laws thereof, escaping into another, shall, in Consequence of any Law or Regulation therein, be discharged from such Service or Labour, but shall be delivered up on Claim of the Party to whom such Service or Labour may be due.

Section 3. New States may be admitted by the Congress into this Union; but no new State shall be formed or erected within the Jurisdiction of any other State; nor any State be formed by the Junction of two or more States, or Parts of States, without the Consent of the Legislatures of the States concerned as well as of the Congress.

The Congress shall have Power to dispose of and make all needful Rules and Regulations respecting the Territory or other Property belonging to the United

States; and nothing in this Constitution shall be so construed as to Prejudice any Claims of the United States, or of any particular State.

Section 4. The United States shall guarantee to every State in this Union a Republican Form of Government, and shall protect each of them against Invasion; and on Application of the Legislature, or of the Executive (when the Legislature cannot be convened), against domestic Violence.

Article V.

The Congress, whenever two thirds of both Houses shall deem it necessary, shall propose Amendments to this Constitution, or, on the Application of the Legislatures of two thirds of the several States, shall call a Convention for proposing Amendments, which, in either Case, shall be valid to all Intents and Purposes, as Part of this Constitution, when ratified by the Legislatures of three fourths of the several States, or by Conventions in three fourths thereof, as the one or the other Mode of Ratification may be proposed by the Congress; Provided that no Amendment which may be made prior to the Year One thousand eight hundred and eight shall in any Manner affect the first and fourth Clauses in the Ninth Section of the first Article; and that no State, without its Consent, shall be deprived of its equal Suffrage in the Senate.

Article VI.

All Debts contracted and Engagements entered into, before the Adoption of this Constitution, shall be as valid against the United States under this Constitution, as under the Confederation.

This Constitution, and the Laws of the United States which shall be made in Pursuance thereof; and all Treaties made, or which shall be made, under the Authority of the United States, shall be the supreme Law of the Land; and the Judges in every State shall be bound thereby, any Thing in the Constitution or Laws of any State to the Contrary notwithstanding.

The Senators and Representatives before mentioned, and the Members of the several State Legislatures, and all executive and judicial Officers, both of the United States and of the several States, shall be bound by Oath or Affirmation, to support this Constitution; but no religious Test shall ever be required as a Qualification to any Office or public Trust under the United States.

Article VII.

The Ratification of the Conventions of nine States, shall be sufficient for the Establishment of this Constitution between the States so ratifying the Same.

DOCUMENT F:
MADISON'S DRAFT AMENDMENTS

Submitted to the House of Representatives on June 8, 1789

The amendments which have occurred to me, proper to be recommended by Congress to the State Legislatures, are these:

First, That there be prefixed to the Constitution a declaration, that all power is originally vested in, and consequently derived from, the people.

That Government is instituted and ought to be exercised for the benefit of the people; which consists in the enjoyment of life and liberty, with the right of acquiring and using property, and generally of pursuing and obtaining happiness and safety.

That the people have an indubitable, unalienable, and indefeasible right to reform or change their Government, whenever it be found adverse or inadequate to the purposes of its institution.

Secondly. That in article 1st, section 2, clause 3, these words be struck out, to wit: "The number of Representatives shall not exceed one for every thirty thousand, but each State shall have at least one Representative, and until such enumeration

Source: Philip B. Kurland and Ralph Lerner, eds., *The Founders' Constitution* (Chicago: University of Chicago Press, 1987), 5:25–26.

shall be made"; and that in place thereof be inserted these words, to wit: "After the first actual enumeration, there shall be one Representative for every thirty thousand, until the number amounts to ____, after which the proportion shall be so regulated by Congress, that the number shall never be less than ____, nor more than ____, but each State shall, after the first enumeration, have at least two Representatives; and prior thereto."

Thirdly. That in article 1st, section 6, clause 1, there be added to the end of the first sentence, these words, to wit: "But no law varying the compensation last ascertained shall operate before the next ensuing election of Representatives."

Fourthly. That in article 1st, section 9, between clauses 3 and 4, be inserted these clauses, to wit: The civil rights of none shall be abridged on account of religious belief or worship, nor shall any national religion be established, nor shall the full and equal rights of conscience be in any manner, or on any pretext, infringed.

The people shall not be deprived or abridged of their right to speak, to write, or to publish their sentiments; and the freedom of the press, as one of the great bulwarks of liberty, shall be inviolable.

The people shall not be restrained from peaceably assembling and consulting for their common good; nor from applying to the Legislature by petitions, or remonstrances, for redress of their grievances.

The right of the people to keep and bear arms shall not be infringed; a well armed and well regulated militia being the best security of a free country: but no person religiously scrupulous of bearing arms shall be compelled to render military service in person.

No soldier shall in time of peace be quartered in any house without the consent of the owner; nor at any time, but in a manner warranted by law.

No person shall be subject, except in cases of impeachment, to more than one punishment or one trial for the same offence; nor shall be compelled to be a witness against himself; nor be deprived of life, liberty, or property, without due process of law; nor be obliged to relinquish his property, where it may be necessary for public use, without a just compensation.

Excessive bail shall not be required, nor excessive fines imposed, nor cruel and unusual punishments inflicted.

The rights of the people to be secured in their persons; their houses, their papers, and their other property, from all unreasonable searches and seizures, shall not be violated by warrants issued without probable cause, supported by oath or affirmation, or not particularly describing the places to be searched, or the persons or things to be seized. In all criminal prosecutions, the accused shall enjoy the right to a speedy and public trial, to be informed of the cause and nature of the accusation, to be confronted with his accusers, and the witnesses against him; to have a compulsory process for obtaining witnesses in his favor; and to have the assistance of counsel for his defence.

The exceptions here or elsewhere in the Constitution, made in favor of particular rights, shall not be so construed as to diminish the just importance of other rights retained by the people, or as to enlarge the powers delegated by the Constitution; but either as actual limitations of such powers, or as inserted merely for greater caution.

Fifthly. That in article 1st, section 10, between clauses 1 and 2, be inserted this clause, to wit: No State shall violate the equal rights of conscience, or the freedom of the press, or the trial by jury in criminal cases.

Sixthly. That, in article 3d, section 2, be annexed to the end of clause 2d, these words, to wit: But no appeal to such court shall be allowed where the value in controversy shall not amount to ___ dollars: nor shall any fact triable by jury, according to the course of common law, be otherwise re-examinable than may consist with the principles of common law.

Seventhly. That in article 3d, section 2, the third clause be struck out, and in its place be inserted the clauses following, to wit: The trial of all crimes (except in cases of impeachments, and cases arising in the land or naval forces, or the militia when on actual service, in time of war or public danger) shall be by an impartial jury of freeholders of the vicinage, with the requisite of unanimity for conviction, of the right of challenge, and other accustomed requisites; and in all crimes punishable with loss of life or member, presentment or indictment by a grand jury shall be an essential preliminary, provided that in cases of crimes committed within any county which may be in possession of an enemy, or in which a general insurrection may prevail, the trial may by law be authorized in some other county of the same State, as near as may be to the seat of the offence.

In cases of crimes committed not within any county, the trial may by law be in such county as the laws shall have prescribed. In suits at common law, between man and man, the trial by jury, as one of the best securities to the rights of the people, ought to remain inviolate.

Eighthly. That immediately after article 6th, be inserted, as article 7th, the clauses following, to wit: The powers delegated by this Constitution are appropriated to the departments to which they are respectively distributed: so that the Legislative Department shall never exercise the powers vested in the Executive or Judicial nor the Executive exercise the powers vested in the Legislative or Judicial, nor the Judicial exercise the powers vested in the Legislative or Executive Departments.

The powers not delegated by this Constitution, nor prohibited by it to the States, are reserved to the States respectively.

Ninthly. That article 7th be numbered as article 8th.

DOCUMENT G:
INITIAL SET OF CONSTITUTIONAL
AMENDMENTS

**Twelve amendments submitted by Congress to the states
on September 25, 1789 (the last ten were ratified by
three-quarters of the states on December 15, 1791)**

Article 1. After the first enumeration, required by the first article of the
Constitution, there shall be one Representative for every thirty thousand,
until the number shall amount to one hundred; after which the proportion
shall be so regulated by Congress, that there shall be not less than one hundred
Representatives, nor less than one Representative for every forty thousand
persons, until the number of Representatives shall amount to two hundred; after
which the proportion shall be so regulated by Congress, that there shall not be less
than two hundred Representatives, nor more than one Representative for every
fifty thousand persons.

Article 2. No law, varying the compensation for the services of the Senators and
Representatives, shall take effect, until an election of Representatives shall have
intervened.

Source: Library of Congress, American Memory, A Century of Lawmaking for a New
Nation, *Senate Journal* 1:96– 97, and National Archives, Charter of Freedom.

Article 3. Congress shall make no law respecting an establishment of religion, or prohibiting the free exercise thereof; or abridging the freedom of speech, or of the press; or the right of the people peaceably to assemble, and to petition the Government for a redress of grievances.

Article 4. A well regulated Militia, being necessary to the security of a free State, the right of the people to keep and bear Arms, shall not be infringed.

Article 5. No Soldier shall, in time of peace be quartered in any house, without the consent of the Owner, nor in time of war, but in a manner to be prescribed by law.

Article 6. The right of the people to be secure in their persons, houses, papers, and effects, against unreasonable searches and seizures, shall not be violated, and no Warrants shall issue, but upon probable cause, supported by Oath or affirmation, and particularly describing the place to be searched, and the persons or things to be seized.

Article 7. No person shall be held to answer for a capital, or otherwise infamous crime, unless on a presentment or indictment of a Grand Jury, except in cases arising in the land or naval forces, or in the Militia, when in actual service in time of War or public danger; nor shall any person be subject for the same offence to be twice put in jeopardy of life or limb; nor shall be compelled in any criminal case to be a witness against himself, nor be deprived of life, liberty, or property, without due process of law; nor shall private property be taken for public use, without just compensation.

Article 8. In all criminal prosecutions, the accused shall enjoy the right to a speedy and public trial, by an impartial jury of the State and district wherein the crime shall have been committed, which district shall have been previously ascertained by law, and to be informed of the nature and cause of the accusation; to be confronted with the witnesses against him; to have compulsory process for obtaining witnesses in his favor, and to have the Assistance of Counsel for his defence.

Article 9. In Suits at common law, where the value in controversy shall exceed twenty dollars, the right of trial by jury shall be preserved, and no fact tried by a jury, shall be otherwise re-examined in any Court of the United States, than according to the rules of the common law.

Article 10. Excessive bail shall not be required, nor excessive fines imposed, nor cruel and unusual punishments inflicted.

Article 11. The enumeration in the Constitution, of certain rights, shall not be construed to deny or disparage others retained by the people.

Article 12. The powers not delegated to the United States by the Constitution, nor prohibited by it to the States, are reserved to the States respectively, or to the people.

DOCUMENT H:
CONSTITUTIONAL
AMENDMENTS 11–27

Amendment XI

Passed by Congress March 4, 1794. Ratified February 7, 1795.

Note: Article III, section 2, of the Constitution was modified by amendment 11.

The Judicial power of the United States shall not be construed to extend to any suit in law or equity, commenced or prosecuted against one of the United States by Citizens of another State, or by Citizens or Subjects of any Foreign State.

Amendment XII

Passed by Congress December 9, 1803. Ratified June 15, 1804.

Note: A portion of Article II, section 1, of the Constitution was superseded by the 12th amendment.

The Electors shall meet in their respective states and vote by ballot for President and Vice-President, one of whom, at least, shall not be an inhabitant of the same

Source: National Archives, Charters of Freedom.

state with themselves; they shall name in their ballots the person voted for as President, and in distinct ballots the person voted for as Vice-President, and they shall make distinct lists of all persons voted for as President, and of all persons voted for as Vice-President, and of the number of votes for each, which lists they shall sign and certify, and transmit sealed to the seat of the government of the United States, directed to the President of the Senate; —the President of the Senate shall, in the presence of the Senate and House of Representatives, open all the certificates and the votes shall then be counted;—The person having the greatest number of votes for President, shall be the President, if such number be a majority of the whole number of Electors appointed; and if no person have such majority, then from the persons having the highest numbers not exceeding three on the list of those voted for as President, the House of Representatives shall choose immediately, by ballot, the President. But in choosing the President, the votes shall be taken by states, the representation from each state having one vote; a quorum for this purpose shall consist of a member or members from two-thirds of the states, and a majority of all the states shall be necessary to a choice. [And if the House of Representatives shall not choose a President whenever the right of choice shall devolve upon them, before the fourth day of March next following, then the Vice-President shall act as President, as in case of the death or other constitutional disability of the President.—]* The person having the greatest number of votes as Vice-President, shall be the Vice-President, if such number be a majority of the whole number of Electors appointed, and if no person have a majority, then from the two highest numbers on the list, the Senate shall choose the Vice-President; a quorum for the purpose shall consist of two-thirds of the whole number of Senators, and a majority of the whole number shall be necessary to a choice. But no person constitutionally ineligible to the office of President shall be eligible to that of Vice-President of the United States.

Amendment XIII
Passed by Congress January 31, 1865. Ratified December 6, 1865.

Note: A portion of Article IV, section 2, of the Constitution was superseded by the 13th amendment.

* *Superseded by section 3 of the 20th amendment.*

Section 1. Neither slavery nor involuntary servitude, except as a punishment for crime whereof the party shall have been duly convicted, shall exist within the United States, or any place subject to their jurisdiction.

Section 2. Congress shall have power to enforce this article by appropriate legislation.

Amendment XIV
Passed by Congress June 13, 1866. Ratified July 9, 1868.

Note: Article I, section 2, of the Constitution was modified by section 2 of the 14th amendment.

Section 1. All persons born or naturalized in the United States, and subject to the jurisdiction thereof, are citizens of the United States and of the State wherein they reside. No State shall make or enforce any law which shall abridge the privileges or immunities of citizens of the United States; nor shall any State deprive any person of life, liberty, or property, without due process of law; nor deny to any person within its jurisdiction the equal protection of the laws.

Section 2. Representatives shall be apportioned among the several States according to their respective numbers, counting the whole number of persons in each State, excluding Indians not taxed. But when the right to vote at any election for the choice of electors for President and Vice-President of the United States, Representatives in Congress, the Executive and Judicial officers of a State, or the members of the Legislature thereof, is denied to any of the male inhabitants of such State, being twenty-one years of age,* and citizens of the United States, or in any way abridged, except for participation in rebellion, or other crime, the basis of representation therein shall be reduced in the proportion which the number of such male citizens shall bear to the whole number of male citizens twenty-one years of age in such State.

Section 3. No person shall be a Senator or Representative in Congress, or elector of President and Vice-President, or hold any office, civil or military, under the

Changed by section 1 of the 26th amendment.

United States, or under any State, who, having previously taken an oath, as a member of Congress, or as an officer of the United States, or as a member of any State legislature, or as an executive or judicial officer of any State, to support the Constitution of the United States, shall have engaged in insurrection or rebellion against the same, or given aid or comfort to the enemies thereof. But Congress may by a vote of two-thirds of each House, remove such disability.

Section 4. The validity of the public debt of the United States, authorized by law, including debts incurred for payment of pensions and bounties for services in suppressing insurrection or rebellion, shall not be questioned. But neither the United States nor any State shall assume or pay any debt or obligation incurred in aid of insurrection or rebellion against the United States, or any claim for the loss or emancipation of any slave; but all such debts, obligations and claims shall be held illegal and void.

Section 5. The Congress shall have the power to enforce, by appropriate legislation, the provisions of this article.

Amendment XV
Passed by Congress February 26, 1869. Ratified February 3, 1870.

Section 1. The right of citizens of the United States to vote shall not be denied or abridged by the United States or by any State on account of race, color, or previous condition of servitude—

Section 2. The Congress shall have the power to enforce this article by appropriate legislation.

Amendment XVI
Passed by Congress July 2, 1909. Ratified February 3, 1913.

Note: Article I, section 9, of the Constitution was modified by amendment 16.

The Congress shall have power to lay and collect taxes on incomes, from whatever source derived, without apportionment among the several States, and without regard to any census or enumeration.

Amendment XVII

Passed by Congress May 13, 1912. Ratified April 8, 1913.

Note: Article I, section 3, of the Constitution was modified by the 17th amendment.

The Senate of the United States shall be composed of two Senators from each State, elected by the people thereof, for six years; and each Senator shall have one vote. The electors in each State shall have the qualifications requisite for electors of the most numerous branch of the State legislatures.

When vacancies happen in the representation of any State in the Senate, the executive authority of such State shall issue writs of election to fill such vacancies: *Provided,* That the legislature of any State may empower the executive thereof to make temporary appointments until the people fill the vacancies by election as the legislature may direct.

This amendment shall not be so construed as to affect the election or term of any Senator chosen before it becomes valid as part of the Constitution.

Amendment XVIII

Passed by Congress December 18, 1917. Ratified January 16, 1919. Repealed by amendment 21.

Section 1. After one year from the ratification of this article the manufacture, sale, or transportation of intoxicating liquors within, the importation thereof into, or the exportation thereof from the United States and all territory subject to the jurisdiction thereof for beverage purposes is hereby prohibited.

Section 2. The Congress and the several States shall have concurrent power to enforce this article by appropriate legislation.

Section 3. This article shall be inoperative unless it shall have been ratified as an amendment to the Constitution by the legislatures of the several States, as provided in the Constitution, within seven years from the date of the submission hereof to the States by the Congress.

Amendment XIX

Passed by Congress June 4, 1919. Ratified August 18, 1920.

The right of citizens of the United States to vote shall not be denied or abridged by the United States or by any State on account of sex.

Congress shall have power to enforce this article by appropriate legislation.

Amendment XX

Passed by Congress March 2, 1932. Ratified January 23, 1933.

Note: Article I, section 4, of the Constitution was modified by section 2 of this amendment. In addition, a portion of the 12th amendment was superseded by section 3.

Section 1. The terms of the President and the Vice President shall end at noon on the 20th day of January, and the terms of Senators and Representatives at noon on the 3d day of January, of the years in which such terms would have ended if this article had not been ratified; and the terms of their successors shall then begin.

Section 2. The Congress shall assemble at least once in every year, and such meeting shall begin at noon on the 3d day of January, unless they shall by law appoint a different day.

Section 3. If, at the time fixed for the beginning of the term of the President, the President elect shall have died, the Vice President elect shall become President. If a President shall not have been chosen before the time fixed for the beginning of his term, or if the President elect shall have failed to qualify, then the Vice President elect shall act as President until a President shall have qualified; and the Congress may by law provide for the case wherein neither a President elect nor a Vice President shall have qualified, declaring who shall then act as President, or the manner in which one who is to act shall be selected, and such person shall act accordingly until a President or Vice President shall have qualified.

Section 4. The Congress may by law provide for the case of the death of any of the persons from whom the House of Representatives may choose a President whenever the right of choice shall have devolved upon them, and for the case of the death of any of the persons from whom the Senate may choose a Vice President whenever the right of choice shall have devolved upon them.

Section 5. Sections 1 and 2 shall take effect on the 15th day of October following the ratification of this article.

Section 6. This article shall be inoperative unless it shall have been ratified as an amendment to the Constitution by the legislatures of three-fourths of the several States within seven years from the date of its submission.

Amendment XXI
Passed by Congress February 20, 1933. Ratified December 5, 1933.

Section 1. The eighteenth article of amendment to the Constitution of the United States is hereby repealed.

Section 2. The transportation or importation into any State, Territory, or Possession of the United States for delivery or use therein of intoxicating liquors, in violation of the laws thereof, is hereby prohibited.

Section 3. This article shall be inoperative unless it shall have been ratified as an amendment to the Constitution by conventions in the several States, as provided in the Constitution, within seven years from the date of the submission hereof to the States by the Congress.

Amendment XXII
Passed by Congress March 21, 1947. Ratified February 27, 1951.

Section 1. No person shall be elected to the office of the President more than twice, and no person who has held the office of President, or acted as President, for more than two years of a term to which some other person was elected President shall be elected to the office of President more than once. But this

Article shall not apply to any person holding the office of President when this Article was proposed by Congress, and shall not prevent any person who may be holding the office of President, or acting as President, during the term within which this Article becomes operative from holding the office of President or acting as President during the remainder of such term.

Section 2. This article shall be inoperative unless it shall have been ratified as an amendment to the Constitution by the legislatures of three-fourths of the several States within seven years from the date of its submission to the States by the Congress.

Amendment XXIII
Passed by Congress June 16, 1960. Ratified March 29, 1961.

Section 1. The District constituting the seat of Government of the United States shall appoint in such manner as Congress may direct:

A number of electors of President and Vice President equal to the whole number of Senators and Representatives in Congress to which the District would be entitled if it were a State, but in no event more than the least populous State; they shall be in addition to those appointed by the States, but they shall be considered, for the purposes of the election of President and Vice President, to be electors appointed by a State; and they shall meet in the District and perform such duties as provided by the twelfth article of amendment.

Section 2. The Congress shall have power to enforce this article by appropriate legislation.

Amendment XXIV
Passed by Congress August 27, 1962. Ratified January 23, 1964.

Section 1. The right of citizens of the United States to vote in any primary or other election for President or Vice President, for electors for President or Vice President, or for Senator or Representative in Congress, shall not be denied or abridged by the United States or any State by reason of failure to pay poll tax or other tax.

Section 2. The Congress shall have power to enforce this article by appropriate legislation.

Amendment XXV
Passed by Congress July 6, 1965. Ratified February 10, 1967.

Note: Article II, section 1, of the Constitution was affected by the 25th amendment.

Section 1. In case of the removal of the President from office or of his death or resignation, the Vice President shall become President.

Section 2. Whenever there is a vacancy in the office of the Vice President, the President shall nominate a Vice President who shall take office upon confirmation by a majority vote of both Houses of Congress.

Section 3. Whenever the President transmits to the President pro tempore of the Senate and the Speaker of the House of Representatives his written declaration that he is unable to discharge the powers and duties of his office, and until he transmits to them a written declaration to the contrary, such powers and duties shall be discharged by the Vice President as Acting President.

Section 4. Whenever the Vice President and a majority of either the principal officers of the executive departments or of such other body as Congress may by law provide, transmit to the President pro tempore of the Senate and the Speaker of the House of Representatives their written declaration that the President is unable to discharge the powers and duties of his office, the Vice President shall immediately assume the powers and duties of the office as Acting President.

Thereafter, when the President transmits to the President pro tempore of the Senate and the Speaker of the House of Representatives his written declaration that no inability exists, he shall resume the powers and duties of his office unless the Vice President and a majority of either the principal officers of the executive department or of such other body as Congress may by law provide, transmit within four days to the President pro tempore of the Senate and the Speaker of the House of Representatives their written declaration that the President is unable to discharge the powers and duties of his office. Thereupon Congress shall decide the issue, assembling within forty-eight hours for that purpose if not in session. If the Congress, within twenty-one days after receipt of the latter written declaration, or, if Congress is not in session, within twenty-one days after Congress is required to assemble, determines by two-thirds vote of both Houses that the President is unable to discharge the powers and duties of his office, the Vice President shall continue to discharge the same as Acting President; otherwise, the President shall resume the powers and duties of his office.

Amendment XXVI
Passed by Congress March 23, 1971. Ratified July 1, 1971.

Note: Amendment 14, section 2, of the Constitution was modified by section 1 of the 26th amendment.

Section 1. The right of citizens of the United States, who are eighteen years of age or older, to vote shall not be denied or abridged by the United States or by any State on account of age.

Section 2. The Congress shall have power to enforce this article by appropriate legislation.

Amendment XXVII
Originally proposed September 25, 1789. Ratified May 7, 1992.

No law, varying the compensation for the services of the Senators and Representatives, shall take effect, until an election of representatives shall have intervened.

ACKNOWLEDGMENTS

I am grateful to Marie Raphael and R. B. Bernstein for meticulous readings of the manuscript; to Pauline Maier, Woody Holton, Edward Larson, James Read, Jack Rakove, JeDon Emenhiser, Charles Biles, and Rebekah Evenson for their helpful comments; to David Rosen for legal tutoring; and to Marc Favreau for his enthusiastic support for the project.

NOTES

When citing Madison's *Notes of Debates in the Federal Convention*, I state the date only, not a page number. There are so many print editions and Internet sources that the date alone will suffice to locate the passage in question. If the date appears in my text, I provide no further reference.

Similarly, when citing *The Federalist*, because readers can access that work in so many ways, I provide only the number of the essay.

Short References

Annals of Congress—*Annals of Congress*, formerly *The Debates and Proceedings in the Congress of the United States, 1789–1824*, Library of Congress, American Memory, A Century of Lawmaking for a New Nation, http://memory.loc.gov/ammem/amlaw/lwae.html.

Most passages cited from *Annals of Congress* also appear by date and chamber of Congress in *DHFFC* (see below).

DHFFC—Linda Grant De Pauw, Charlene Bangs Bickford, Kenneth R. Bowling, Helen E. Veit, eds., *Documentary History of the First Federal Congress, March 4, 1789–March 3, 1791* (Baltimore: Johns Hopkins University Press, 1972–2012).

DHRC—Merrill Jensen et al., eds., *Documentary History of the Ratification of the Constitution* (Madison: State Historical Society of Wisconsin, 1976–). Jenson also founded and co-edited *Documentary History of the First Federal Elections, 1788–1790* (Madison: University of Wisconsin Press, 1976–1990).

Farrand, *Records of Federal Convention*: Max Farrand, ed., *The Records of the Federal Convention of 1787* (New Haven, CT: Yale University Press, 1911). Farrand includes not only Madison's notes but also the convention's official journal and less comprehensive notes taken by Robert Yates, Rufus King, James McHenry, William Pierce, William Paterson, Alexander Hamilton, and George Mason, as well as committee reports, printed drafts, and numerous letters from delegates. Farrand can also be accessed at Library of Congress, American Memory, A Century of Lawmaking for a New Nation, http://memory.loc.gov/ammem/amlaw/lwfr.html.

Franklin, *Papers*—Leonard W. Labaree and William B. Willcox, eds., *The Papers of Benjamin Franklin* (New Haven, CT.: Yale University Press, 1959–).

Hamilton, *Papers*—Harold C. Syrett, ed., *The Papers of Alexander Hamilton* (New York: Columbia University Press, 1961–87).

Hamilton, Madison, and Jay, *The Federalist*—originally published as *The Federalist: A Collection of Essays, Written in Favour of the New Constitution, As Agreed Upon by the Federal Convention, September 17, 1787* (New York: John and Archibald M'Lean, 1788), in Early American Imprints, Series I, Evans (1639–1800), document 21127. On the Internet: Avalon Project, Yale Law School, http://avalon.law.yale.edu/subject_menus/fed.asp.

Journals of Continental Congress—*Journals of the Continental Congress*, Library of Congress, American Memory, A Century of Lawmaking for a New Nation, http://memory.loc.gov/ammem/amlaw/lwjclink.html.

Jefferson, *Papers*—Julian P. Boyd, Charles T. Cullen, John Catanzariti, and Barbara B. Oberg, eds., *The Papers of Thomas Jefferson* (Princeton, N.J.: Princeton University Press, 1950–).

Kurland and Lerner, *Founders' Constitution*—Philip B. Kurland and Ralph Lerner, eds., *The Founders' Constitution* (Chicago: University of Chicago Press, 1987), http://press-pubs.uchicago.edu/founders/tocs/toc.html.

Madison, *Notes of Debates*—James Madison, *Notes of Debates in the Federal Convention of 1787*, ed. Adrienne Koch (New York: W. W. Norton, 1987). On the Internet: Avalon Project, Yale Law School, http://avalon.law.yale.edu/subject_menus/debcont.asp.

Madison, *Papers*—Robert A. Rutland et al., eds., *The Papers of James Madison* (Chicago: University of Chicago Press, 1962–; and Charlottesville: University Press of Virginia, 1977–). The volumes are arranged in four series: Congressional, Secretary of State, Presidential, and Retirement.

Schwartz, *Bill of Rights*—Bernard Schwartz, ed., *The Bill of Rights: A Documentary History* (New York: Chelsea House, 1971).

Statutes at Large—*United States Statutes, at Large*, on the Web at Library of Congress, American Memory, Lawmaking Home, http://memory.loc.gov/ammem/amlaw/lwsl.html.

Veit, *Bill of Rights*—Helen E. Veit, Kenneth R. Bowling, and Charlene Bangs Bickford, eds., *Creating the Bill of Rights: The Documentary Record from the First Federal Congress* (Baltimore: Johns Hopkins University Press, 1991).

Washington, *Papers*—W. W. Abbot and Dorothy Twohig, eds., *The Papers of George Washington* (Charlottesville: University Press of Virginia, 1983–). The volumes are numbered in separate series: Colonial, Revolutionary War, Confederation, Presidential, and Retirement. Although this is the most recent and authoritative collection, it is unfinished and can be augmented by the older Fitzpatrick collection (listed below) and the Washington papers in the Library of Congress.

Washington, *Writings*—John C. Fitzpatrick, ed., *The Writings of George Washington from the Original Manuscript Sources, 1745–1789* (Washington, D.C.: U.S. Government Printing Office, 1931–44), http://etext.virginia.edu/washington/fitzpatrick/.

Preface: The Historical Constitution

1. Wendy L. Wall, *Inventing the "American Way": The Politics of Consensus from the New Deal to the Civil Rights Movement* (New York: Oxford University Press, 2008), 227–40. At the high-profile cities of Memphis and Birmingham, officials at the American Heritage Foundation, which organized and administered the project, called off the stops rather than submit to local demands for segregation. At other stops, though, informal compromises allowed segregated viewing, so long as separate lines did not form in segregated waiting rooms and the groups entering the train were in fact given equal time. For the Freedom Train's documents, the American Heritage Foundation website, "The Story of the 1947–1949 Freedom Train," Memorabilia, Documents of the Freedom Train, http://www.freedomtrain.org/freedom-train-m-documents-02.htm.

2. Madison, *Notes of Debates*, 17; DHRC; DHFFC.

3. For Madison's evolution, see chapter 5, and for Hamilton's, chapter 6. Jefferson is perhaps the most quoted founder of all, yet rarely are his words placed in context. We hear what he wrote about the role of government, individual rights, slavery, and so on, often with no mention of when he wrote it, what he was responding to, or who his audience was. His pronouncements on public matters spanned more than half a century, which included the years of unrest before the Revolution, declaring independence, the war to defend that independence, the hard times after the war, the framing and ratification of the Constitution, the turbulent politics of the 1790s, a quasi-war with France, a second war with Great Britain, and life in the new republic under six different presidents, including himself. During that time Jefferson drafted the Declaration of Independence, served as governor of Virginia while the state was under British assault, represented the United States in France, served as the nation's first secretary of state, became the leading critic of the ruling Federalist Party and the leading spokesman for the opposition Republican Party, advocated the right of states to nullify federal law, lost an election for the presidency, served as vice president under the man who beat him, and praised the French Revolution, only to see it result in the Reign of Terror and the rise of Napoleon Bonaparte. During the two terms he served as president, Jefferson almost doubled the size of the nation (although he worried that this was unconstitutional) and he assumed nearly dictatorial powers to enforce the Embargo Acts of 1807–1808, the most extreme exercise of federal power until the Civil War.

All of these events, and Jefferson's relationship to them, make a difference. When we interpret some statement he made about "liberty," it makes a world of difference whether his words were meant to justify the fight against British tyranny, to promote opposition to a law passed by Congress and signed by the president of the United States, or with respect to his suppression of the anti-Embargo resistance.

Jefferson's public and private life intersected with the institution of slavery on many levels. In 1769 he tried to make it easier for masters to free their slaves. In 1776 he proposed that "no person hereafter coming into this country [Virginia] shall be held in slavery under any pretext." In 1783 he advocated the gradual emancipation of all slaves in Virginia after 1800. In 1784 he advocated the exclusion of slavery in the West. But he also argued that blacks were inherently inferior to whites (*Notes on the State of Virginia*, drafted in 1781 and published in 1785), tightened Virginia's slave codes, offered a slave as a bounty for any white man who joined the army, claimed ownership of over 600 human beings during his lifetime (about 200 at a given moment), bred slaves for profit ("I consider the labor of a breeding woman as no object, and that a child raised every 2 years is of more profit than the crop of the best laboring man," he wrote to his plantation manager in 1819), sold more than 100 men, women, and children to finance his architectural schemes at Monticello, and in 1820 vigorously opposed the Missouri Compromise because it invoked federal power to prohibit slavery in the Northwest. To take one statement and assume that it represented the whole of his relationship with slavery, or even the dominant stream of his thinking, is simply not possible.

4. The following day in Connecticut, on the road from Norfolk (now home to Xerox Corporation) to Fairfield (where General Electric is headquartered), he noted: "We found all the farmers busily employed in gathering, grinding, and expressing the juice of their apples; the crop of which they say is rather above mediocrity. The average wheat crop they add, is about 15 bushels to the acre from their fallow land—often 20 & from that to 25. . . . The principle export from Norwalk & Fairfield is horses and cattle—salted beef & porke, lumber & Indian corn, to the West Indies—and in a small degree wheat and flour." Donald Jackson and Dorothy Twohig, eds., *The Diaries of George Washington* (Charlottesville: University Press of Virginia, 1979), 5:461–62. I treat the differences between then and now, particularly with respect to the presidency, more extensively in Ray Raphael, *Mr. President: How and Why the Founders Created a Chief Executive* (New York: Knopf, 2012), 268–80.

5. One explicit example: Article IV, Section 4 guarantees that the United States government, at the request of a state legislature, will offer protection against "domestic violence." Today, "domestic violence" denotes intrafamily conflict such as spousal abuse; then, it meant riots or insurrection.

6. This iconic opening line from L.P. Hartley's 1953 novel *The Go-Between* yields over one-half a million Google entries (accessed August 21, 2012).

1. A Revolution in Favor of Government

1. At http://www.jamesmadison.com/about.html (accessed January 10, 2012).

2. *Redwood Times* (CA), March 22, 2011.

3. Prior to the congressional Declaration of Independence, scores of state and local bodies issued their own declarations, proclaiming they were ready to break from Britain and instructing their representatives to higher bodies to act accordingly. As they did so, however, they insisted on the right of self-governance at the state level; they were not about to relinquish their political independence, even to other Americans. "Sole and exclusive right" comes from the Congress of North Carolina, April 12, 1776, reprinted in Peter Force, ed., *American Archives, Fourth Series: A Documentary History of the English Colonies in North America from the King's Message to Parliament of Marcy 7/74, to the Declaration of Independence by the United States* (New York: Johnson Reprint Company, 1972; first published 1833–46), 5:860.

4. Delegates used the word "vigor," always referring to what they wanted from government, a dozen times, and "energy" or "energetic" twenty-five times. See the searchable Farrand, *Records of Federal Convention*, http://oll.libertyfund.org/?option=com_staticxt&staticfile=show .php%3Ftitle=1785&Itemid=27.

5. Quoted in the frontispiece to Max M. Edling, *A Revolution in Favor of Government: Origins of the U.S. Constitution and the Making of the American State* (New York: Oxford University Press, 2003).

6. Avalon Project, Yale Law School, http://avalon.law.yale.edu/17th_century/mayflower .asp.

7. Kenneth Colegrove, "New England Town Mandates," Colonial Society of Massachusetts, *Publications* 21 (1919): 428–37 (accessible online through Google Books at http://is.gd/ivsat); Edmund S. Morgan, *Inventing the People: The Rise of Popular Sovereignty in England and America* (New York: Norton, 1988), 212–13; William Lincoln, *History of Worcester, Massachusetts, from Its Earliest Settlement to September, 1836* (Worcester, MA: Charles Hersey, 1862), 66–68. For a more complete discussion of instructions from New England town meetings, see Ray Raphael, "The Democratic Moment: The Revolution and Popular Politics," in Edward G. Gray and Jane Kamensky, eds., *The Oxford Handbook to the American Revolution* (New York: Oxford University Press, 2012).

8. Evarts B. Greene, *The Provincial Governor in the English Colonies of North America* (New York: Russell & Russell, 1966), 67–68.

9. For the move to Raleigh Tavern, see William J. Van Schreeven, Robert L. Scribner, and Brent Tarter, eds., *Revolutionary Virginia: The Road to Independence; A Documentary Record* (Charlottesville: University Press of Virginia, 1973), 1:69–77; for the Salem incident, see Ray Raphael, *The First American Revolution* (New York: The New Press, 2002), 90–95.

10. For Worcester's instructions, see Raphael, *First American Revolution*, 159. For the state and local declarations of independence, see Pauline Maier, *American Scripture: Making the Declaration of Independence* (New York: Vintage, 1998).

11. See note 2 above.

12. *Journals of Continental Congress*, 1:15–24. Even Congress's Continental Association, which called for a boycott of British goods, was no more a "law" than were previous local associations. It was an agreement among subscribing members, who in this case were delegates representing the provincial assemblies, congresses, and conventions in their respective colonies. For any of Congress's measures to be considered laws, Congress would have to declare itself a government, which of course it was not ready to do.

13. William Lincoln, ed., *The Journals of Each Provincial Congress of Massachusetts in 1774 and 1775, and of the Committee of Safety, with an Appendix, containing the Proceedings of the County Conventions* (Boston: Dutton and Wentworth, 1838), 231.

14. Dickinson's draft appears in *Letters of Delegates to Congress*, Library of Congress, American Memory, http://memory.loc.gov/ammem/amlaw/lwdglink.html, 4:432–50.

15. Gouverneur Morris to Matthew Ridley, August 6, 1782, quoted in James J. Kirschke, *Gouverneur Morris: Author, Statesman, and Man of the World* (New York: St. Martin's Press, 2005), 146.

16. "His Excellency General Washington's LAST LEGACY," broadside printed on June 11, 1783, reproduced in Library of Congress, American Memory, Printed Ephemera, search for "legacy," http://memory.loc.gov/cgi-bin/query.

17. The legacy letter also appears in Washington, *Writings*, 26:483–96, or above as appendix B.

18. Washington to James Warren, October 7, 1785, Washington, *Papers* (CS), 3:299–300. To Warren, Washington expressed his amazement that antigovernment sentiments would continue, now that citizens chose their own rulers: "[I]t is one of the most extraordinary things in nature, that we should Confederate for National purposes, and yet be afraid to give the rulers thereof who are the creatures of our own making—appointed for limited and short duration—who are amenable for every action—recallable at any moment—and subject to all the evils they may be instrumental in producing, sufficient powers to order & direct the affairs of that Nation." Note the phrases "appointed by limited and short duration" and "recallable at any moment." According to the Articles of Confederation, state legislatures were to select their delegates to Congress annually and could recall them "at any time within the year." Further, "no person shall be capable of being a delegate for more than three years in any term of six years."

19. David Szatmary, *Shays' Rebellion: The Making of an Agrarian Insurrection* (Amherst: University of Massachusetts Press, 1980), 57–59, 123–26.

20. Washington to Knox, December 26, 1786, and February 3, 1787, Washington, *Papers* (CS), 4:481 and 5:7–8.

21. *Journals of Continental Congress*, 32:73–74. Congress was responding to a call for a convention issued by a prior convention, held in Annapolis the preceding September. Only twelve delegates from five states had attended the first attempt to consider revisions to the Articles of Confederation, but the fears stirred by civil unrest that fall and winter led to a wider response to the second convention.

22. Knox to Washington, January 14, 1787, Washington, *Papers* (CS), 4:520–22.

23. Washington to Knox, February 3, 1787, Washington, *Papers* (CS), 5:9.

24. Washington to Knox, April 2, 1787, and Knox to Washington, April 9, 1787, Washington, *Papers* (CS), 5:119 and 134. For a full rendering of Washington's decision to attend, see Pauline Maier, *Ratification: The People Debate the Constitution, 1787–1788* (New York: Simon & Schuster, 2010), 18–23.

25. Madison, *Notes of Debates*, May 29.

26. Ibid., May 30.

27. Ibid., May 30.

28. Washington to James Warren, October 7, 1785, and Washington to John Jay, August 15, 1786, Washington, *Papers* (CS), 3:300 and 4:212.

2. Taxes

1. At http://minnesotaindependent.com/27718/live-video-cpac-emcee-bachmann-slams-stimulus-as-taxation-with-representation.

2. At http://biggovernment.com/tdelbeccaro/2010/04/15/top-10-anti-tax-quotations-annotated/.

3. Parliament could and did levy impost duties to regulate commerce, but it was not supposed to do this with the chief goal of raising revenue.

4. A broader statement would be, "To taxes and the desire to regulate commerce we owe our Constitution," but taxes and commercial regulation were intricately intertwined.

5. Alvin Rabushka, *Taxation in Colonial America* (Princeton, NJ: Princeton University

Press, 2008), 168–71, 234–35, 244, 268; Sidney Ratner, *American Taxation: Its History as a Social Force in Democracy* (New York: Norton, 1942), 51–52.

6. E. James Ferguson, *The Power of the Purse: A History of American Public Finance, 1776–1790* (Chapel Hill: University of North Carolina Press, 1961), 7–10.

7. Ferguson, *Power of the Purse*, 27–32.

8. Benjamin Franklin to Samuel Cooper, April 22, 1779, quoted in Ferguson, *Power of the Purse*, 48.

9. Robert Morris, *The Papers of Robert Morris, 1781–1784*, ed. E. James Ferguson (Pittsburgh: University of Pittsburgh Press, 1973), 1:70, 397. While the impost of 1783 encountered resistance in Rhode Island and Virginia, New York was the final holdout (*DHRC*, 13:147).

10. Edling, *Revolution in Favor of Government*, 154–55; Woody Holton, *Unruly Americans and the Origins of the Constitution* (New York: Hill and Wang, 2007), 65–82; *Journals of Continental Congress*, 30:72.

11. Madison, *Papers*, 9:348. Washington thought the weakness of Congress and its inability to raise money were ruining the nation's credit, and with it the nation's future: "That our resources are ample, & encreasing, none can deny. But whilst they are grudgingly applied, or not applied at all, we give the vital stab to the public credit, and must sink into contempt in the eyes of Europe" (Washington to James Warren, October 7, 1785, Washington, *Papers* [CS], 3:299).

12. The precise definition of "direct tax" caused some confusion. Did the term denote poll and property taxes (the common usage at the time), or did it refer to the relationship between the taxing body and those whom it taxed? The delegates themselves had some difficulty deciphering what they meant by "direct tax." On August 20 Madison jotted this curious entry into his notes: "Mr KING asked what was the precise meaning of *direct* taxation. No one answered."

13. *DHRC*, 15:19 and 22. In Delaware, which ratified the Constitution five days before Pennsylvania, there was no significant opposition.

14. For the various amendments relevant to taxation proposed at state ratification conventions, see Veit et al., *Bill of Rights*, 14, 15, 16, 19, 24; Schwartz, *Bill of Rights*, 2:665, 713, 757, 760, 841, 843, 914–15, and 969.

15. *DHRC*, 9:1045, 1063.

16. Virginia Convention, June 11 in *DHRC*, 9:1156–57. Also in Kurland and Lerner, *Founders' Constitution*, 2:438–39 (Article 1, Section 8, Clause 1, Document 16).

17. Virginia Convention, June 7, *DHRC*, 1016–28. Also in Kurland and Lerner, *Founders' Constitution*, 2:433–35 (Article 1, Section 8, Clause 1, Document 16).

18. *DHRC*, 10:1548–54. Also in Veit et al., *Bill of Rights*, 17–19; Schwartz, *Bill of Rights*, 2:841, 843.

19. *Annals of Congress*, 1:803–4.

20. Ibid., 1:807 (House vote) and 1:78 (Senate vote). The "antitax crusaders," as I call them, were not opposed to all taxes, just federal taxes; in fact, one of their major complaints was that federal taxation would hamper the ability of the states to levy and collect taxes. Politically, though, they can be viewed as antecedents to antitax crusaders of today, whose resistance to taxation is colored by the desire to limit federal authority. Even after the matter appeared settled, some opponents of unrestricted federal taxation refused to accept Congress's decision as the final word. Later that year Hardin Burnley wrote to Madison, "Whatever may be the fate of the

amendments submitted by Congress it is probable that an application for further amendments will be made by this assembly [Virginia], for the opposition to the Foederal Constitution is in my opinion reduced to a single point, the power of direct taxation" (Burnley to Madison, November 28, 1789, in Schwartz, *Bill of Rights*, 2:1188). Since the framers had taken care to provide for two different ways of initiating amendments, through Congress or through state legislatures, the state legislators could have kept the issue of taxation alive, but they didn't, and the Constitution, as drafted by the framers and approved by a sufficient number of ratification conventions, remained unaltered.

21. Hamilton was not the first to suggest liquor as a source of income for the federal government. Back in 1750, when Benjamin Franklin first contemplated an American confederacy that would soon be called the Albany Plan, he proposed to finance the costs of administration by duties on imported liquor, license fees for public houses, and an excise tax on all liquor, foreign or domestic. Both Franklin and Hamilton considered liquor taxes the easiest to impose; theoretically, people who didn't want to pay the tax could cease consuming alcohol, but in fact they wouldn't, so government coffers could be filled. Franklin to James Parker, March 20, 1750 or 1751, in Franklin, *Papers*, 4:119.

22. The framers of the Constitution had hoped to prevent this, but they hadn't. The document they created required the liquor excise to be uniform throughout the states, which it was. The tax on "spirits" did vary according to the strength of the brew, from nine cents to twenty-five cents per gallon, but it did not vary according to the place it was produced or sold. It might have been unfair and politically destructive, but it was not unconstitutional (*Statutes at Large*, 1st Cong., 3rd sess., 1:203).

23. David P. Currie, *The Constitution in Congress: The Federalist Period, 1789–1801* (Chicago: University of Chicago Press, 1997), 183–86; *Annals of Congress*, 4:644–45; *Hylton v. U.S.*, 3 U.S. 171 (1796), http://caselaw.lp.findlaw.com/scripts/getcase.pl?court=US&vol=3&invol=171.

24. Unlike Congress in 1798, colonial assemblies did not establish progressively higher rates, but even so, the very nature of property taxes, the major source of revenue in the North, was to levy increased taxes for larger holdings. In the South, landed interests that held political power relied more on regressive poll taxes.

25. In 1780 Gouverneur Morris had proposed the idea of a specific tax on windows, and on March 8, 1783, Superintendent of Finance Robert Morris had suggested to Congress a sharply graduated tax on the number of glazed windows: no tax for the first five, 50 cents for fewer than ten, and then increasing steadily, peaking at $100 for a seventy-window mansion (Morris, *Papers*, 7:525–30, 537).

26. *Statutes at Large*, 5th Cong., 2nd sess., 1:597–604.

27. Ratner, *American Taxation*, 53–56; *Statutes at Large*, 37th Cong., 2nd sess., 12:473. The Civil War income tax was an integral component of a sweeping tax bill that included a stamp tax, an inheritance tax, and all sorts of excises and licensing fees. In 1881, in *Springer v. United States*, the Supreme Court stated explicitly that income taxes were to be considered indirect, not direct. This decision was based in part on earlier holdings that only poll and property taxes could be considered direct: *Hylton v. United States* (1796), *Pacific Insurance Co. v. Soule* (1868), *Veazie Bank v. Fenno* (1869), and *Scholey v. Rew* (1874). For *Springer*, see http://

caselaw.lp.findlaw.com/scripts/getcase.pl?case=/us/102/586.html&court=US&navby=
search.

28. *Pollock v. Farmers' Loan and Trust Company*, Legal Information Institute, Cornell University Law School, http://www.law.cornell.edu/supct/html/historics/USSC_CR_0157_
0429_ZO.html.

29. Robin Leigh Einhorn, *American Taxation, American Slavery* (Chicago: University of Chicago Press, 2006), 159. Chief Justice Melville Fuller, in the majority opinion for the *Pollock* case, contended, "Nothing can be clearer than that what the Constitution intended to guard against was the exercise by the general government of the power of directly taxing persons and property within any State through a majority made up from the other States. It is true that the effect of requiring direct taxes to be apportioned among the States in proportion to their population is necessarily that the amount of taxes on the individual taxpayer in a State having the taxable subject matter to a larger extent in proportion to its population than another State has would be less than in such other State, but *this inequality must be held to have been contemplated, and was manifestly designed to operate to restrain the exercise of the power of direct taxation to extraordinary emergencies, and to prevent an attack upon accumulated property by mere force of numbers*" (emphases added). This explanation is purely conjectural and makes no sense. Writers of constitutions do not knowingly mandate two principles that contradict each other with the mere hope that this will rarely come to pass. In fact, both provisions resulted from compromises (see chapter 3), and it is altogether possible that delegates failed to notice that adherence to one contradicted the spirit of the other. Technically, there is one interpretation by which the two provisions would not *directly* contradict each other. Article I, Section 8, Clause 1 states only that "all Duties, Imposts, and Excises shall be uniform throughout the United States"—it does not use the word "taxes" here, although it does refer to taxes earlier in the sentence when outlining the powers of Congress. It is conceivable that this omission was purposive in order to allow nonuniformity for taxes that might be apportioned but, if so, the framers probably did not envision that apportionment would result in citizens from some states being taxed at twice the rate of others merely by virtue of their place of residence.

30. Washington to the People of the United States, September 19, 1796, http://avalon.law
.yale.edu/18th_century/washing.asp.

3. Politics

1. Thomas Jefferson to John Adams, August 30, 1787, Jefferson, *Papers*, 12:69, or Lester J. Cappon, ed., *The Adams-Jefferson Letters: The Complete Correspondence between Thomas Jefferson and Abigail and John Adams*, 2 vols. (Chapel Hill: University of North Carolina Press for the Institute of Early American History and Culture, 1959), 1:196. Also at http://teachingamerican
history.org/library/index.asp?document=1887.

2. John Robert Irelan, *The Republic, or, A History of the United States of America* (Chicago: Fairbanks and Palmer, 1888), 15:164.

3. Joseph Ellis, *Founding Brothers: The Revolutionary Generation* (New York: Knopf, 2000), 13.

4. Madison, *Notes of Debates*, May 29.

5. Madison to Thomas Ritchie, Sept 15, 1821, Kurland and Lerner, *Founders' Constitution*, 1:74, document 28.

6. Jefferson to John Adams, August 30, 1787, Jefferson, *Papers*, 12:69, or Cappon, *Adams-Jefferson Letters*, 1:196. On general ideas of secrecy and what we call "the public's right to know" in this period, see Daniel N. Hoffman, *Governmental Secrecy and the Founding Fathers: A Study in Constitutional Controls* (Westport, CT: Greenwood Press, 1981).

7. Paterson's quote is from Robert Yates's notes, not Madison's, for June 16 (Farrand, *Records of Federal Convention*, 1:258). Ellsworth's quote is from Madison, *Notes of Debates*, June 29.

8. The instructions for each state appear in Farrand, *Records of Federal Convention*, 3:559–86.

9. Farrand, *Records of Federal Convention*, 3:575. See also the notes of Madison and Yates, ibid., 1:4 and 1:6; Mason to George Mason Jr., May 27, 1783, ibid., 3:28; Luther Martin, "The Genuine Information, delivered to the Legislature of the State of Maryland, relative to the Proceedings of the General Convention, held at Philadelphia, in 1787," ibid., 3:173. Census figures from Thomas L. Purvis, *Revolutionary America, 1763 to 1800*, Almanacs of American Life Series (New York: Facts on File, 1995), 124.

10. Madison, *Notes of Debates*, May 30.

11. Ibid., June 29. For the political challenge, see Clinton Rossiter, *1787: The Grand Convention* (New York: Macmillan, 1966), 182–96.

12. Madison, *Notes of Debates*, June 25.

13. Ibid., June 27.

14. Ibid., June 30. Five days later, on July 5, Bedford offered a nonapology apology that did nothing to lessen the small-state, large-state divide: "He found that what he had said as to the small States being taken by the hand, had been misunderstood; and he rose to explain. He did not mean that the small States would court the aid & interposition of foreign powers. He meant that they would not consider the federal compact as dissolved untill it should be so by the Acts of the large States. In this case the consequence of the breach of faith on their part, and the readiness of the small States to fulfill their engagements, would be that foreign Nations having demands on this Country would find it their interest to take the small States by the hand, in order to do themselves justice. This was what he meant. But no man can foresee to what extremities the small States may be driven by oppression. He observed also in apology that some allowance ought to be made for the habits of his profession [Bedford was a lawyer] in which warmth was natural & sometimes necessary. But is there not an apology in what was said by [Mr. Govr. Morris] that the sword is to unite: by Mr. Ghorum that Delaware must be annexed to Penna. and N. Jersey divided between Pena. and N. York. To hear such language without emotion, would be to renounce the feelings of a man and the duty of a Citizen."

15. Ibid., July 5.

16. Ibid., June 29.

17. Many commentators suggest that Franklin was using the ploy to bring his colleagues to their senses. For a thoroughly researched discussion, see William G. Carr, *The Oldest Delegate: Franklin in the Constitutional Convention* (Newark, DE: University of Delaware Press, 1990), 96–101.

18. Madison, *Notes of Debates*, June 29.

19. Membership on the committee predetermined the results. Leading advocates of

proportional representation in both houses—James Madison, James Wilson, Gouverneur Morris, and Rufus King—were not included; instead, delegations from the three largest states appointed delegates who had already expressed a desire to compromise—George Mason, Benjamin Franklin, and Elbridge Gerry. Meanwhile, Maryland sent Luther Martin, Delaware sent Gunning Bedford, New Jersey sent William Paterson, and New York sent Robert Yates—all firm opponents of proportional representation. Connecticut sent Oliver Ellsworth, who had offered the motion for equal representation in the second house, and Georgia sent Abraham Baldwin, whose vote for Ellsworth's motion had divided his state's delegation and deadlocked the Convention. These delegates were not going to opt for proportional representation in the upper house, nor could they deny proportional representation in the lower house, an indispensable feature of the overall plan (see chapter 4). Whereas the committee's compromise was politically dictated, it was handy philosophically as well. "Dual sovereignty" was a difficult concept to grasp: how could citizens owe allegiance to two governments at once, the state and the national? Put another way, was the United States to have a truly national government, with all parts subservient to the whole; a confederation, with the whole subservient to the parts; or a new form of confederated government, in which state governments retained some representation? The compromise implied a solution to this matrix of problems: one house of the legislature represented people directly and was therefore apportioned by population, while the other house represented states, which would each receive an equal vote. It would be a hybrid government, simultaneously national and federal.

20. Madison, *Notes of Debates*, July 5.

21. Ibid.

22. Ibid.

23. Ibid., July 10.

24. Washington to Hamilton, July 10, 1787, Washington, *Papers* (CS), 5:257. Hamilton left the Convention because he was consistently outvoted by his New York colleagues Robert Yates and John Lansing Jr.

25. *Journals of Continental Congress*, 24:223, Madison, *Notes of Debates*, July 11. In 1783 Congress cleverly used only euphemisms to denote slaves. Funds for the federal treasury were to be "supplied by the several states in proportion to the whole number of white and other free citizens and inhabitants of every age, sex and condition, including those bound to servitude for a term of years, and three-fifths of all other persons not comprehended in the foregoing description, except Indians, not paying taxes, in each state." Delegates to the Federal Convention followed this precedent.

26. Only Delaware joined South Carolina and Georgia in voting to consider slaves on a par with free people; other delegations remained content with three-fifths. Delaware's vote was curious. Although 18 percent of its population was enslaved, it did not normally side with South Carolina and Georgia on issues involving slavery. Possibly, it voted to count slaves on a par with free citizens to undermine the general concept of proportional representation.

27. Madison, *Notes of Debates*, July 13.

28. Ibid., July 14 (Martin) and July 12 (Davie).

29. As with any vote on multiple issues, it is difficult to dissect the returns, but judging from previous and subsequent positions, it appears that a bloc of small states was happy to achieve

equal representation in the second branch, whereas Virginia and Pennsylvania, not ready to compromise, refused to concede and voted against the measure. South Carolina and perhaps Georgia also resisted compromise, with at least some delegates holding out for full slave representation. Delegates from Massachusetts divided over the slavery compromise, while three of the four North Carolina delegates thought compromise on all issues was in order. At first glance the five-to-four tally might have seemed inconclusive, subject to being overturned in the future. But two states were not present, and both likely would have approved: New Hampshire because it was a small state and New York because it appeared to give the states legal representation in Congress. Tiny Rhode Island, not present at the Convention, would also have favored equal representation for small states, and Georgia, had all its delegates been present, might well have voted yes rather than no. The vote was not as close as it might appear. Richard Beeman, *Plain, Honest Men: The Making of the American Constitution* (New York: Random House, 2010), 219–22.

30. On August 22, Elbridge Gerry of Massachusetts noted that "we had nothing to do with the conduct of the States as to Slaves, but ought to be careful not to give any sanction to it." This was the most forthright explanation of the delegates' decision to avoid use of the terms "slavery" and "slaves" in the Constitution's text.

31. Martin owned six slaves at the time, and he also represented the state of Maryland, with approximately one hundred thousand slaves (one-third of its population), but he was clearly disturbed by the institution, and he would soon help found the Maryland Society for the Abolition of Slavery. Even so, he did not speak out against the three-fifths compromise, which increased Maryland's representation in Congress, and he seems to have gone along with the rest of his delegation in voting for it. Was that also "inconsistent with the principles of the revolution" and a "dishonorable" feature of the Constitution? (Beeman, *Plain, Honest Men*, 320.) Mason, while denouncing slavery, refused to take any responsibility for it. Slavery, he argued, was not caused by people like himself or Washington or any of the nineteen framers whose livelihoods depended on slave labor, nor the nine other delegates, like Martin, known to have owned slaves. Instead, Mason looked to cast the blame for slavery onto slave traders: "This infernal trafic originated in the avarice of British Merchants. The British Govt. constantly checked the attempts of Virginia to put a stop to it." Those antislavery Virginians were also thwarted in their attempts by "some of our Eastern brethren," New England merchants who "from a lust of gain embarked in this nefarious traffic." Only by cutting off further importation, Mason argued, could the spread of slavery be curtailed. Mason's argument paralleled Thomas Jefferson's argument in the famous passage of his draft of the Declaration of Independence attacking slavery, which blamed George III for foisting slavery on the helpless colonies. For a listing of slaveholders at the Federal Convention, see Ray Raphael, *The Complete Idiot's Guide to the Founding Fathers and the Birth of Our Nation* (New York: Alpha Books, 2011), 146–47.

32. C.C. Pinckney's words are from McHenry's notes, Farrand, *Records of Federal Convention*, 2:378, and from Madison, *Notes of Debates*, August 22.

33. Ibid., August 21 and 22. Charles Cotesworth Pinckney, too, predicted that his state would never assent to a document that left slave importation vulnerable. "S. Carolina & Georgia cannot do without slaves," he stated, so a failure to protect slave importation would amount to "an exclusion of S. Carola. from the Union." John Rutledge delivered the same message: "The true question at present is whether the Southn. States shall or shall not be parties to the Union."

34. Ibid., August 21 and 22. Likewise, Roger Sherman, also of Connecticut, said that "no public good" would be achieved by taking away "the right to import slaves," even though he personally "disapproved of the slave trade." Elbridge Gerry, of Massachusetts, "thought we had nothing to do with the conduct of the States as to Slaves."

35. In 1785, John Jay had sought authorization from the Confederation Congress to negotiate a treaty with Spain that would have signed away American shipping rights on the Mississippi River in return for privileged trading status. The deal was welcomed in the commercial North but detested in the South, since it would inhibit westward expansion. Fortunately for the South, the Articles of Confederation required nine of the thirteen states to approve an act that affected commerce, and five southern states (Maryland, Virginia, North Carolina, South Carolina, and Georgia) declared that they would reject any treaty negotiated on that basis. Jay's proposed treaty was one of the hot-button issues of the day, and it explains why the framers paid such attention to whether enacting navigation acts should require a simple majority or a supermajority.

36. Ibid., August 22.

37. Not all small-state delegates agreed with Dayton. Delegates from New Hampshire and Delaware, thinking that separate ballots would prove too cumbersome, broke ranks with their small-state brethren.

38. For Morris's opposition to legislative selection of the president, see Ray Raphael, *Mr. President: How and Why the Founders Created a Chief Executive* (New York: Knopf, 2012), 78–120 and 281–85, and for and the devious methods used by Morris and the New Jersey delegation to get the matter into committee, see ibid., 101–6.

39. Madison, *Notes of Debates*, September 4 and 5. In the floor debates on the committee report, several delegates disapproved of the Senate's playing such a significant role and suggested that the runoff occur in the House instead, but small states rebuffed that idea because they would lose their influence. Finally, the Convention transferred the runoff to the House but with each state delegation, whether large or small, having one vote, thereby preserving the small-state advantage. For a more complete discussion of issues and committee negotiations, see Raphael, *Mr. President*, 107–12.

40. On September 5, committee member Rufus King "observed that the influence of the small States in the Senate was somewhat balanced by the influence of the large States in bringing forward the candidates; and also by the concurrence of the small States in the Committee in the clause vesting the exclusive origination of money bills in the House of Representatives." To this observation Madison appended a footnote: "This explains the compromise mentioned above by Mr. Govr. Morris. Col. Masson Mr. Gerry & other members from large States set great value on this privilege of originating money bills. Of this the members from the small States, with some from the large States who wished a high mounted Govt endeavored to avail themselves, by making that privilege, the price of arrangements in the constitution favorable to the small States, and to the elevation of the Government."

41. Samuel Tilden in 1876, Benjamin Harrison in 1888, and Albert Gore in 2000 won the popular vote but lost in the Electoral College. Andrew Jackson won a plurality of votes in 1824, but since no candidate received a majority of electoral votes, the presidency was decided in the House of Representatives, which chose John Quincy Adams over Jackson.

42. Mason to Jefferson, May 26, 1788, George Mason, *The Papers of George Mason*, ed. Robert A. Rutland, 3 vols. (Chapel Hill: University of North Carolina Press, 1960), 3:1045.

43. Mason's "Objections," in *DHRC*, 8:45 or 13:350; Washington to Stuart, November 30, 1787, *DHRC*, 8:193.

44. Madison, *Notes of Debates*, August 29.

45. Ibid., September 17. Morris's and Franklin's comments in the succeeding paragraphs are also from that date.

46. Washington to Patrick Henry, Benjamin Harrison, and Thomas Nelson (former governors of Virginia), September 24, 1787, *DHRC*, 8:15.

47. Farrand, *Records of Federal Convention*, 2:677. Toward the end of the ratification controversy, John Jay turned the framers' ability to compromise into his closing argument for the proposed Constitution. In April 1788, although eight states had already ratified the Constitution, one state shy of the required minimum, opponents of the Constitution in New York wanted several changes before ratifying, and they pushed for a second constitutional convention (see chapter 7). That was a terrible idea, Jay argued in an influential pamphlet, *An Address to the People of the State of New York, on the Subject of the Constitution*, which he published under the pseudonym "A Citizen of New-York." Delegates to the Federal Convention, Jay said, did not present their proposed Constitution "as the best of all possible ones, but only as the best which they could unite in and agree to." Perhaps, after seven months of public discussion, a second convention could come up with some better ideas, but it did not follow that delegates to that convention "would be equally *disposed to agree*" (Jay's emphasis). In fact, because of the intensity of the ratification debates, the spirit of compromise that not only permeated but in a sense defined the Federal Convention had been abandoned; without that spirit, Americans would not be able to agree on a different plan, even if they chose to shun the proposed Constitution and try to start again from scratch. In an emotive passage with an eerie resonance for today, Jay described precisely how the partisanship of the ratification debates precluded constructive solutions that opposing parties "could unite in and agree to": "You must have observed that the same temper and equanimity which prevailed among the people on former occasions, no longer exist. We have unhappily become divided into parties; and this important subject has been handled with such indiscreet and offensive acrimony, and with so many little, unhandsome artifices and misrepresentations, that pernicious heats and animosities have been kindled, and spread their flames far and wide among us. When, therefore, it becomes a question who shall be deputed to the new convention, we cannot flatter ourselves that the talents and integrity of the candidates will determine who shall be elected. Federal electors will vote for federal deputies, and anti-federal electors for anti-federal ones. Nor will either party prefer the most moderate of their adherents; for, as the most stanch and active partisans will be the most popular, so the men most willing and able to carry points, to oppose and divide, and embarrass their opponents, will be chosen.

"A convention formed at such a season, and of such men, would be but too exact an epitome of the great body that named them. The same party views, the same propensity to opposition, the same distrusts and jealousies, and the same unaccommodating spirit, which prevail without, would be concentred and ferment with still greater violence within. Each deputy would recollect who sent him, and why he was sent, and be too apt to consider himself bound in honor to contend and act vigorously under the standard of his party, and not hazard their displeasure by preferring compromise to victory. As vice does not sow the seed of virtue, so neither does passion cultivate the fruits of reason. Suspicions and resentments create no disposition to conciliate; nor do they infuse a desire of making partial and personal objects bend to general union and the common good." (*DHRC*, 20:936).

By contrast, the Federal Convention, driven by the spirit of political compromise, seemed downright patriotic, and quite arguably it was. The full text of Jay's pamphlet, which deserves to be better known, is available online: http://teachingamericanhistory.org/library/index .asp?document=1791. A lengthy excerpt, including this passage, is accessible on the Web under the title "John Jay and the Constitution," http://www.columbia.edu/cu/lweb/digital/exhibi tions/constitution/address/address.html.

One more quotation from the pamphlet distills Jay's argument into one sentence: "While reason retains her rule, while men are as willing to receive as to give advice, and as willing to be convinced themselves as to convince others, there are few political evils from which a free and enlightened people cannot deliver themselves."

4. Principles

1. "Texas Essential Knowledge and Skills for Social Studies: Middle School," http://ritter .tea.state.tx.us/rules/tac/chapter113/ch113b.html.

2. At http://wiki.answers.com/Q/7_principles_of_the_constitution (accessed April 2, 2012).

3. Jonathan Elliot, *The Debates in the Several State Conventions on the Adoption of the Federal Constitution* (New York: Burt Franklin, 1888), 3:608; and *Founders' Constitution*, 1:268 (chap. 8, doc. 21), both cited in Gordon Wood, *Creation of the American Republic* (Chapel Hill: University of North Carolina Press, 1969), 499–500.

4. Elliot, *Debates*, 3:66, cited in Wood, *Creation of the American Republic*, 544.

5. In 1789 James Madison, when suggesting amendments that would later turn into the Bill of Rights, included a proposition that would have made the separation of powers overt: "The powers delegated by this Constitution are appropriated to the departments to which they are respectively distributed: so that the Legislative Department shall never exercise the powers vested in the Executive or Judicial, nor the Executive exercise the powers vested in the Legislative or Judicial, nor the Judicial exercise the powers vested in the Legislative or Executive Departments." Congress rejected this proposal. "Separation of powers" was to be inferred from the structure of the Constitution, not stated explicitly (*Annals of Congress*, 1:453; reprinted in Veit et al., *Bill of Rights*, 14). The final provision of the Massachusetts Declaration of Rights, drafted by John Adams in 1779 and adopted in 1780 as part of the Massachusetts Constitution, stated: "In the government of this commonwealth, the legislative department shall never exercise the executive and judicial powers, or either of them; the executive shall never exercise the legislative and judicial powers, or either of them; the judicial shall never exercise the legislative and executive powers, or either of them; to the end it may be a government of laws, and not of men" (Schwartz, *Bill of Rights*, 1:344).

6. The *general* principle of limited government is often used to support *particular* limitations on governmental activities. The dissent by Justices Antonin Scalia, Anthony Kennedy, Clarence

Thomas, and Samuel Alito in the 2012 Supreme Court decision upholding most provisions of the Affordable Care Act (*National Federation of Independent Businesses v. Sebelius*) stated: "What is absolutely clear, affirmed by the text of the 1789 Constitution, by the Tenth Amendment ratified in 1791, and by innumerable cases of ours in the 220 years since, is that there are structural limits upon federal power—upon what it can prescribe with respect to private conduct, and upon what it can impose upon the sovereign States. Whatever may be the conceptual limits upon the Commerce Clause and upon the power to tax and spend, they cannot be such as will enable the Federal Government to regulate all private conduct and to compel the States to function as administrators of federal programs" (Legal Information Institute, Cornell University Law School, http://www.law.cornell.edu/supremecourt/text/11-393).

7. Randolph to Washington, February 12, 1791, Washington, *Papers* (PS), 7:337.

8. Jefferson to Washington, February 15, 1791, Washington, *Papers* (PS), 7:352 (emphases in the original).

9. Madison to Washington, February 21, 1791, Washington, *Papers* (PS), 7:395.

10. Hamilton to Washington, February 23, 1791, Washington, *Papers* (PS), 7:425, 429, 430 (emphases in the original). In *Mr. President: How and Why the Founders Created a Chief Executive* (New York: Knopf, 2012), I treat this sequence of events in the context of presidential powers. Washington's veto, had he delivered it, would have been the nation's first.

11. Hamilton to Washington, February 23, 1791, Washington, *Papers* (PS), 7:443, 450.

12. In *Mr. President*, I treat the debate over the national bank in the context of presidential powers. Washington's veto, had he delivered it, would have been the nation's first.

13. Veit et al., *Bill of Rights*, 14; Schwartz, *Bill of Rights*, 2:712. New Hampshire's ratification convention proposed the exact same amendment. South Carolina declared that powers "not expressly relinquished" by the states remained with them. New York's proposed amendment stated that "every power, Jurisdiction, and right, which is not by the said Constitution clearly delegated to the Congress of the United States, or the departments of the Government thereof, remains to the people of the several States, or to the their respective State Governments." Virginia and North Carolina proposed slightly milder versions, without the intensifying adverbs "expressly" or "clearly." A committee of Maryland's convention first echoed Massachusetts: "Congress shall exercise no power but what is expressly delegated by this Constitution," and then proclaimed this amendment was necessary to "restrain . . . the general powers given to Congress" under the sweeping first clause in Article I, Section 8, which gave Congress authority to "provide for the common Defence and general Welfare" of the nation, as well as the potentially expansive "necessary and proper" clause that closed that section. Even the critical clause in Article V that declared the Constitution and the laws passed by Congress "the supreme Law of the Land" needed to be "restrained," the Maryland committee held. While the committee's proposal never came to a vote in the full convention, this passage demonstrates an extreme desire to *expressly* limit the powers of the federal government. Veit et al., *Bill of Rights*, 15, 16, 19, 21–22; Schwartz, *Bill of Rights*, 2:732, 757, 760, 842, 911–12, 968.

14. *Annals of Congress*, 1:453, 790 (June 8 and August 18, 1789); also in Veit et al., *Bill of Rights*, 14 and 197.

15. Ibid., 1:797 (August 21, 1789); also in Veit et al., *Bill of Rights*, 199, with the roll-call vote omitted.

16. Later, as we will see in chapter 5, Madison would modify this stance, but at the time Congress approved his amendment, that is the meaning he and his colleagues attributed to it. That is the amendment Thomas Tudor Tucker had hoped to alter.

17. "Laws and Ordinances . . . of the City of Albany, MDCCLXXIII," http://www.nysm .nysed.gov/albany/doc/laws.html. For a valuable discussion of the ideal of the "well-regulated society" reigning from late colonial times until the years following the Civil War, see William J. Novak, *The People's Welfare: Law and Regulation in Nineteenth-Century America* (Chapel Hill: University of North Carolina Press, 1996).

18. "Determinatus," *Boston Gazette*, January 8, 1770, in *The Writings of Samuel Adams*, ed. Harry Alonzo Cushing (New York: G. P. Putnam's Sons, 1906), 2:5.

19. With the prospect of peace, Alexander Hamilton used a different rationale to argue that the good of the whole could take precedence over the liberty "to do as you please." In 1782, as the fighting neared an end and the bankrupt nation was trying to recover, he argued that timely regulations would help promote commerce, not restrain it. "Commerce, like other things, has its fixed principles, according to which it must be regulated. If these are understood and observed, it will be promoted by the attention of government; if unknown, or violated, it will be injured" ("The Continentalist No. V," April 18, 1782, in Hamilton, *Papers*, 7:76).

20. Madison, *Papers*, 9:348–53.

21. Martin's comment is from Yates's note for June 27 (Farrand, *Records of Federal Convention*, 1:441). In this case Martin was arguing against proportional representation and the presidential veto, but he still contended that those features endangered the "public good" because the will of the people, represented by ten smaller states, could be negated.

22. In *The Federalist No. 1*, even while supporting liberty and trying to appease fears that the new federal government might be too strong, Alexander Hamilton warned against "an over-scrupulous jealousy of danger to the rights of the people" and predicted that an obsession with liberty could undermine the nation and its people. "A dangerous ambition more often lurks behind the specious mask of zeal for the rights of the people than under the forbidden appearance of zeal for the firmness and efficiency of government. History will teach us that the former has been found a much more certain road to the introduction of despotism than the latter, and that of those men who have overturned the liberties of republics, the greatest number have begun their career by paying an obsequious court to the people; commencing demagogues, and ending tyrants." That is precisely why people needed government, Hamilton argued—a government such as provided by the newly minted Constitution, which he was urging people to accept. Although he was only one participant in the struggle for ratification and later debates over the meaning of the Constitution, and although some of his contemporaries might have disagreed with his statement here, and although his argument could be seen as a way to denigrate his opposition, Hamilton's strong pronouncement demonstrates that the ongoing discussion concerning liberty and government did not always favor liberty at the expense of government, as Americans commonly assume today.

23. Consider James Wilson's argument, offered early in the deliberations of the Federal Convention, for the direct popular election of federal representatives: "He wished for vigor in the Govt., but he wished that vigorous authority to flow immediately from the legitimate source of all authority. The Govt. ought to possess not only 1st. the force, but 2dly. the mind or sense

of the people at large" (Madison, *Notes of Debates*, June 6). For a broader discussion of this idea in the period 1776–80, see Donald S. Lutz, *Popular Consent and Popular Control: Whig Political Theory in the Early State Constitutions* (Baton Rouge: Louisiana State University Press, 1980).

24. Madison, *Notes of Debates*, May 31. To keep citizens at some distance, Sherman wanted federal representatives to be chosen by state legislatures, as they were under the Articles of Confederation, rather than by the people. Gerry admitted he had been "too republican heretofore," but now, after the uprising in his home state of Massachusetts, he had been "taught by experience the danger of the levelling spirit."

25. Madison, *Notes of Debates*, May 31. Wilson, unlike most other delegates, also favored popular election of senators and the president.

26. Madison, *Notes of Debates*, June 12 (Randolph), July 19 (Morris), and June 26 (Madison). Even in the lower house of Congress, the relationship between the people and their representatives was not intended to be *too* direct. In late colonial and Revolutionary America, lower public bodies such as New England town meetings, as legal embodiments of "the people," typically issued specific instructions to their representatives in higher bodies, telling them what actions they should initiate and how to vote on specific issues (see chapter 1). The Constitution said nothing about citizens issuing instructions, but the silence was noticed. Ratification conventions in four states (Virginia, New York, North Carolina, and Rhode Island) proposed amendments to guarantee the people's right "to instruct their representatives," and the First Federal Congress, when considering amendments that would eventually become the Bill of Rights, debated the right to issue instructions. Virginia's John Page tied the right of instructions directly to the fundamental notion of popular sovereignty: "Our Government is derived from the people, of consequence the people have a right to consult for the common good; but to what end will this be done, if they have not the power of instructing their representatives? Instruction and representation in a republic appear to me to be inseparably connected." But Pennsylvania's Thomas Hartley, like the framers of the Constitution, preferred to give representatives full discretion: "Representation is the principle of our government; the people ought to have confidence in the honor and integrity of those they send forward to transact their business. . . . [H]appy is that Government composed of men of firmness and wisdom to discover, and resist popular error." For the better part of a day, congressmen declared for a representative government, in which elected leaders were free to deliberate and decide on their own, or for a pure democracy, in which the people led and leaders followed, or something in between, in which people maintained the right to issue instructions, but representatives could reject them with good cause. Perhaps this debate should have occurred during the Federal Convention, but because no framer treated the notion of popular sovereignty quite so literally, the issue never arose. The matter was finally settled in the Federalist-dominated First Federal Congress, when the motion for an amendment to guarantee the right of instructions failed by a vote of ten to forty-one. The debate over instructions in the First Federal Congress, on August 15, 1789, is in *Annals of Congress*, 1:759–76. For more on instructions, see Michael Zuckerman, *Peaceable Kingdoms: New England Towns in the Eighteenth Century* (New York: Knopf, 1970), 166, 212–13; Ray Raphael, "The Democratic Moment: The Revolution and Popular Politics," in *The Oxford Handbook to the American Revolution* (New York: Oxford University Press, 2012); Ray Raphael, "Instructions: The People's Voice in Revolutionary America," *Common-Place* 9:1 (October 2008), http://www.common-place

.org/vol-09/no-01/raphael/. Some states continued to attempt to instruct their senators, but this practice faded away in the first years of the nineteenth century.

27. Whereas the opening of the Preamble, "We the People," is a sincere expression of popular sovereignty, too much is made of the last minute decision by the Committee of Style and its designated draftsman, Gouverneur Morris, to change the text from the Committee of Detail's original draft—"We the people of the States of New Hampshire, Massachusetts, Rhode-Island and Providence Plantations . . ." and so on, listing the states north to south—to the more succinct "We the People of the United States." This was not a dramatic ideological pronouncement in favor of democratic nationalism, but rather a political necessity. Rhode Island, which had refused to send delegates, might refuse to ratify the proposed Constitution, as might other states. In that case, the original preamble would become a farcical reminder of the lack of unanimity and the Constitution would need to be amended to take account of the missing state or states. The listing of the separate states made no sense, so it simply had to go.

28. Yale Law School professor Akhil Reed Amar, for example, claims that "the abiding heart and spirit of the document [the Constitution] lay in the structure of its rules for political participation and political power, and these rules were . . . generally populist." Through mechanisms the framers established, Amar says, the people keep their government in check (Akhil Reed Amar, *America's Constitution: A Biography* [New York: Random House, 2005], 159). In his reading, which downplays the intentional filtrations, popular sovereignty joins separation of powers and checks and balances to form an overarching ideology focused on limiting government. This "democratic" interpretation of the Constitution, though, downplays or ignores key historical contexts. As I argue in *Mr. President*, 306–7: "The absence of federal property qualifications for the franchise, which some claim was a reflection of democratic principles, was actually a political necessity. Any attempt to impose such uniform standards would have created a host of troublesome problems, such as how to count (or not count) slaves. The absence of property qualifications for national office-holders, allegedly another democratic move, was also a political necessity because of the dissimilarity among state economies; further, it was not deemed necessary, for the framers assumed that only men of means would ever be considered for such positions. The direct election of House members, truly a democratic element, met the minimum standard for republican government, but the framers insured that no other federal office holders would be elected by the people. Instead of insisting that presidential electors be chosen by the people, they left the matter in the hands of state legislatures; this was a states' rights issue, not a democratic one. In sum, the Constitution itself did not 'pull . . . America toward a populist presidency,' in Amar's words (p. 152); later events did, and as they did, they undermined the basic intentions of the framers. Mass campaigning and pandering to voters, hallmarks of modern democracy and a 'populist presidency,' were anathema to the men who wrote the Constitution. Such phenomena they would view as signs of decay, the beginning of the end of true republican government. Gouverneur Morris, when recalling the mood among the framers, later wrote, 'History, the parent of political science, had told them, that it was almost as vain to expect permanency from democracy, as to construct a palace on the surface of the sea' (Morris to Robert Walsh, February 5, 1811, Farrand, *Records of Federal Convention*, 3:418). There is one respect in which the Constitution was indeed democratic. The ratification process called for conventions in each state to legitimate the proceedings in an uncontestable fashion. Here, the framers remained

true to the basic premise of popular sovereignty: only the people themselves had the right to establish a constitution. Even this move, though, was motivated in part by the need to bypass state legislatures, which had good reasons to oppose the new Constitution because it usurped the authority of state governments and therefore the political power of each state legislator."

29. For constitutional arguments through the 1790s in Congress and among the population, see David P. Currie, *The Constitution in Congress: The Federalist Period, 1789–1801* (Chicago: University of Chicago Press, 1997), and Larry D. Kramer, *The People Themselves: Popular Constitutionalism and Judicial Review* (New York: Oxford University Press, 2004).

5. The Father

1. At http://en.wikipedia.org/wiki/James_Madison (accessed January 10, 2012). The titles of two prominent books play on the notion that Madison was uniquely responsible for the Constitution by referring to him as "*The* Founder" and "*The* Founding Father": Marvin Myers, ed., *The Mind of the Founder: Sources of the Political Thought of James Madison* (Indianapolis: Bobbs-Merrill, 1973), and Robert Allen Rutland, *James Madison: The Founding Father* (New York: Macmillan, 1987).

2. At http://www.jamesmadison.com/about.html (accessed January 10, 2012).

3. Farrand, *Records of Federal Convention*, 3:94.

4. A few other delegates took notes, sent letters, or offered later recollections, but none of these other records come close to the daily records of every debate that Madison kept. Also, the Convention's secretary, Major William Jackson of Georgia, kept an official journal, but he recorded only motions and votes, not debates, and often made mistakes. All these, together with Madison's voluminous notes, are compiled chronologically in Farrand, *Records of Federal Convention*, and in Charles C. Tansill, ed., *Documents Illustrative of the Formation of the Union of the American States* (Washington, DC: Government Printing Office, 1927). James H. Hutson has argued that Madison managed to record only five to ten percent of what was said in the Convention. James H. Hutson, "The Creation of the Constitution: The Integrity of the Documentary Record," *Texas Law Review* 65:1 (November 1986): 1–39.

5. For Gouverneur Morris's push to transform the presidency, see Raphael, *Mr. President: How and Why the Founders Created a Chief Executive* (New York: Knopf, 2012), 78–120 and 281–85.

6. Madison to William Cogswell, March 10, 1834, Farrand, *Records of Federal Convention*, 3:533.

7. Melanie Randolph Miller, *An Incautious Man: The Life of Gouverneur Morris* (Wilmington, DE: ISI Books, 2008), 63; Madison, *Notes of Debates*, September 7.

8. Madison to Jefferson, September 6, 1787, Madison, *Papers*, 10:163.

9. Madison to Jefferson, March 19, 1787, Madison to Randolph, April 7, 1787, and Madison to Washington, April 16, 1787, in Madison, *Papers*, 9:317–22, 368–71, 382–87.

10. Madison to Washington, April 16, 1787, in Madison, *Papers* 9:383–85.

11. Jay to Washington, January 7, 1787, and Knox to Washington, January 14, 1787, in Washington, *Papers* (CS), 4:502–4, 521–22; 5:163–66; Pauline Maier, *Ratification: The People Debate the Constitution* (New York: Simon & Schuster, 2010), 18–19, 26; Jack N. Rakove, *Original*

Meanings: Politics and Ideas in the Making of the Constitution (New York: Random House, 1996), 59. For meetings of the Virginia caucus, see George Mason to George Mason Jr., May 20, 1787, in Farrand, *Records of Federal Convention*, 3:23. For common use of the term "Madison's Plan," see the Wikipedia entry "Constitutional Convention," heading "James Madison's Blueprint," http://en.wikipedia.org/wiki/Constitutional_Convention_(United;_sfStates)#James_Madison.27s_blueprint (accessed March 24, 2012).

12. Whereas his fellow Virginians did include Madison's national veto of state legislation, they wisely refrained from the combative phrase "in all cases whatsoever"—the very words Parliament had used in the Declaratory Act of 1766, when it claimed the absolute right to tax Americans.

13. Before voting on the committee report, the Convention addressed the question of composition in the first house of Congress for its first session: exactly how many members should each state get? This matter was sent to committee, and once again Madison evidenced displeasure with the committee's report, which he noted was not based on any firm principle. Seizing the moment, he offered "a proper ground of compromise" that would give small northern states even less of a voice in the Senate than they had in the House: "In the first branch the States should be represented according to their number of free inhabitants; and in the 2d. which had for one of its primary objects the guardianship of property, according to the whole number, including slaves." This was hardly a "compromise," for it would leave the small northern states at a greater disadvantage than any other proposal. Madison's suggestion was not seriously considered (Madison, *Notes of Debates*, July 9).

14. Neither defeat was total, despite Madison's disappointment. One house of Congress still would have proportional representation, and the Convention soon would make the supremacy of the national government over state governments explicit. On August 6 the five-man Committee of Detail, in its expanded version of the working draft, inserted some important new delineations of state and national powers. First, it stated that all treaties and acts of Congress "shall be the supreme law of the several States, and of their citizens and inhabitants; and the judges in the several States shall be bound thereby in their decisions; any thing in the Constitutions or laws of the several States to the contrary notwithstanding." Next, it required congressional approval for state legislation in a list of key areas: "No State, without the consent of the Legislature of the United States, shall emit bills of credit, or make any thing but specie a tender in payment of debts; nor lay imposts or duties on imports; nor keep troops or ships of war in time of peace; nor enter into any agreement or compact with another State, or with any foreign power." Madison did not serve on that committee, but James Wilson, who also supported a federal veto of state laws, was on the committee, and the draft containing these clauses is in his handwriting. Wilson undoubtedly pushed their cause to the furthest extent he deemed possible. For Wilson's draft of these measures in the Committee of Detail report, see Farrand, *Records of Federal Convention*, 2:169.

15. On August 22, the day before Pinckney and Madison pushed to reconsider the issue, Virginia delegate James McClurg wrote to Madison: "I have still some hope that I shall hear from you of the reinstatement of the *Negative*—as it is certainly the only mean by which the several Legislatures can be restrain'd from disturbing the order & harmony of the whole, & the Governmt. render'd properly *national*, & *one*. I should suppose that some of its former opponents

must by this time have seen the necessity of advocating it, if they wish to support their own principles" (McClurg to Madison, August 22, 1787, Madison, *Papers*, 10:154). We do not know when he read McClurg's letter, but Madison was certainly thinking along the same lines.

16. Madison to Washington, April 16, 1787, Madison, *Papers*, 9:384–85.

17. Immediately, Gouverneur Morris seized on the idea of requiring three-quarters rather than two-thirds for an override. Morris had favored an absolute veto but was rejected; now, he saw a chance to strengthen the executive by making an override next to impossible. Morris prevailed, evidently with Madison's approval. Later, in the last week of the Convention, Madison opposed returning to two-thirds, but he was outvoted.

18. Madison, *Notes of Debates*, September 7. An executive council was pushed vociferously by George Mason and supported by luminaries Franklin, Wilson, Dickinson, and Madison, yet it still failed, possibly because delegates were in a hurry to be done with their business.

19. Madison, *Notes of Debates*, September 7 and 8. Madison's motion to require a simple majority for treaties of peace initially passed without dissent, but the next day the Convention reversed that decision. His motion to permit the Senate, without the president, to conclude treaties of peace lost by three states to eight.

20. Madison, *Notes of Debates*, September 8.

21. Madison to Jefferson, September 6, 1787, Madison, *Papers*, 10:163–64; Jack N. Rakove, *James Madison and the Creation of the American Republic* (Glenview, IL.: Scott Foresman/Little, Brown, 1990), 68.

22. Madison to Jefferson, October 24, 1787, Madison, *Papers*, 10:207–14. A national negative, Madison continued, was necessary not only to grant "the whole" a check over "its parts," but also "to secure individuals agst. encroachments on their rights." Individual rights would be "more secure under the Guardianship of the General Government than under the State Governments," because oppressive majorities were less likely to coalesce on a national scale. Precisely because there was "such an infinitude of legislative expedients" that could produce "injustice" in state and local jurisdictions, state law needed to be "controuled by some provision which reaches all cases whatsoever"—again, those strong words. Abusive state legislation was in fact one of the proximate causes of the Federal Convention: "The mutability of the laws of the States is found to be a serious evil. The injustice of them has been so frequent and so flagrant as to alarm the most stedfast friends of Republicanism. I am persuaded I do not err in saying that the evils issuing from these sources contributed more to that uneasiness which produced the Convention, and prepared the public mind for a general reform, than those which accrued to our national character and interest from the inadequacy of the Confederation to its immediate objects." Without a sweeping national veto over state legislation, even in matters of seemingly local concern, states would be able to "oppress the weaker party within their respective jurisdictions." The absence of a national negative was a serious flaw in the Constitution and perhaps a fatal one, he concluded. Madison had offered a similar argument at the Convention on June 6.

23. The balance of powers is emphasized in *The Federalist Nos. 47–51*, shared sovereignty in *The Federalist Nos. 39* and *45–46*.

24. Madison to Washington, April 16, 1787, in Madison, *Papers* 9:383.

25. "Vices of the Political System of the United States," an unpublished essay penned in April 1787 (Madison, *Papers*, 9:355–57); Madison, *Notes of Debates*, June 6; Madison to Jefferson,

October 24, 1787 (Madison, *Papers*, 10:212–14). For the version of this argument in his letter to Jefferson, see note 22 above.

26. For the full results, see http://www.ourdocuments.gov/content.php?flash=true& page=vote. For the process and the announcement of the results, see "The National Archives Announces Results of 'The People's Vote,' " American Historical Association, January 2004 "Perspectives," http://www.historians.org/perspectives/issues/2004/0401/0401new7.cfm (accessed April 11, 2012).

27. Newspaper reprints: *DHRC*, 19:542–43, 547. Publication of the second volume of *The Federalist*: *DHRC*, 18:83–85, 20:1116–18. Most commentators today assume that because Madison's argument is so clever, other Federalist leaders must have used it and the public must have bought into it. Gordon Wood, in his seminal *The Creation of the American Republic, 1776–1787* (1969; repr., Chapel Hill: University of North Carolina Press, 1998), assigns the argument to "the Federalists" (502) or "several Federalists and Madison in particular" (504), but other than Madison, he cites only one obscure work as using this argument. For the obscurity of Wood's citation, see *DHRC*, 18:326–31.

28. Maier, *Ratification*, 270–71.

29. J. Allen Smith, *The Spirit of American Government* (New York: Macmillan, 1907), 42–43, 205–6; Charles A. Beard, *An Economic Interpretation of the Constitution of the United States* (New York: Macmillan, 1913), 153–61. See in particular the discussion by Douglass Adair, "The Tenth Federalist Revisited," *William and Mary Quarterly*, 3rd ser., 8:1 (January 1951); 48–67, conveniently reprinted as chapter 3 of Douglass Adair, *Fame and the Founding Fathers: Essays of Douglass Adair*, ed. Trevor Colbourn (New York: Norton for the Institute of Early American History and Culture, 1974; repr., Indianapolis, IN: Liberty Fund, 1998). In that essay, Adair also analyzes the neglect of *The Federalist No. 10* through the nineteenth century.

30. For Supreme Court citations of *The Federalist*, see Ira C. Lupu, "The Most-Cited Federalist Papers," *Constitutional Commentary* 15 (1998): 403–10; W.B. Allen with Kevin A. Cloonan, *The Federalist Papers: A Commentary—The Baton Rouge Lectures* (New York: Peter Lang, 2000), 399–429; Melvyn R. Durchslag, "The Supreme Court and the Federalist Papers: Is There Less Here Than Meets the Eye?" *William & Mary Bill of Rights Journal* 14 (2005); 316–49. Justice William O. Douglas's concurring opinion in *Gibson v. Florida Legislative Investigation Committee* (1963) reveals the obvious appeal of *The Federalist No. 51* for late-twentieth-century Americans: "Madison too knew that tolerance for all ideas across the spectrum was the only true guarantee of freedom of the mind: 'Whilst all authority in it will be derived from and dependent on the society, the society itself will be broken into so many parts, interests and classes of citizens, that the rights of individuals, or of the minority, will be in little danger from interested combinations of the majority. In a free government the security for civil rights must be the same as that for religious rights. It consists in the one case in the multiplicity of interests, and in the other in the multiplicity of sects. The degree of security in both cases will depend on the number of interests and sects.' "

31. The resolutions passed the House of Delegates by a vote of 100 to 63 and the Virginia Senate by 14 to 3. Madison's political ally Thomas Jefferson, in a similar but more strongly worded set of resolutions he submitted to the Kentucky legislature, proclaimed that a state could declare an unconstitutional act of Congress "void and of no force." The Virginia and Kentucky

Resolutions, though, were not endorsed by other states. For the background of Madison's resolutions, including his communications with Jefferson, see the editorial note in Madison, *Papers*, 17:185–88. The text of the Virginia Resolutions follows on pages 188–91. Early in 1800 Madison issued a detailed report to the House of Delegates explaining and defending the controversial Virginia Resolutions, which had come under attack from other states. Again in this "vindication," his positions differed considerably from those he had espoused at the Federal Convention. In 1787, he had argued against the weaknesses of the Articles of Confederation, but in 1800 he referred to the Articles and the Constitution in the same breath as "the two great federal charters," and he used the "original" compact to elucidate the meaning of the "existing" one. At issue was the term "general welfare," which he noted was used in both documents. Because nobody thought "general welfare" implied an open-ended mandate for Congress under the Articles of Confederation, he argued, the appearance of that phrase in the Constitution must be viewed in the same light. If the sovereignty of the United States were extended "to all cases of the 'general welfare,' that is to say, to *all cases whatsoever*," the states would be consolidated "into one sovereignty," and that in turn would lead to "monarchy" (emphasis in the original). Earlier, Madison insisted on national supremacy in all cases; now he demonstrated what a dangerous concept that was. "The Report of 1800," in Madison, *Papers*, 17:313–16. The 1787 quotation is from Madison to Washington, April 16, 1787, Madison, *Papers*, 9:383.

32. *Annals of Congress*, 1:178–79; David P. Currie, *The Constitution in Congress: The Federalist Period, 1789–1801* (Chicago: University of Chicago Press, 1997), 71.

33. *Annals of Congress*, 1:183; Currie, *Constitution in Congress*, 70. Even at the Federal Convention, at least one framer wondered whether lighthouses would be covered under the commerce clause. On September 4, James McHenry of Maryland mused, "Upon looking over the constitution it does not appear that the national legislature can erect light houses or clean out or preserve the navigation of harbours. This expence ought to be borne by commerce-of course by the general treasury into which all the revenue of commerce must come." Farrand, *Records*, 2:504.

34. *Annals of Congress*, 1:1115, 1145–46; Currie, *Constitution in Congress*, 19–20. Madison also supported the appointment of a congressional committee to investigate an executive officer, although that did not appear in the Constitution's list of powers granted to Congress. *Annals of Congress*, 1:1515; Currie, *Constitution in Congress*, 20–21.

35. Madison's speeches in the House of Representatives, February 2 and 8, *Annals of Congress*, 2:1944–52, 2008–12. In the first session of Congress, when Madison presented amendments that would evolve into the Bill of Rights (see chapter 7), he took a more charitable stance toward "implications." One of his proposals set forth the principle of enumerated powers— "The powers not delegated by this constitution, nor prohibited by it to the States, are reserved to the States respectively"—but that statement was not clear enough for South Carolina representative Thomas Tudor Tucker, who moved to insert the key word "expressly" before "delegated" (see chapter 4). Madison opposed the *explicit* limitation. "It was impossible to confine a Government to the exercise of express powers; there must necessarily be admitted powers by implication, unless the Constitution descended to recount every minutia" *Annals of Congress*, 1:453, 790 June 8 and August 18, 1789; also in Veit et al., *Bill of Rights*, 14 and 197. See above, chapter 4. Elbridge Gerry, at the Federal Convention, assumed that the commerce clause *did* permit granting

charters to corporations. On September 15 he listed his reasons for not signing the Constitution, among which was this: "The Power given respectg. Commerce will enable the Legislature to create corporations and monopolies." (This is from Rufus King's notes, reprinted in Farrand, *Records of Federal Convention*, 2:635. Madison's rendition reads, "*Under* the power over commerce, monopolies may be established.") Admittedly, the convention was winding down, but even so, Madison makes no record of any attempt that he made to counter this claim, either on the floor or as a footnote to his notes. Further, when Madison gathered the amendments proposed by state ratification conventions while preparing his own list, he certainly noted that most of the states proposing amendments sought to prevent Congress from granting monopolies or giving any "exclusive advantages of commerce" to a single company; apparently, they thought something on the order of a national bank *would* be permitted under the commerce clause unless the Constitution were amended. This is not to suggest that Madison's view was mistaken, but only that the view he expressed in 1791 was not the assumed interpretation at the time of the Constitution's drafting and ratification.

36. For Madison's transformation, see Gordon Wood, "Is There a James Madison Problem?" in David Womersely, ed., *Liberty and American Experience in the Eighteenth Century* (Indianapolis: Liberty Fund, 2006), 425–47, reprinted in Gordon S. Wood, *Revolutionary Characters: What Made the Founders Different* (New York: Penguin Press, 2006), 141–72. For visions of nationalism, see Max M. Edling, *A Revolution in Favor of Government* (New York: Oxford University Press, 2003).

37. Numbers for the Google search are for December 20, 2011. Madison's 1794 quotation on the relief for San Domingo refugees, within the context of the congressional debate, is in *Annals of Congress*, 4:170.

38. Madison's sponsorship of powers of incorporation, on August 18 and September 14, would take a peculiar twist. During the national bank debate in 1791, he claimed that Congress lacked the authority to incorporate, and to prove it, he "well recollected that a power to grant charters of incorporation had been proposed in the General Convention but rejected." (*Annals of Congress*, 2:1945 [February 2, 1791]; Rakove, *Original Meanings*, 351.) He had turned full circle, and he used his earlier defeat to demonstrate, in his mind, that the framers did not intend to give Congress the power to incorporate. In this debate, Madison came as close to breaking his oath of secrecy about the Convention's deliberations as he had ever done. (See chapter 8 for more on Madison's citation of his own previous motion, but to reverse effect.)

39. Here is Madison's full distilling of a speech he made in favor of national control of the militia on August 23: "As the greatest danger is that of disunion of the States, it is necessary to guard agat. it by sufficient powers to the Common Govt. and as the greatest danger to liberty is from large standing armies, it is best to prevent them, by an effectual provision for a good Militia."

40. Supreme Court of the United States, *National Federation of Independent Businesses v. Sebelius, Secretary of Health and Human Services* (2012), Scalia, Kennedy, Thomas, and Alito, JJ., dissenting, 3, http://www.supremecourt.gov/opinions/11pdf/11-393c3a2.pdf.

6. *The Federalist Papers*

1. At http://www.saveourcountrynow.net/archives/tag/tea-party.

2. At http://www.law.cornell.edu/supct/html/95-1478.ZD1.html.

3. For authorship of the essays, see *DHRC*, 13:488–90. In addition to Publius, several writers published serial essays in the newspapers under pseudonyms that were also drawn from Roman history: Caesar, Brutus, Cato, Fabius, Cincinnatus.

4. Hamilton, *Papers*, 4:287–88; Madison, *Papers*, 10:259–60; *DHRC*, 13:486–88. Duer's essays later appeared in New York newspapers under the pen name "Philo-Publius."

5. In this chapter, as throughout the book, when I cite any essay from *The Federalist* by number, I offer no further reference. There are countless print editions and ways to access *The Federalist* on the Internet, and readers will undoubtedly have their own preferences. I find the one posted by the Avalon Project, from the Yale Law School, easy to navigate: http://avalon.law.yale.edu/subject_menus/fed.asp.

6. Hamilton's naming the letters "The Federalist" was itself a political move. Late in 1786 and early in 1787, those who urged a stronger confederation labeled themselves "Federalists" and called those more wary of change "narrow-soul'd, antifederal politicians in the several States." Fortuitously, the 1787 Convention, charged with revising and upgrading the Articles of *Confederation*, was dubbed "the *federal* convention." Afterward, supporters of the Convention's proceedings used this nomenclature to solidify their claim to the word "Federalist," which meant of course that those who opposed them were "Anti-Federalists"—negative obstructionists at best. Ironically, this rhetorical ploy reversed the use of the term "Federalist" at the Convention, where "Federalists" were those who wanted the states to continue as sovereign entities, as opposed to nationalists, who wanted a strong national government (see the Preface, above). "A union of the states merely federal" was not enough, Gouverneur Morris had maintained at the start of the Convention, for it was no more than "a mere compact, resting on the good faith of the parties." The federal model, he said, should be supplanted by a "national, supreme government" (see chapter 1). Afterward, opponents of the proposed Constitution stayed true to use of the word at the Convention and declared themselves the true "Federalists." On October 17, "A Democratic Federalist" penned a lengthy rebuttal to James Wilson's famous speech in favor of the Constitution (see below). Ten days later, Hamilton published his first essay as Publius, adopting the title "The Federalist" to support views similar to Wilson's and to oppose those of such writers as "A Democratic Federalist." Subsequently, on November 8, "Federal Farmer" published what are now considered among the most effective "Anti-Federalist" letters, and on November 28, "A Republican Federalist" followed with his own reasons for opposing ratification of the Constitution unless there were amendments. In the tussle over the name, however, Hamilton's side prevailed: supporters of the Federal Convention, in popular usage, became "Federalists," like Publius (*DHRC*, 13:89, 193, 387 and 14:255).

7. For numbers printed and left unsold, see *DHRC*, 19:141.

8. Douglass Adair, "The Authorship of the Disputed Federalist Papers," *William and Mary Quarterly*, 3rd ser., 1:2 (1944): 97–122 and 1:3, 235–64, reprinted as chap. 2 of Douglass Adair, *Fame and the Founding Fathers: Essays of Douglass Adair*, ed. Trevor Colbourn (New York:

Norton for the Institute of Early American History and Culture, 1974; repr., Indianapolis, IN: Liberty Fund, 1998).

9. There were four separate editions published in 1961, two under the revised title *The Federalist Papers*: Clinton Rossiter, ed., *The Federalist Papers* (New York: New American Library/Mentor Books, 1961); Roy P. Fairfield, ed., *The Federalist Papers* (Garden City, NY: Anchor Books/Doubleday, 1961); Benjamin F. Wright, ed., *The Federalist* (Cambridge, MA: Belknap Press of Harvard University Press/John Harvard Library, 1961); Jacob E. Cooke, ed., *The Federalist* (Middletown, CT: Wesleyan University Press, 1961). Whereas Fairfield's edition had little impact, Rossiter's became a classic and remains in print today. On these editions and their relative merits, see Douglass G. Adair, "The Federalist Papers," *William and Mary Quarterly*, 3rd ser., 22 (1965): 131–39, reprinted as chap. 13 of Adair, *Fame and the Founding Fathers*. Adair never discusses the innovative title. Cooke's Wesleyan University Press's edition, unlike that of the New American Library, was based faithfully on the newspaper versions, complete with the repetitive salutations for every essay: "To the People of the State of New-York." While Cooke's version is treated to this day as authoritative, it is not widely circulated outside scholarly circles, nor is any reprint under the original title, *The Federalist*.

Outside of publishing, the term "Federalist Papers" has an interesting etymology. The authors themselves referred to their separate essays as "papers," although they never hinted that the word should become part of the title. Starting in 1912 (in both *Kiernan v. Portland* and *Pacific States Tel. & Tel. Co. v. Oregon*), Supreme Court justices used the lowercased "papers" after "Federalist" to denote essays written under the "Federalist" title. From there, in a seemingly natural but not entirely logical evolution, they eventually capitalized "Papers," effectively including it in the title—first in *United States v. South Eastern Underwriters Association* in 1944 and several dozen times since then. Although the previous conjoining of "Federalist" with "papers" did provide the editors at New American Library with a trace of a precedent, their decision to give the book a new title after more than one and a half centuries was certainly a brazen move.

10. For Justice Thomas's reference to "*The Federalist Papers*," see *McIntyre v. Ohio Elections Commission* (1995), *Missouri v. Jenkins* (1995), *Loving v. United States* (1996), and *Gonzales v. Raich* (2005).

11. The 1788 bound volumes can be accessed through Early American Imprints, series I, Evans (1639–1800), doc. 21127.

12. For a listing of editions of *The Federalist* in the century following its publication, see Paul Leicester Ford, *Pamphlets on the Constitution of the United States* (Brooklyn, NY, 1888), 397–406, and Henry Cabot Lodge's introduction, written in 1886, to *The Federalist* (G.P. Putnam's Sons, 1892), xxxvi–xlii. In later years, and particularly with the addition of the word "Papers," the title is left on its own, without a subtitle.

13. There is some justification for this omission. The original bound volumes had also dropped the repetitive salutations—but in their stead, vol. 1 opened with an introduction by Hamilton that stated, "It is supposed that a collection of the papers which have made their appearance in the Gazettes of this City, under the title of The FEDERALIST, may not be without effect in assisting the public judgment on the momentous question of the Constitution of the United States." Further, on the first page of the opening essay, in large font, were the words,

"Addressed to the People of the State of New-York," thereby eliminating the need for repetition in other essays. Both features were dropped in many reprints based on the bound volumes, downplaying the local emphasis.

14. Rossiter, *Federalist Papers*, xii–xiii.

15. Rossiter, *Federalist Papers*, xi.

16. New York: Basic Books, 2008, p. 139. Rossiter, in his 1961 introduction to *The Federalist Papers*, took care not to make this leap. "Publius, by his own admission, spoke to a select audience of reasonable, responsible and established men," most of whom already supported the Constitution. The "chief usefulness of *The Federalist*," he concluded, "was as a kind of debaters handbook in Virginia and New York." Note Rossiter's continued use of the old title, even as his publishers tacked on a new one (Rossiter, *Federalist Papers*, xi).

17. Washington to Hamilton, August 28, 1788, Washington, *Papers* (CS), 6:480–81.

18. *DHRC*, 13:493–94. Rufus King, a Federalist from Massachusetts who had taken an active role at the Federal Convention, commented on Publius's lack of popular appeal after Publius's first twenty-six essays: "The 'Landholder' will do more service our way, than the elaborate works of Publius." "Landholder"—Oliver Ellsworth, another Federalist veteran of the Convention—did not shy from addressing his opponents directly, calling them out by their names, and readers, or at least newspaper editors, preferred this style. The sixth of Landholder's thirteen essays, which probably inspired King's comment, was reprinted in eighteen newspapers in eight states outside of Connecticut, Ellsworth's home state. *The Federalist No. 19*, published two days earlier, was reprinted in only one state outside of Publius's putative home state of New York, and *The Federalist No. 20*, published one day after *Landholder VI*, was not published in a single out-of-state paper. Rufus King to Jeremiah Wadsworth, December 23, 1787, *DHRC*, 15:71. For the authorship of Landholder, see *DHRC*, 13:561. For Landholder's essays published shortly before King's comment, see *DHRC*, 14:231–35, 334–39, and 398–403. For circulation numbers, see *DHRC*, 14:533.

19. *DHRC*, 13:490 for Madison's and Washington's attempt to circulate *The Federalist* in Virginia. *DHRC*, 19:540–49 for newspaper publication of Publius's essays.

20. *DHRC*, 13:337–38 and 344 for newspaper publication of Wilson's speech. For reprinting of more than 800 essays and articles from the ratification debates, see the appendices in *DHRC*, vol. 13–18. For a visual representation of how Publius compares to the others, note in particular 15:575–79, 16:597–600, and 18:407; there, if a piece appears in only one state, the odds are strong that it's one of Publius's. It can be argued that newspapers didn't reprint Publius once bound volumes were promised, but given that the second volume, which included the majority of the essays (numbers 37 through 85), did not appear until very late in the game (see below), this excuse cannot be used to promote their impact.

21. The numbers for *Common Sense* most often cited—100,000, 120,000, and 150,000—come from Paine's boastful pronouncements. They are estimates only, for Paine had little to do with most of the printings. There is no independent corroboration, and in-depth analysis of the evidence points to a lower figure. Even so, it seems likely that somewhere in the neighborhood of fifty thousand is realistic, one hundred times the number for *The Federalist*. (Trish Loughran, *The Republic in Print: Print Culture in the Age of Nation-Building, 1770–1870* (New York: Columbia University Press, 2009), 40–58, 452–60.

22. *DHRC*, 18:83–85, 20:878–80, 1116–18.

23. *New York Journal*, June 12, 1788, in *DHRC*, 21:1582. The landslide against the Constitution might have been slightly exaggerated by the sympathetic *New York Journal*, but the *Albany Gazette*, June 5, 1788, gives a preliminary report of a 2-to-1 majority for the Constitution's opponents (*DHRC*, 21:1581). Publius's newspaper articles had not effectively stemmed that landslide. Following *The Federalist No. 21*, only one of the remaining sixty-four essays appeared in any of the state's papers north of the city (*DHRC*, 19:540–49).

24. Jay's *Address to the People of New-York, on the Subject of the Constitution* was published two weeks before New York's elections for delegates, and contemporary reports suggest that had it not been published, the majority of the convention opposed to the Constitution would have been greater yet. For its influence, see Maier, *Ratification*, 336–38, and *DHRC*, 20:922–42. Webster quote: *DHRC*, 20:924. The conversion quotation, one of several testifying to Jay's influence, is from Samuel Blachley Webb to Joseph Barrell, April 27, 1788, ibid., 924. Jay's *Address* was reprinted in its entirety in serial form in seven out-of-state newspapers, a mark no group of Publius's essays ever achieved. Federalists focused specifically on circulating it in New Hampshire, which soon became the ninth and deciding state to ratify the Constitution. For Jay's *Address* see also chap. 3, n. 47.

25. Reprints of *The Federalist No. 85*: *DHRC*, 18:137. To win enough opposition votes for ratification in New York, Federalist delegates did allow the New York Convention to call for a second constitutional convention, but this new convention would be only to consider proposed amendments. The final quote is from Glenn Beck, *The Original Argument:* The Federalists' *Case for the Constitution Adapted for the 21st Century* (New York: Mercury Radio Arts, 2011), 11. Jay's concern was that to call a second convention without first approving the results of the first would produce political bedlam, and in light of the political discord already displayed in the ratification debates, that argument, in the words of Federalist Noah Webster, was "altogether unanswerable" (*DHRC*, 20:924).

26. Despite the vow of secrecy, rumors of Hamilton's June 18 speech at the Convention (see the following paragraph in the text) had leaked out and were used by the Constitution's opponents to discredit the proposed Constitution. Also, some opponents speculated that Hamilton was Publius, but that was not confirmed.

27. "Conjectures about the New Government," an unpublished and undated manuscript in Hamilton's handwriting, probably written sometime between September 17 and September 30 (Hamilton, *Papers*, 4:276).

28. Quotations in these paragraphs are from Hamilton's speech to the Federal Convention on June 18 and from *The Federalist No. 69*.

29. Hamilton's notes are from Hamilton, *Papers*, 4:178–87. This quote is on 186.

30. Jay makes the same mistake in *The Federalist No. 64*: "They [delegates to the Federal Convention] have directed the President to be chosen by select bodies of electors, to be deputed by the people for that express purpose." Madison got it right. In *Federalist No. 44* he wrote, "The election of the President and Senate, will depend, in all cases, on the legislatures of the several States," and in *Federalist No. 45*, "Without the intervention of the State Legislatures, the President of the United States cannot be elected at all. They must in all cases have a great share in his appointment, and will perhaps in most cases of themselves determine it."

31. For Hamilton's obsession with electors and the need to place them at a considerable remove from the people, note the convoluted and nearly incomprehensible electoral plan he penned near the close of the convention, transcribed in Hamilton, *Papers*, 4:259–61. Some historians suggest that the framers rejected popular election of the president for mechanical reasons, not because they disapproved of popular elections per se. It would have been impossible to create an election machinery on a national scale, they say, and any attempt to develop a uniform franchise requirement would have torn the Convention asunder. This begs the question. The framers could have called for popular elections in each state without a federal machinery; such elections could be conducted by state governments and open to voters enfranchised by local standards. They had no difficulty in reverting to state standards in legislative elections, and they could have done the same for executive elections. Further, to prevent a state from achieving undue influence by expanding its electorate and boosting its vote totals, they could have weighted each state's popular votes according to a preexisting formula, just as they did with their elector plan, and that formula might well have been the same as that of the final system, based on the total number of representatives and senators from each state. One handy way of doing this would have been to give each state a certain number of electors, but rather than allow these electors to make their own decisions, bind them to the results of popular elections, as is the custom today. Expecting representatives to follow instructions from their constituents was common in New England and practiced to some extent elsewhere during the Revolutionary era, so it would not have been a stretch to build on this custom and have the populace instruct electors. (See Ray Raphael, "The Democratic Moment: The Revolution in Popular Politics," in Edward G. Gray and Jane Kamensky, eds., *The Oxford Handbook of the American Revolution* [New York: Oxford University Press, 2012].) In sum, there was no objective or mechanical reason to institute an intermediate level of decision makers between the people and the president; that was a discretionary decision to keep the people from voting directly for the president. For a full treatment of the issues surrounding the selection of the presidency at the Convention, see Ray Raphael, *Mr. President*, chap. 3–5.

32. "Unreasonableness of the people": Hamilton, *Papers*, 4:185. "Popular views": *DHRC*, 22:1768. Tillinghast quote: *DHRC*, 22:1796. At the New York convention, Hamilton, who had expressed such harsh words about republican government at the Federal Convention, now embraced it: "After all, Sir, we must submit to this idea, that the true principle of a republic is, that the people should choose whom they please to govern them." *DHRC*, 22:1773. See also Maier, *Ratification*, 355.

33. Gregory E. Maggs, "A Concise Guide to the Federalist Papers as a Source of the Original Meaning of the United States Constitution," George Washington University Law School, Public Law Research Paper No. 258, March 9, 2007, 838, 831, 840, http://www.bu.edu/law/central/jd/organizations/journals/bulr/documents/MAGGS.pdf. The "haste" excuse is politically naive. Maggs plays the innocent when he states without evidence that Hamilton, Madison, and Jay "did not have time to adjust their vocabulary" or to modify "how they spoke in the *Federalist Papers* because of their own political goal of obtaining ratification of the Constitution." If the avowed purpose of the project was to push for ratification, what advocate would *not* weigh his words with that end in mind? The authors "probably had little reason to want to misrepresent what the Convention intended," Maggs contends, but in fact they had a very good

reason: to make the proposed new government appear less threatening so people would accept it (837–38).

34. In *The Federalist No. 59,* Hamilton reported that a quorum in the Senate would "consist of sixteen members," although at the time he wrote eleven states had ratified the Constitution, yielding twenty-two senators, and according to Article I, Section 5, Clause 1, quorum was to be a simple majority, in this case twelve. If all thirteen states were counted, the majority of twenty-six senators would be fourteen. In *The Federalist No. 84,* Hamilton wrote, "The two branches of the legislature are, in the first instance, to consist of only sixty-five persons, which is the same number of which Congress, under the existing Confederation, may be composed." This was actually the number of representatives only, listed in a state-by-state enumeration in Article I, Section 2, Clause 3, and did not include senators; once all thirteen states had ratified, the total number in both houses of Congress would total ninety-one. In *Federalist No. 68,* Hamilton explained the runoff for executive officers in case the electors did not produce a majority: "The Vice-President is to be chosen in the same manner with the President; with this difference, that the Senate is to do, in respect to the former, what is to be done by the House of Representatives, in respect to the latter." This was not the case. According to Article I, Section 2, Clause 3, the House, not the Senate, chose the vice president as well as the president if electors produced no majority winner, and only if the House produced two or more runners-up with equal votes would the Senate break that tie. The first two of these mistakes, whether intentionally or not, furthered arguments Hamilton was making at those moments. A larger quorum in the Senate produced greater security from intrigue, and a smaller number of representatives and senators would reduce the expenses of the federal government. See Seth Barrett Tillman, "The Federalist Papers as Reliable Historical Source Material for Constitutional Interpretation," *West Virginia Law Review* 105 (March 2003): 603–13. Regarding Hamilton's prevarication: Selection of the president had been a major focus of debate on several different occasions over the course of the Federal Convention. Although Hamilton had missed some of those sessions, he was present when delegates overwhelmingly rejected Wilson's idea for popular selection on June 2, and he had returned in time to participate in the floor discussion of the elector scheme presented by the Committee of Eleven in early September. He had been one of five delegates appointed on September 8 to the Committee of Style, charged with fine-tuning the wording of the entire Constitution in the final days, and in that capacity he must have read and considered the clause in the Committee of Eleven's report and adopted by the Convention: "Each State shall appoint in such manner as its Legislature may direct, a number of electors . . ." Hamilton's Committee of Style made one small change in this provision, substituting a more legalistic "the Legislature thereof" for "its Legislature."

35. Rossiter, *Federalist Papers,* xiii. For calling Hamilton's position on removal an "error," see Maggs, "Concise Guide," 837–38. For more on what historians call "the great removal debate," see Raphael, *Mr. President,* 161–66. For the debate itself, see *Annals of Congress,* 1:473–599.

36. See Seth Barrett Tillman, "The Puzzle of Hamilton's Federalist No. 77," *Harvard Journal of Law and Public Policy* 33:1 (2010): 149–67. Tillman tries to untangle the puzzle by making a purely legalistic distinction between the words "displace" (Hamilton's term) and "removal" (the term used in the congressional debates). This subtle distinction supposedly makes Hamilton's

views logically consistent, but that is not even necessary. There is no political or historical reason why Hamilton's words to one audience in one context should not contradict his words to another audience in a different context.

37. R. B. Bernstein identifies seven arguments for how to resolve the Constitution's troublesome silence on dismissals. "The Constitution As an Exploding Cigar and Other 'Historian's Heresies' About a Constitutional Orthodoxy," *New York Law School Law Review* 55 (2010–11): 1042–43. It took Hamilton little time to discover a different error in the Constitution, not just an omission but a genuine "defect." On January 25, 1789, ten days before electors were to cast their votes for the first president and vice president under the new Constitution, he wrote to James Wilson: "Every body is aware of that defect in the constitution which renders it possible that the man intended for Vice President may in fact turn up President." Since electors were to cast two votes but were not directed to distinguish between president and vice president, those preferring the second candidate on a ticket to the top candidate could "throw away a few votes" for the presidential candidate, thereby allowing his running partner to become president. The system could be gamed, and Hamilton himself attempted to do so in the elections of 1789, 1796, and 1800. See Raphael, *Mr. President*, 199–206, and Joanne B. Freeman, *Affairs of Honor: National Politics in the New Republic* (New Haven, CT: Yale University Press, 2001), chap. 5.

38. *Annals of Congress*, 1:474; William Loughton Smith to Edward Rutledge, June 21, 1789, in *South Carolina Historical Magazine* 69 (1968), 6, 8, cited in Tillman, "Puzzle of Hamilton's *Federalist* No. 77," 162. Tillman dismisses Hamilton's disavowal because it does not live up to legal standards of proof, but historical standards are quite different. Smith's letter to Rutledge, written at the time, is extant. Benson's report of the communication with Hamilton is plausible, while any conjecture that this conversation was manufactured is implausible. While Hamilton's exact words are admittedly open to question, the basic message, that he repudiated his words in *The Federalist No. 77*, is not only plausible but also consistent with all other evidence. The only inconsistency lies with Hamilton's stated views in diverse contexts; legally this might create a problem, but historically it does not.

39. This argument set up Hamilton's opposition to a Bill of Rights, the subject of his next essay, *The Federalist No. 84*: protections against nonenumerated powers would be pointless (see chapter 7).

40. Hamilton to Washington, February 23, 1791, Hamilton, *Papers*, 8:98, 100, 103. Here is Hamilton's more complete statement of his argument reversing the burden of proof: "The very general power of laying & collecting taxes & appropriating their proceeds—that of borrowing money indefinitely—that of coining money & regulating foreign coins—that of making all needful rules and regulations respecting the property of the United States—these powers combined, as well as the reason & nature of the thing speak strongly this language: That it is the manifest design and scope of the constitution to vest in congress all the powers requisite to the effectual administration of the finances of the United States. As far as concerns this object, there appears to be no parsimony of power. To suppose then, that the government is precluded from the employment of so usual as well as so important an instrument for the administration of its finances as that of a bank, is to suppose, what does not coincide with the general tenor & complexion of the constitution, and what is not agreeable to impressions that any mere spectator would entertain concerning it. Little less than a prohibitory clause can destroy the strong presumptions

which result from the general aspect of the government. Nothing but demonstration should exclude the idea, that the power exists" (*Papers*, 8:132).

41. In fact, many Americans were scared by the mere possibility of such a thing as the incorporation of a national bank. Six of the eight states that proposed amendments to the Constitution at their ratification conventions (Massachusetts, New Hampshire, Virginia, New York, North Carolina, and Rhode Island) wanted to prohibit the government from granting exclusive advantages of commerce, such as would be enjoyed by investors in the Bank of the United States.

42. Morton J. Frisch, ed., *The Pacificus-Helvidius Debates* (Indianapolis: Liberty Fund, 2007), 1, 11–13.

43. Ibid., 64.

44. Scalia's remarks were reported by Representative Jan Schakowsky (D-IL), in Huffington Post, January 25, 2011. Souter's quotation from *Printz v. United States* (1997), Cornell University Law School, Legal Information Institute, http://www.law.cornell.edu/supct/html/historics/USSC_CR_0521_0898_ZD1.html. Citation numbers are from Melvyn R. Durchslag, "The Supreme Court and the Federalist Papers: Is There Less Here Than Meets the Eye?" *William & Mary Bill of Rights Journal* 14 (2005): 346, 344. Multiple citations are also discussed in Pamela C. Corley, Robert M. Howard, and David C. Nixon, "The Supreme Court and Opinion Content: The Use of the Federalist Papers," *Political Research Quarterly* 58:2 (June 2005): 329–40. Citations from *The Federalist* in *Printz* are discussed by William N. Eskridge Jr.: "*The Federalist* cannot be understood without exploring the larger historical context. Even if Madison's and Hamilton's essays were not strategic documents and were representative views of citizens at the time, scholars must refer to other contemporary documents and current theories of the ideological debate during the founding period to understand the essays' meanings. This would involve mastery of a massive body of scholarship that is not evidenced by either judges or many law professors at this time. In *Printz*, for example, Justices Scalia and Souter sparred over the proper construction of Hamilton's *The Federalist* No. 27. Souter read this essay to defend the proposition that state officials would be 'incorporated' into national programs at the discretion of Congress, a reading disputed by Scalia. Missing in the heated exchange was any historical context: To what Anti-Federalist argument was Hamilton responding? How did the argument mesh with Hamilton's theory of state versus national sovereignty (a terribly complicated issue but one critical to one's reading of *The Federalist* No. 27)? How widely was Hamilton's theory of sovereignty held? His views about national supremacy? The Justices did not address the primary documents and historiographical literature addressing these issues." "Textualism and Original Understanding: Should the Supreme Court Read *The Federalist* but Not Statutory Legislative History?" *George Washington Law Review* 66 (1998): 1309–10.

45. Jack N. Rakove, "Early Uses of *The Federalist*," in Charles R. Kesler, ed., *Saving the Revolution: The Federalist Papers and the American Founding* (New York: The Free Press, 1987), 237–47.

46. Maggs, "Concise Guide," 802, 819; Rakove, "Early Uses of *The Federalist*," 234–49. For increased use in recent years, see Ira C. Lupu, "Time, the Supreme Court, and The Federalist," *George Washington Law Review* 66 (1998): 1324–35. William H. Manz tabulates citations of *The Federalist* for the October 1996 term, not only in majority opinions but also in petitioners' briefs, respondents' briefs, and amicus briefs, and he compares these with citations from legislative

and other historical sources. Manz, "Citations in Supreme Court Opinions and Briefs: A Comparative Study," *Law Library Journal* 94 (2002): 282–83. See also Buckner F. Melton Jr., "The Supreme Court and *The Federalist*: A Citation List and Analysis, 1789–1996," *Kentucky Law Journal* 85 (1996): 243–345, and supplements for 1996–2001 (90 [2001]: 415–40) and 2001–2006 (95 [2006]: 749–64). Nomination proceedings: Dan T. Coenen, "A Rhetoric for Ratification: The Argument of *The Federalist* and Its Impact on Constitutional Interpretation," *Duke Law Review* 56 (2006): 472.

47. Pamela C. Corley, Robert M. Howard, and David C. Nixon, "The Supreme Court and Opinion Content: The Use of the Federalist Papers," *Political Research Quarterly*, 58:2 (June 2005): 336.

48. Rakove, *Original Meanings*, 17. As early as 1952, Alpheus T. Mason argued persuasively that strategic considerations drove the ratification debates in various directions: "To quiet the fears of opponents, advocates of ratification said things which, in later years, proved embarrassing to themselves and misleading to scholars. On the other hand, certain of the Constitution's enemies turned alarmist, portraying the proposed national charter in the most extreme terms. The strategy obscured positions on all sides and made the Constitution's meaning less than crystal clear." Mason, "*The Federalist*—A Split Personality," *American Historical Review* 57:3 (April 1952): 625–43, reprinted in John P. Roche, ed., *Origins of American Political Thought* (New York: Harper and Row, 1967), 163, 168, quoted in Peter J. Smith, "Sources of Federalism: An Empirical Analysis of the Court's Quest for Original Meaning," *UCLA Law Review* 52 (2004), n. 159. Other works discussing the grounds for the alleged authoritative stature of *The Federalist* include (among many others) Coenen, "Rhetoric for Ratification," 469–543; James W. Ducayet, "Publius and Federalism: On the Use and Abuse of The Federalist in Constitutional Interpretation," *New York University Law Review* 68 (1993): 821–69; Eskridge, "Should the Supreme Court Read *The Federalist*?" 1301–23; Tillman, "Federalist Papers as Reliable Historical Source Material," 601–19; Durchslag, "Supreme Court and the Federalist Papers," 243–349. John F. Manning argues persuasively that even an originalist judge (see chapter 8) basing his opinion of textual evidence alone cannot cite *The Federalist* as determinative of the meaning of a specific passage: "Modern readers should approach *The Federalist* the same way a reasonable ratifier would have. A textualist judge must never simply conclude that 'the Constitution means X because this or that number of *The Federalist* said that it means X.' To be sure, *The Federalist* has significant interpretive value as a detailed, contemporaneous exposition of the Constitution by authors who were intimately familiar with its legal and political background. *The Federalist* is nonetheless a piece of political advocacy, whose contents may at times reflect the exigencies of debate, rather than a dispassionate account of constitutional meaning." "Textualism and the Role of The Federalist in Constitutional Adjudication," *George Washington Law Review* 66 (1998): 1339.

49. The quote is from Coenen, "Rhetoric for Ratification," 528. The taxonomy of justifications that follows is based on Coenen, 528–40.

50. Antonin Scalia, *A Matter of Interpretation: Federal Courts and the Law* (Princeton: Princeton University Press, 1997), 38.

51. Coenen offers a more sophisticated alternative to these traditional justifications: "Precisely because Publius's purpose was to gain support from a broad and diverse audience with arguments based on reason, the views set forth in the Papers could be neither sloppy nor personal

nor idiosyncratic. Rather, Publius's depiction of the Constitution had to reflect a broadly acceptable view of the document's meaning. And because that depiction had to reflect a broadly acceptable view, it seems fair to conclude that it articulated something that approximated a consensus" (Coenen, "Rhetoric for Ratification," 539). There is a germ of truth in this, but only a germ. Yes, Publius's arguments were rational, and yes, they were aimed at a broad public; yet so too were other essays written for and against the Constitution. Why are some rational arguments, on one side only, to be considered authoritative and others not? The notion that there was any sort of "consensus" on the Constitution would be big news to the people of those times. The Constitution's supporters and opponents tugged mightily for the soul of the nation. The war of words was occasionally punctuated by physical skirmishes. The American nation was young and malleable, without a firm sense of national tradition, and in this moment of decision the stakes were unimaginably high.

52. We learn from Publius that despite residual localism and fears of centralization, the idea of "Union," featured in the first fourteen essays, could be politically attractive. In the next set of essays, Publius detailed the failures of the Articles of Confederation and of confederations generally, opening the way for a truly national government "with the power of extending its operations to individuals" rather than through the intermediary of state governments. Due to deep traditions of colonial provincialism this embrace of national government was a revolutionary notion, but it was vital to the Constitution so Publius tackled it forthrightly. Likewise, because Publius devoted the next seven essays (30 through 36) to the single issue of national taxation, we can infer that he sensed great resistance in that regard but had no choice but to confront it, for without the power to tax the federal government could not function (see chapter 2). The emphasis in essays 37 through 46—the shared sovereignty between the federal and state governments—suggests that people would never accept the new plan unless they were convinced that state governments would survive in some meaningful manner. The following twenty essays touted the cross-checking mechanisms of the various branches, with an emphasis on the distinctions between the two houses of Congress; this argument too was geared to alleviate fears of concentrated power (see chapter 4). Essays 67–78 attempted to ease concerns over the seemingly greatest concentration of power: the presidency. People hoped to have a say in the choice of the president and they wanted to circumscribe his powers, Publius observed, and he wrote these essays with those desires in mind. In the final set of essays, Publius tried to balance the need for a supreme judicial authority with concerns that such a body would undermine state judicial systems or individual liberties. In sum, by watching Hamilton, Madison, and Jay allay people's fears, giving ground on some counts but holding firm on others, we see how the Constitution's radical enlargement of centralized power could be presented in such a way that sufficient numbers of Americans might accept the proposed new plan.

53. Madison to Thomas Ritchie, September 15, 1821, Farrand, *Records of Federal Convention*, 3:447–48. Madison never claimed that his essays should be used to define the Constitution, as the title to a recent book by Michael I. Meyerson states: *Liberty's Blueprint: How Madison and Hamilton Wrote the Federalist Papers, Defined the Constitution, and Made Democracy Safe for the World* (New York: Basic Books, 2008). Indeed, it seems doubtful such a thought would even occur to him, and a simple glance at *The Federalist No. 37* explains why not. Questions of constitutional interpretation, Madison explained, could not be decided in advance by *any* assemblage of words

or philosophies, even the Constitution itself. "Experience has instructed us that no skill in the science of government has yet been able to discriminate and define, with sufficient certainty, its three great provinces—the legislative, executive, and judiciary; or even the privileges and powers of the different legislative branches," he wrote. "Questions daily occur in the course of practice, which prove the obscurity which reins in these subjects, and which puzzle the greatest adepts in political science." Such questions, he concluded, could only be worked out on the ground, *after* implementation. "All new laws, though penned with the greatest technical skill, and passed on the fullest and most mature deliberation, are considered as more or less obscure and equivocal, until their meaning be liquidated and ascertained by a series of particular discussions and adjudications."

The context for these remarks was to show that the Federal Convention could not possibly create a perfect plan with absolute clarity. Madison explained further: "Besides the obscurity arising from the complexity of objects, and the imperfection of the human faculties, the medium through which the conceptions of men are conveyed to each other adds a fresh embarrassment. The use of words is to express ideas. Perspicuity, therefore, requires not only that the ideas should be distinctly formed, but that they should be expressed by words distinctly and exclusively appropriate to them. But no language is so copious as to supply words and phrases for every complex idea, or so correct as not to include many equivocally denoting different ideas. Hence it must happen that however accurately objects may be discriminated in themselves, and however accurately the discrimination may be considered, the definition of them may be rendered inaccurate by the inaccuracy of the terms in which it is delivered. And this unavoidable inaccuracy must be greater or less, according to the complexity and novelty of the objects defined. When the Almighty himself condescends to address mankind in their own language, his meaning, luminous as it must be, is rendered dim and doubtful by the cloudy medium through which it is communicated."

If we accept Publius at face value, as many insist we must, we have no choice to heed what he says in that essay: the final meaning of the Constitution, as determined by its practical application, cannot be decided in advance by prior conjectures, even his own, but only by "a series of particular discussions and adjudications" once the new rules take effect. *The Federalist No. 37*, by denying its own authority, gives the lie to all rationales for relying on Publius to settle practical disputes over constitutional law.

54. Clinton Rossiter, in the introduction to his 1961 classic edition of *The Federalist*, states, "*The Federalist* stands third only to the Declaration of Independence and the Constitution itself among all the sacred writings of American political history. It has a quality of legitimacy, of authority and authenticity, that gives it the high status of a public document" (Rossiter, *Federalist Papers*, vii). Publius's writing, however brilliant, does not in itself make the work any more legitimate or authentic than other contemporary sources by private citizens.

55. Publius conveniently ignored the complicated compromise involving the temporary ban on slave importation, the fugitive slave clause, and the requirements for commercial treaties (see chapter 3). Although he had to admit to the three-fifths compromise, central to the key issue of representation, he did so begrudgingly. In *The Federalist No. 54* Madison placed a justification of that provision within quotations and then added, "Such is the reasoning which an advocate for the Southern interests might employ on this subject; and although it may appear to be a little

strained in some points, yet, on the whole, I must confess that it fully reconciles me to the scale of representation which the convention have established." This was as close as Publius came to addressing the framers' most consequential haggling. While he did refer to other political compromises, he dispatched them as briefly as he possibly could, preferring to portray the Constitution as a cohesive whole firmly grounded on republican theory.

56. Durchslag, "The Supreme Court and the Federalist Papers," 315.

57. Ibid., 313. The cases, with the justices who made the citations, are listed on pages 316–49. In several cases Publius was cited in two or more opinions.

58. Chicago Tea Party website: Resources, Issues, Limited Government, http://teaparty chicago.netboots.net/node/175 (accessed February 16, 2012).

59. Beck, *Original Argument*, 12. One trouble with the Charles/Beck translation is that neither writer understands the original language. Lacking the historical context, they frequently distort and even invert the text. In *The Federalist No. 85*, for example, Hamilton condemned the campaign against the Federalists: "The charge of a conspiracy against the liberties of the people, which has been indiscriminately brought against the advocates of the plan, has something in it too wanton and too malignant, not to excite the indignation of every man who feels in his own bosom a refutation of the calumny. The perpetual changes which have been rung upon the wealthy, the well-born, and the great, have been such as to inspire the disgust of all sensible men. And the unwarrantable concealments and misrepresentations which have been in various ways practiced to keep the truth from the public eye, have been of a nature to demand the reprobation of all honest men." In the second of these three interrelated sentences, Hamilton was possibly referring to debtor relief legislation at the state level, and he was certainly referencing the political attacks by the Constitution's opponents against respectable, prominent men—"the wealthy, the well-born, and the great"—who supported the Constitution and were on his side. But Charles and Beck, with no understanding of Hamilton's political, social, and intellectual connection to the mercantile class, give the passage their own populist twist. Under the heading "Original Quote," they reverse Hamilton's condemnation of mindless attacks on men of standing: "The constant favors and special treatment which have been common for the wealthy, the well-born, and the great, must surely disgust all reasonable men, just as the numerous misrepresentations and concealments of the truth from the public eye deserve the disapproval of all honest men." Then, immediately following, they proclaim the "Relevance for Today": "We should have equal protection before the law, but Congress continues to pass legislation and get special treatment. Senior government officials, for example, are exempt from TSA pat-downs at the airport. And some government officials don't have to comply with all elements of the Health Care Reform Act" (*Original Argument*, 36). How any of this contributes to an understanding of our Constitution or its "relevance for today" is a mystery, yet merely by citing *The Federalist* Beck and Charles garner support from the founding fathers.

From *The Federalist No. 41*, Beck and Charles choose for their featured quotation: "The clearest marks of this prudence are stamped on the proposed Constitution. The Union itself, which it cements and secures, destroys every pretext for a military establishment which could be dangerous. America united, with a handful of troops, or without a single soldier, exhibits a more forbidding posture to foreign ambition than America disunited, with a hundred thousand veterans ready for combat." Strangely, Beck and Charles see in this passage support for their call to establish English as an official language, a nonissue in the founding era. Its "relevance for today," they say, is this: "A united America is more powerful than an army. But too many actions by the federal government now serve to divide us rather than to bring us together. We need a common language, a common national identity, and common equality before the law" (*Original Argument*, 80). A common language was never a priority for the founders. National leaders at the time, all of whom favored national expansion, favored immigration from diverse European nations. Without immigrants who didn't speak English, speculators in westward lands (this includes most of the famous founders) would never be able to populate them.

Beck and Charles are not alone. According to the Chicago Tea Party, cited above in n. 58, "The *Constitution* (whose provisions, and original intent thereof, are informed by the *Declaration of Independence* and the writings of the Founders in the *Federalist Papers*) is the supreme law of the land." How the Constitution was "informed" by the so-called *Federalist Papers*, which were written afterward, is curious. Those essays, it says, "were written by the Founders to set forth their rationale for the various provisions in the Constitution." In this rendering, "the Founders" are reduced to James Madison, Alexander Hamilton (who absented himself from most of the Federal Convention), and John Jay (who never attended). It's a common ploy.

The "basic philosophy" of the Ravalli Republic website starts with this: "Adherence to Constitutional government as defined in the Constitution of the United States and the Bill of Rights as explained in the Federalist Papers." Here the *Federalist Papers* "explain" the Bill of Rights, yet another complete reversal. *The Federalist*, of course, was written over a year before the first ten amendments were even drafted, and Publius's only mention of a possible Bill of Rights was in *The Federalist No. 84*, in which Hamilton argued in the strongest possible terms *against* amending the Constitution to add a bill or declaration of rights. Ravalli Republic website: http:// ravallirepublic.com/news/opinion/viewpoint/article_863912c8-efc0-11e0-9ff2-001cc4c03286 .html#ixzz1adVzZpC5 (accessed February 16, 2012).

60. Publius-Huldah's blog: Understanding the Constitution: http://publiushuldah.word press.com/2011/01/24/why-states-must-nullify-unconstitutional-acts-of-congress-instruc tions-from-hamilton-madison-jefferson/ (accessed February 16, 2012).

61. *McCulloch v. Maryland*, Cornell University Law School, http://www.law.cornell.edu/ supct/html/historics/USSC_CR_0017_0316_ZO.html.

7. Bill of Rights

1. At http://www.sodahead.com/united-states/did-god-give-us-the-bill-of-rights/ques tion-452661/?page=4#comments (posted June 23, 2009, and accessed January 9, 2012). These two options are not mutually exclusive. "The Bill of Rights exists for no other purpose than to make sure we have the right to practice what the Creator told us to do," said prolific author David Barton (*Original Intent: The Courts, the Constitution, & Religion; Separation of Church and State: What the Founders Meant; The Second Amendment*) on the Glenn Beck show, August 6, 2010, http://www.foxnews.com/story/0,2933,598802,00.html.

2. At http://wiki.answers.com/Q/Who_was_the_author_of_the_Bill_of_Rights (ac cessed January 9, 2012).

3. At http://www.lewrockwell.com/gregory/gregory49.html (accessed January 9, 2012).

4. Avalon Project, Yale Law School, http://avalon.law.yale.edu/17th_century/england .asp.

5. The various state constitutions and declarations of rights appear in Schwartz, *Bill of Rights* 1:231–379. Only the last of these, New Hampshire's in 1784, called the list of rights a "bill of rights." The rest used the term "declaration of rights."

6. Schwartz, *Bill of Rights*, 1:49–175.

7. Ibid., 1:71–84.

8. Leonard W. Levy, "Bill of Rights," in Leonard W. Levy, ed., *Essays on the Making of the Constitution* (New York: Oxford University Press, 1987), 268–69; Schwartz, *Bill of Rights*, 1:231–50, 256–379. Vermont, which was not yet a state, also passed a Declaration of Rights, modeled after that of Pennsylvania but with the notable addition of a prohibition against slavery. Two states, Connecticut and Rhode Island, did not draft new constitutions, but Connecticut did enact a short list of rights (Schwartz, *Bill of Rights*, 1:289–90). For the difference between constitutional commands and codification of principles, see William E. Nelson and Robert C. Palmer, *Liberty and Community: Constitution and Rights in the Early American Republic* (Dobbs Ferry, NY: Oceana Publications, 1987), and Richard B. Bernstein, *Amending America: If We Love the Constitution So Much, Why Do We Keep Trying to Change It?* (New York; Times Books/ Random House, 1993; paperback, Lawrence: University Press of Kansas, 1995), 14–47.

9. Mason had drafted Virginia's 1776 Declaration of Rights, which served as a model for the "declaration or bill of rights" proposed by Virginia's ratifying convention. Mason no doubt assumed a national bill of rights could be based on these existing documents.

10. Mason also offered a related argument: "The laws of the U.S. are to be paramount to State Bills of Rights." During the debates over ratification, opponents of the proposed Constitution seized on this idea and warned that the new federal government could in effect nullify the state declarations of rights.

11. *DHRC*, 8:43–45 or 13:348–50.

12. Ibid., 13:339–40.

13. Hamilton made one additional argument against a bill of rights in *The Federalist No. 84*. His argument was intriguing but easily rebutted. "Bills of rights are, in their origin, stipulations between kings and their subjects, abridgements of prerogative in favor of privilege, reservations of rights not surrendered to the prince," he wrote. "They have no application to constitutions professedly founded upon the power of the people, and executed by their immediate representatives and servants. Here, in strictness, the people surrender nothing; and as they retain every thing they have no need of particular reservations." Kings, however, were not the only tyrants to be guarded against, as Americans at the time knew too well. It was Parliament that passed the oppressive laws leading up to the Revolution, and colonials had for a decade addressed their grievances against Parliament to the Crown. More recently, state legislatures had passed laws that the framers thought violated the rights of a minority (creditors) in favor of the majority (debtors). What would happen if the new national legislature, without a monarch, trampled the rights of citizens? Were no precautions in order? Again, Hamilton's argument failed to convince.

14. Madison to Jefferson, October 17, 1788, Madison, *Papers*, 11:297.

15. Madison, *Notes*, September 15.

16. Southborough: *DHRC*, 5:1032–33. "Language adopted to slaves": *DHRC*, 5:834.

17. Revolutionary War and Beyond website: http://www.revolutionary-war-and-beyond .com/history-bill-of-rights.ht ml. The final sentence is incorrect on two counts. First, as shown below, this was not "a Bill of Rights." Second, Federalist delegates at the Massachusetts ratifying convention could not promise a so-called Bill of Rights "would be added," only that they would work toward that goal.

18. The Massachusetts amendments are in Schwartz, *Bill of Rights*, 2:712–23; *DHRC*, 6:1381–82; or Avalon Project, http://avalon.law.yale.edu/18th_century/ratma.asp.

19. Schwartz, *Bill of Rights*, 2:756–57, 760–61, 840–45, 911–18, 966–71; Avalon Project: South Carolina: http://avalon.law.yale.edu/18th_century/ratsc.asp; New Hampshire: http:// avalon.law.yale.edu/18th_century/ratnh.asp; Virginia: http://avalon.law.yale.edu/18th_ century/ratva.asp; New York: http://avalon.law.yale.edu/18th_century/ratny.asp; North Carolina: http://avalon.law.yale.edu/18th_century/ratnc.asp. The Maryland Convention did not formally propose amendments, but a committee of the convention did vote to approve thirteen suggestions for amendments. A minority of that committee presented fifteen others that the majority rejected. Rather than join the intracommittee squabble over which amendments to include, the convention ratified without officially adopting the committee's report (Schwartz, *Bill of Rights*, 2:732–38; *DHRC*).

20. New York's official ratification statement also expressed its "full confidence" that "until a Convention shall be called and convened for proposing Amendments," the federal government would not send New York militia out of state for longer than six weeks, Congress would not control congressional elections within New York, Congress would not levy any excise taxes ("Ardent Spirits excepted") within New York, and, most significantly, Congress would not "lay direct taxes within this state" unless imposts and excises had proved insufficient and New York had failed to comply with its requisition. New York stopped just shy of demanding these amendments as a condition of ratification, changing the words "on condition" to "in full confidence" by a vote of thirty-one to twenty-nine (Maier, *Ratification*, 392–93, 397; Elliot, *Debates*, 2:412–14; *DHRC*, 22: 2326–30.)

21. Madison to Hamilton and Madison to Washington, June 27, 1788; Madison to Jefferson, August 23, 1788; Madison to Washington, August 11, 1788, Madison, *Papers*, 11:181–83, 238, 230.

22. Washington to Madison, August 17, 1788, Madison, *Papers*, 11:234.

23. Madison to Richard Peters, August 19, 1789, Veit et al., *Bill of Rights*, 282.

24. Jon Butler, "James Ireland, John Leland, John 'Swearing Jack' Waller, and the Baptist Campaign for Religious Freedom in Revolutionary Virginia," in Alfred F. Young, Gary B. Nash, and Ray Raphael, eds., *Revolutionary Founders: Rebels, Radicals, and Reformers in the Making of the Nation* (New York: Knopf, 2011), 182; Madison to George Eve, January 2, 1789, Madison, *Papers*, 11:404–5.

25. Washington's First Inaugural Address to Congress, April 30, 1789, Washington, *Papers* (PS), 2:176.

26. Washington to Jefferson, August 31, 1788, Washington, *Writings*, 30:83.

27. Washington to Madison, ca. May 31, 1789, Washington, *Papers* (PS), 2:419.

28. *Annals of Congress*, 1:449–50. After listing his proposed amendments, Madison continued his seemingly faint praise of declarations of rights. "The people of many States have

thought it necessary to raise barriers against power in all forms and departments of Government, and I am inclined to believe, if once bills of rights are established in all the States as well as the federal constitution, we shall find, that, although some of them are rather unimportant, yet, upon the whole, they will have a salutary tendency. It may be said, in some instances, they do no more than state the perfect equality of mankind. This, to be sure, is an absolute truth, yet it is not absolutely necessary to be inserted at the head of a Constitution." Ibid., 1:454. Madison's speech, with his proposed amendments, is reprinted in *The Founders' Constitution*, 1:479–84, and Veit et al., *Bill of Rights*, 11–14, 77–86.

29. *Annals of Congress*, 1:445.

30. Ibid., 1:685–86, 730; Thomas Harley to Jasper Yeates, August 16, 1789, Veit et al., *Bill of Rights*, 279.

31. *Annals of Congress*, 1:734–35. Sherman based his argument on the premise that the original Constitution was the product of the people's exercise of their constituent power—the power to constitute a government—and that any amendments, the products of the Article V amending process, should follow to make their origins and history clear and distinct. Several representatives supported Sherman: Congress could amend but not alter the original text, which must "remain a monument to justify those who made it," and besides, since the Constitution was already "lodged in the archives of the late Congress, it was impossible for this House to take, and correct, and interpolate that without making it speak a different language." The original must "remain inviolate, and not be patched up, from time to time, with various stuffs resembling Joseph's coat of many colors." Further, if they altered it, they would have to expunge the signatures of Washington and the other framers, who had not at that moment signed on to such changes, and nullify the ratification of the state conventions, which likewise did not approve the amendments at that time.

Others supported Madison: the Constitution, as amended, should form "one complete system." A document with numerous amendments tacked onto the end would appear "like a careless written letter," with "more attached to it in a postscript than was contained in the original composition." Further, separate amendments would invite embarrassing comparisons with the original document, leaving it unclear how to resolve any apparent conflicts, and, finally, an isolated list would confuse the document's meaning. Madison had placed his amendments in specific places, making it easier to understand their intent. Several amendments, for instance, were to be inserted in Article I, Section 9, which specified limitations on the powers of Congress. Restrictions against intrusions of rights by the states, on the other hand, were to be placed in Article I, Section 10, where similar constraints on state authority were listed. Madison wanted freedom of conscience and the press, along with trial by jury in criminal cases, to be protected from state as well as federal abuse, a provision he called "the most valuable amendment in the whole lot," but the House eventually struck his proposal from the list (*Annals of Congress*, 1:734–44 for the debate on placement and 1:1145–46 for Madison's quotation).

When the question was called, Madison's position prevailed. The amendments, if adopted, would appear within the Constitution, not listed separately at the end—until six days later, when the House repeated its earlier debate but reversed its decision. A *separate* listing of rights, seen then as a matter of form rather than substance, squeaked in at the last moment, over and above the strenuous objections of James Madison, their primary promoter within Congress, but much to the pleasure of Roger Sherman, a leading opponent of amendments (*Annals of Congress*, 1:795).

Madison remained disgruntled over this decision. On August 24, immediately after the House approved the amendments and sent them to the Senate, he wrote to Alexander White (a Federalist representative from Virginia who had been absent from these debates), "It became an unavoidable sacrifice to a few who knew their concurrence to be necessary, to the dispatch if not the success of the business, to give up the form by which the amendts. when ratified would have fallen into the body of the Constitution, in favor of the project of adding them by way of appendix to it. It is already apparent I think that some ambiguities will be produced by this change, as the question will often arise and sometimes be not easily solved, how far the original text is or is not necessarily superceded, by the supplemental act." Veit et al., *Bill of Rights*, 287–88; Schwartz, *Bill of Rights* 2:1139–40.

32. *Annals of Congress*, 1:774–75 (August 15). Items that did not evolve into what we now call the Bill of Rights included a preamble reminiscent of that in the Declaration of Independence (but with no mention of equality), a general call for the separation of powers, a limitation on the number of people a congressman could represent, and a prohibition against Congress raising its own compensation until after the subsequent election. (The full text is in appendix F below.) The first two were dropped by Congress, the last two were not ratified by three-quarters of the states. The compensation amendment was revived two centuries later and in 1992 became the Twenty-seventh Amendment to the Constitution. See Richard B. Bernstein, "The Sleeper Wakes: The History and Legacy of the Twenty-Seventh Amendment," *Fordham Law Review* 61:3 (December 1992): 497–557.

33. *Annals of Congress*, 1: 786–92 (Gerry and Tucker, August 18); 1:761–76 (right of instruction, August 15); 1:790 ("expressly delegated," August 18); 1:780–81 (standing army, August 17); 1:797–802 (federal control of elections, August 21).

34. *Annals of Congress*, 1:803–7.

35. Butler to Iredell, August 11, 1789, Veit et al., *Bill of Rights*, 274; Morris to Francis Hopkinson and Morris to Richard Peters, August 24, 1789, Veit et al., *Bill of Rights*, 278, 288. Madison was not pleased with the Senate's changes: "The Senate have sent back the plan of amendments with some alterations which strike in my opinion at the most salutary articles." For Madison's particular objections, see Madison to Edmund Peterson, September 14, 1789, and Madison to Edmund Pendleton, September 23, 1789, Veit et al., *Bill of Rights*, 296–98. In the end, the Senate approved twelve amendments. First on the list was the limitation on the number of people that a congressman could represent, next came the stipulation against Congress augmenting its own compensation unless an election of representatives shall have intervened, and then the ten amendments we know today as the Bill of Rights. Differences between the House and Senate versions were ironed out in conference, accepted by both chambers, and passed on to the president on September 25. One week later, on undated single sheets of parchment signed by the Speaker of the House and president of the Senate, copies of the twelve amendments were sent to the eleven states then in the union for ratification. (North Carolina and Rhode Island had not yet ratified the Constitution.)

36. Madison to Richard Peters, August 19, 1789, Veit et al., *Bill of Rights*, 281–82. Lee to Francis Lightfoot Lee, September 13, 1789, and to Patrick Henry, September 14 and 27, 1789;

Maier, *Ratification*, 461 (for Henry's complaint); Grayson to Patrick Henry, September 29, 1789, in Veit et al., *Bill of Rights*, 299–300, 294, 295, 299, 300.

37. John Adams to Abigail Adams, July 3, 1776, Charles Francis Adams, ed., *Familiar Letters of John Adams and his Wife Abigail Adams, during the Revolution* (New York: Hurd and Houghton, 1876).

38. Francis Hopkinson, *Account of the Grand Federal Procession, Philadelphia, July 4, 1788* (Philadelphia: M. Carry, 1788); "Order of Procession," broadside printed by Hall and Sellers, 1788; Van Horne, "Federal Procession of 1788"; John C. Van Horne, "The Federal Procession of 1788," website for Carpenters' Hall, http://www.ushistory.org/carpentershall/history/procession.htm (consulted May 27, 2012).

39. Jefferson to governors, March 1, 1792, Schwartz, *Bill of Rights*, 2:1203.

40. For the lack of contemporary denotations of the first amendments as the "Bill of Rights," see Maier, *Ratification*, 459–63.

8. Originalism

1. Clarence Thomas, Wriston Lecture to the Manhattan Institute, October 16, 2008, *Wall Street Journal*, October 20, 2008, http://online.wsj.com/article/SB122445985683948619.html.

2. Antonin Scalia, *A Matter of Interpretation: Federal Courts and the Law* (Princeton: Princeton University Press, 1997), 45. Justice Scalia does qualify this remark: "Sometimes (though not very often) there will be disagreement regarding the original meaning; and sometimes there will be disagreement as to how that original meaning applies to new and unforeseen phenomena." As I argue below, the term "not very often" is not a fair empirical assessment of the number and intensity of disagreements.

3. A weaker version of originalism features the framers but bypasses the troublesome notion of intent: when examining a particular motion put forth at the Federal Convention, we don't need to know the intent of its author to learn how his fellow delegates understood it, which is the key question. Even here, though, we confront problems. How, exactly, are we to surmise a delegate's understanding? The vow of secrecy curtailed private correspondence, whereas the delegates' speeches, recorded by Madison and others, must be viewed in a political light. Inferring the intentions of delegates to the ratification conventions is also problematic. Jack Rakove explains the problems of focusing on intent in any form: "Both the framing of the Constitution in 1787 and its ratification by the states involved processes of collective decision-making whose outcomes necessarily reflected a bewildering array of intentions and expectations, hopes and fears, genuine compromises and agreements to disagree. The discussions of both stages of this process consisted largely of highly problematic predictions of the consequences of particular decisions. In this context, it is not immediately apparent how the historian goes about divining the true intentions or understandings of the roughly two thousand actors who served in the various conventions that framed and ratified the Constitution, much less the larger electorate they claimed to represent" (Jack Rakove, *Original Meanings: Politics and Ideas in the Making of the Constitution* (New York: Random House, 1996), 6.

4. This is true, of course, for all political speech. Today, when we hear some public statement, we are quick to factor in the probable intentions of the author. When addressing alleged

"commentaries" on the Constitution by the founders, however, we sometimes let down our guard, accepting statements at face value.

5. In the extreme version of the "single tablet" approach, the source was God himself. For example: "We have to learn the basic truth about the Constitution: God wrote it. It comes directly from the government instituted by Moses when he led the Children of Israel out of Egypt. That system was re-instituted in England around 450 A.D. by the Anglo-Saxon rulers Hengist and Horsa. The Founding Fathers, led by Thomas Jefferson, copied the Constitution directly from the 'ancient constitution' of the Anglo-Saxons" (http://www.theatlantic.com/national/archive/2010/10/all-patriots-know-that-moses-wrote-the-constitution/65353/).

6. *Annals of Congress*, 1:574, 544 (June 18, 1789).

7. See Ray Raphael, *Mr. President: How and Why the Founders Created a Chief Executive* (New York: Knopf, 2012), 166–69.

8. Ibid., 182–88.

9. Ibid., 188–93. In a related matter, the House demanded the president send it papers relating to the treaty, but Washington refused to do so, claiming executive privilege over the presidency's own affairs.

10. For Congress interpreting the Constitution, see David P. Currie, *The Constitution in Congress: The Federalist Period, 1789–1801* (Chicago: University of Chicago Press, 1997). For "popular constitutionalism," see Larry D. Kramer, *The People Themselves: Popular Constitutionalism and Judicial Review* (New York: Oxford University Press, 2004). For competing Fourth of July celebrations, see Len Travis, *Celebrating the Fourth: Independence Day and the Rites of Nationalism in the Early Republic* (Amherst: University of Massachusetts Press, 1997), 69–106.

11. Madison, *Papers*, 16:295. Madison suggested a similar position in 1791, when arguing against a national bank: "In controverted cases, *the meaning of the parties to the instrument*, if to be collected by reasonable evidence, *is a proper guide*. Contemporary and concurrent expositions are a reasonable evidence of the meaning of the parties" (Rakove, *Original Meanings*, 352 [emphasis added]). In 1821, he repeated it forcefully: "As a guide in expounding and applying the provisions of the Constitution, the debates and incidental decisions of the Convention can have no authoritative character. . . . [T]he legitimate meaning of the Instrument must be derived from the text itself; or if a key is to be sought elsewhere, it must be not in the opinions or intentions of the Body which planned & proposed the Constitution, but in the sense attached to it by the people in their respective State Conventions where it recd. all the authority which it possesses" (Madison to Thomas Ritchie, September 15, 1821, Farrand, *Records*, 3:447–48).

12. Madison to Ritchie, September 15, 1821, Farrand, *Records*, 3:447. Even one-third of a century after the fact, Madison scrawled "Confidential" on his letter to Ritchie. He said "it has not been my intention that they [his notes] should remain for ever under the veil of secresy," but "of the time when it might not be improper for them to see the light," he had "formed no particular determination," although he thought it "might be best to let the work be a posthumous one." That, in the end, is what happened. Madison arranged for the publication of his notes after he and all the other framers had passed. He died in 1836, having outlived his peers from the Convention; his notes were published in 1840.

13. *Annals*, 2:2004–5 (February 7, 1791). Gerry was speaking in support of a national bank, which Madison opposed, and his comments here were in response to Madison's contention that

"the meaning of the parties to the instrument, if to be collected by reasonable evidence," could be "a proper guide" in resolving constitutional issues (see n. 11 above). Through the 1790s, other representatives and senators cited evidence from the ratification conventions, which they believed rested on firmer ground than evidence gleaned from proceedings of the Federal Convention. During the debate over Jay's Treaty, Benjamin Bourne, a representative from Rhode Island, said, "the real inquiry was, what opinion was entertained on this subject by those who ratified the Constitution" (Rakove, *Original Meanings*, 359).

14. *Annals*, 2:1954 (February 3, 1791). Ames was speaking in favor of Hamilton's national bank. Here is the full passage: "If Congress may not make laws conformably to the powers plainly implied, though not expressed in the frame of Government, it is rather late in the day to adopt it as a principle of conduct. A great part of our two years' labor is lost, and worse than lost to the public, for we have scarcely made a law in which we have not exercised our discretion with regard to the true intent of the Constitution. Any words but those used in that instrument will be liable to a different interpretation. We may regulate trade; therefore we have taxed ships, erected light-houses, made laws to govern seamen, &c., because we say that they are the incidents to that power. The most familiar and undisputed acts of Legislation will show that we have adopted it as a safe rule of action to legislate beyond the letter of the Constitution."

15. *Annals*, 2:1945 (February 2, 1791); Rakove, *Original Meanings*, 351. Although the Federal Convention rejected Madison's motion to grant Congress powers of incorporation, the debate on September 14 was primarily about canals and only incidentally about banks. Two arguments against incorporation clearly referred to canals. Roger Sherman said, "The expence in such cases will fall on the U. States, and the benefit accrue to the places where the canals may be cut," and Rufus King noted, "The States will be prejudiced and divided into parties by it," since they would fight over where canals should be built. Incorporating banks did worry some delegates, though. King said, "In Philada. & New York, It will be referred to the establishment of a Bank, which has been a subject of contention in those Cities. In other places it will be referred to mercantile monopolies." George Mason added that he was "was afraid of monopolies of every sort." James Wilson, meanwhile, thought "mercantile monopolies" were "already included in the power to regulate trade," while Mason did not think "by any means" the mercantile monopolies were "already implied by the Constitution." The range of the discussion reveals the problems inherent in trying to determine the sense of the full Convention, as Elbridge Gerry aptly noted.

16. Hamilton, unlike Madison, was not shy about using the Federal Convention as a guide. In 1796, when Madison argued that the House as well as the Senate needed to approve Jay's Treaty, Hamilton, writing under a pseudonym, inquired rhetorically how treaty making "was understood by the Convention, in framing it, and by the people, in adopting it." He challenged Madison to deny that the framers thought treaty-making powers were "sufficiently guarded" by the president and the Senate (Rakove, *Original Meanings*, 357–58). Madison, of course, could not do this, knowing full well that on September 7 the Convention had resoundingly rejected James Wilson's motion to include the House in the ratification process. Madison himself, on September 7 and 8, had participated actively in determining exactly what fraction of the Senate must concur for a treaty to be ratified. Washington, too, appealed to the Federal Convention when claiming Jay's Treaty did not need to be approved by the House. He wrote formally to the House of Representatives: "Having been a member of the General Convention, and knowing the principles on

which the Constitution was formed, I have ever entertained but one opinion on this subject, . . . that the power of making treaties is exclusively vested in the President, by and with the advice and consent of the Senate, provided two thirds of the Senators present concur" (Washington to House of Representatives, March 30, 1796, Washington, *Writings*, 35:3–4).

17. *Dred Scott v. Sandford*, 60 U.S. 393 (1856), http://www.law.cornell.edu/supct/html/historics/USSC_CR_0060_0393_ZO.html.

18. *Reynolds v. United States*, 98 U.S. 145 (1878), http://law2.umkc.edu/faculty/projects/ftrials/conlaw/reynoldsvus.html. Chief Justice Waite, writing for the Court, determined that while there was indeed a "wall of separation between church and state," a federal law prohibiting bigamy in United States Territories did not in fact violate that First Amendment, as Jefferson conceived it.

19. Woodrow Wilson, "What Is Progress," from *The New Freedom II*, 1913, http://teaching americanhistory.org/library/index.asp?documentprint=2553. Black's dissent in Griswold at http://www.law.cornell.edu/supct/html/historics/USSC_CR_0381_0479_ZD.html.

20. Johnathan George O'Neill, *Originalism in American Law and Politics: A Constitutional History* (Baltimore: Johns Hopkins University Press, 2005), 138.

21. Edwin Meese III, speech before the American Bar Association, July 9, 1985; "The Supreme Court of the United States: Bulwark of a Limited Constitution," *South Texas Law Review* 27 (1986): 464; "Toward a Jurisprudence of Original Intent," *Harvard Journal of Law and Public Policy* 11 (1988): 8. All three quotations are from Gregory E. Maggs, "Which Original Meaning of the Constitution Matters to Justice Thomas?" *New York University Journal of Law & Liberty* 4:494 (2009): 501, 552, 553.

22. Legal Information Institute, Cornell University Law School, http://www.law.cornell .edu/supct/html/93–1260.ZC1.html (accessed June 3, 2012).

23. Maggs, "Justice Thomas," 507–14.

24. Legal Information Institute, Cornell University Law School, http://www.law.cornell .edu/supct/html/93–986.ZC1.html; http://www.law.cornell.edu/supct/html/07–5439.ZC3 .html; http://www.law.cornell.edu/supct/html/08–1448.ZD.html.

25. For Justice Thomas's selective application of originalism, see Mark Graber, "Clarence Thomas and the Perils of Amateur History," in *Rehnquist Justice: Understanding the Court Dynamic*, ed., Earl M. Maltz (Lawrence: University of Kansas Press, 2003), 70–72.

26. Madison, *Notes*, July 2. Morris's response to this danger was to create an independent president, chosen by special electors who would meet at a designated moment in the separate states so they would not be subject to influence—the so-called Electoral College.

27. Adams to John Taylor, April 15, 1814, Charles Francis Adams, ed., *The Works of John Adams* (Boston: Little, Brown, 1856), 6:456–57. By voting with the majority in *Citizens United*, Justice Thomas did endorse two peripheral arguments based on originalism, neither of which addressed the core issues of money, influence, and corporate power. "There is simply no support for the view that the First Amendment, as originally understood, would permit the suppression of political speech by media corporations," the majority argued. Logically, this claim carried little weight, because media corporations were specifically exempted from the restrictions in question, but alluding to the great newspaper debates of the times allowed Justice Thomas and four other justices to preach about the founders' love of a free press, an uncontested point. Even more

marginal was a bizarre appeal to Madison's *The Federalist No. 10*: "By suppressing the speech of manifold corporations, both for-profit and non-profit, the Government prevents their voices and viewpoints from reaching the public and advising voters on which persons or entities are hostile to their interests. . . . Factions should be checked by permitting them all to speak." Was Madison really talking about *global corporations*, which somehow would neutralize one another's influence in elections? And did others at the time understand him this way? In his concurring opinion, rather than offering an originalist variant on the majority opinion, Justice Thomas challenged one of the Court's findings. While overturning most of the ban on corporate campaigning thirty days prior to an election, the Court upheld the requirement for posting or broadcasting disclosures, and Justice Thomas, citing his own endorsement of anonymous campaigning in *McIntyre v. Ohio Elections Commission*, objected to this restriction because it facilitated personal reprisals: "I cannot endorse a view of the First Amendment that subjects citizens of this Nation to death threats, ruined careers, damaged or defaced property, or pre-emptive and threatening warning letters as the price for engaging in core political speech, the 'primary object of First Amendment protection.' " From an originalist point of view, it was a strangely squeamish argument. In the founding era, a man subjected to defamation or death threats for his stated political views could fight back in the press, and should that not suffice, if he were a man of honor, he might challenge the aggressor to a duel rather than hide behind the sort of governmental protection Thomas now urged. On this contentious politics, shaped by considerations of honor and reputation, see Joanne B. Freeman, *Affairs of Honor: National Politics in the New Republic* (New Haven, CT: Yale University Press, 2001).

28. Even without this originalist perspective, Bush's standing to bring the case before the Court was highly questionable. "The majority never even bothered to ask whether Governor Bush had constitutional standing to raise his ultimately triumphant equal protection claim against Florida on behalf of certain unidentified Florida voters. In equal protection cases involving racial minorities, the Court has been adamant that plaintiffs seeking a hearing may assert neither the rights of others nor abstract principles of fairness, but rather must establish their own standing to bring a claim by showing that they have suffered a concrete personal injury that is traceable to the government and redressable by the courts. Thus, in *Allen v. Wright*, the Court denied standing to African-American parents who wanted to compel the Internal Revenue Service to deny tax exemptions to private schools that discriminate on the basis of race. Justice O'Connor stated that citizens have no general right to make the government comply with the law and found that the African-American plaintiffs were not personally injured by the 'abstract stigmatic injury' associated with white flight allegedly facilitated by the IRS policy. But in *Bush v. Gore*, the majority did not question whether (much less explain how) Governor Bush was personally injured by the order of a manual recount. Assuming that there was a threatened injury to a certain subclass of pregnant chad voters, it would have been an injury visited on them, not on Governor Bush, Vice President Gore, or anyone else with standing to raise their claims for them. If Bush's claim was that he would have been personally injured as a candidate if all ballots were not in fact counted, this might have been a plausible, if speculative, argument on the theory that the winning candidate acts as a proxy for the right of the majority to govern. The problem is that the relief Governor Bush was seeking, and the relief that was ordered, was not the counting of all the pregnant and dimpled chad ballots but the counting of none of them. Thus, he would have

had to allege a hypothetical injury arising out of the counting of a class of ballots that the Court ultimately determined should have been counted. And even if we assume, bizarrely, that Governor Bush was going to be prospectively injured by the hypothetical possibility that anonymous third party citizens not in the case might have their pregnant chad ballots counted differently in one part of Florida than in another, how could stopping the vote-counting sufficiently redress these third party injuries? If your vote is in danger of not being counted, how does it help you for the Supreme Court to make sure that someone else's vote is not counted along with it?" Jamin B. Raskin, "Symposium: Litigating the Presidency: The Election 2000 Decision and its Ramifications for the Supreme Court," *Maryland Law Review* 61 (2002):652–61.

Instead of offering an originalist argument, Justice Thomas sided with the majority, which argued that some Floridians had been denied the fundamental right to vote for president by the decision to recount ballots from some jurisdictions but not others. The obvious remedy, of course, would have been to require a manual recount from *all* jurisdictions, but the majority, which included Justices Thomas and Scalia, argued pragmatically that that would be impossible—an argument based on consequences, which originalists theoretically eschew.

29. Clarence Thomas, Wriston Lecture (see note 1 above).

30. Jeffrey Toobin, "Partners: Will Clarence and Virginia Thomas Succeed in Killing Obama's Health Care Plan?" *New Yorker*, August 29, 2011, 42.

31. Ibid., 43.

32. Scalia, *Matter of Interpretation*, 38.

33. Ibid.

34. For a related use of the contrast between discovery and construction, see Lawrence H. Tribe, "Comment," in Scalia, *Matter of Interpretation*, 71.

35. Legal Information Institute, Cornell University Law School, http://www.law.cornell.edu/supct/html/95-1478.ZO.html#FN9. See also Peter J. Smith, "Sources of Federalism: An Empirical Analysis of the Court's Quest for Original Meaning," *UCLA Law Review* 52 (2004): 219. To his credit, Justice Scalia admits that the search for original meaning is "a task sometimes better suited to the historian than the lawyer," but in practice, although he was trained in law and not history, he assumes the job nonetheless (Antonin Scalia, "Originalism: The Lesser Evil," *University of Cincinnati Law Review* 57 [1989]: 857). Other justices, like Justice Scalia, comb the sources selectively. One study of the Supreme Court since 1970 concluded, not surprisingly, that in cases involving federalism, justices promoting the authority of the federal government preferred to cite Federalists, while those favoring state authority tended to cite the Constitution's opponents. There were exceptions, but these are easily explained. Justices who sided with states occasionally cited Federalists who were trying to appease their adversaries, and justices siding with the national government might cite opponents of the Constitution who, for political reasons, highlighted the strength of the national government under the proposed Constitution. When considering the state ratifying conventions, justices on opposite sides cited the same sources but drew contradictory conclusions. Pro-state justices took complaints by the Constitution's adversaries seriously, saying delegates would never have voted for ratification if fears of centralization had not been satisfactorily appeased. Pro-national justices dismissed these same complaints because the majority adopted the Constitution without any changes (Smith, "Sources of Federalism," 217–287; Maggs, "Justice Thomas," 503).

36. Scalia, "Originalism: The Lesser Evil," 863–64.

37. "Scalia seeks to *deactivate* the Court's previous activism," argues Kevin Ring in *Scalia Dissents: Writings of the Supreme Court's Wittiest, Most Outspoken Justice* (Washington, DC: Regnery, 2004), 16.

38. Thomas, "Wriston Lecture"; Scalia, *Matter of Interpretation*, 38; Scalia, conversation with Peter Robinson, February 23, 2009, Hoover Institution, Stanford, CA, http://www.huffingtonpost.com/2012/07/04/antonin-scalia_n_1649211.html?utm_hp_ref=politics.

39. Tribe, "Comment," 73, 85, 70.

40. Stephen Breyer, *Active Liberty: Interpreting Our Democratic Constitution* (New York: Knopf, 2005), 124, 37, 15. Justice Breyer's methodology, though comprehensive, simplifies the historical record. Even if we agree with Justice Breyer's insistence on identifying the document's "critical values," his emphasis on democracy, which presented complex problems for the framers (see chapter 4), reveals the perils of inferring values from a document presented largely in the form of rules. The declarations of rights prepared by the states, and later the federal Bill of Rights, might be more suggestive of values, but the state declarations were preambles, affixed to constitutions that established concrete government structures and procedures.

41. Scalia, *Matter of Interpretation*, 137, 142.

42. Ibid., 45.

43. Ronald Dworkin, "Comment," in Scalia, *Matter of Interpretation*, 120–22. After drawing the distinction between rules and principles, Dworkin takes his antioriginalist argument one step further: "The Constitution insists that our judges do their best collectively to construct, reinspect, and revise, generation by generation, the skeleton of freedom and equality of concern that its great clauses, in their majestic abstraction, command." It is difficult to locate precisely which clause within the Constitution makes this insistence, however. Distinguishing between rules and abstractions does not tell us how abstractions are to be treated (Ibid., 123).

Justice Scalia admits that some provisions are more abstract than others, but he treats this distinction very differently. Because *some* provisions, including all the concrete rules, are clearly fixed in time, and because it is difficult to ascertain *which* provisions the framers might have intended as rules and which as abstract "aspirations" (a term Professor Tribe uses), Justice Scalia concludes that we are obliged to treat them *all* in the most literal way. That the authors of the Seventh Amendment would go so far as to stipulate a lower limit for jury trials in civil cases—precisely twenty dollars—proves to him that they had fixed ideas about the freedoms they protected in the Bill of Rights, ideas we are now obligated to respect (Scalia's oral reply, as reported by Tribe, to his Tanner Lecture on Human Values, Princeton University, March 8–9, 1995, *Matter of Interpretation*, 88–89). Historically, Scalia's argument seems forced. The twenty-dollar minimum was tacked on at the very last minute by the Senate with no dissent, after the House had passed the amendment without specifying a lower limit. There was no recorded discussion about whether the limit was too high, too low, or whether there should be a limit at all; the matter was too small to bother with. We cannot base the way we treat the Bill of Rights and the Constitution on an incidental move to procure a few final votes. (The documentary evidence for the evolution of the Seventh Amendment and the insertion of the twenty-dollar threshold is in Veit et al., *Bill of Rights*, 13, 40, 47, 49, 196.)

Justice Scalia is correct in noting the difficulty in ascertaining the difference between rules and principles. The Bill of Rights contains several principles, but even there, some provisions state rules, not principles: "No soldier shall, in time of peace be quartered in any house, without the consent of the Owner" and "In suits at common law, where the value in controversy shall exceed twenty dollars, the right of trial by jury shall be preserved." Whereas these provisions might embody principles, they function within the document as laws that must be followed to the tee.

In fact, the Constitution's "grammar" needs to be refined. There are several different types of provisions, not only two:

Goals, as stated in the preamble.

Procedures, such as how to select officers, the lengths of their terms, and how a bill becomes law.

Qualifications for representatives, senators, and the president.

Grants of power to the legislative and executive branches and *definitions of authority* for the judicial branch. Some grants of power entail specified procedures that define and in some cases limit that power. The president is authorized to "make Treaties" with the "Advice and Consent of the Senate," provided "two-thirds of the Senators present concur."

Prohibitions that define the limits of federal or state authority.

Declarations of rights, which can be phrased as prohibitions of governmental authority.

Charges that instruct the government or its officers to perform certain acts or achieve specified results. Most charges overlap with procedures and grants of power, as in Article II, Section 3: "He [the president] shall from time to time give to the Congress Information of the State of the Union, and recommend to their Consideration such Measures as he shall judge necessary and expedient." Others require a result without specifying a procedure, most notably Article IV, Section 4: "The United States shall guarantee to every State in this Union a Republican Form of Government." Article VI, Section 1, which requires the federal government to assume all prior debts of the United States, can also be considered a charge.

Self-reflexive assertions of constitutional authority. Three provisions make metastatements about the Constitution itself. The opening and closing words of the preamble—"We the People of the United States . . . do ordain and establish this Constitution for the United States of America"—establish the Constitution as a contract. Article VI, Section 2, declares the Constitution to be "the supreme Law of the Land." Article VII states how the Constitution is to be ratified, a process very different from the existing rules for amending the Articles of Confederation as set forth in that document's Article 13.

Some categories present more interpretative difficulties than others. Goals are the most problematic, not only because they are cast with broad strokes but also because they are not tied to specific procedures, grants of power, and so on. The Constitution itself gives no guidance as to how "general Welfare" contributes to any particular provision, yet because those words are featured so prominently and declared as a major goal, we can hardly ignore them. Historically, most disputes have centered on the limits of congressional authority (grants of power and prohibitions of federal authority), allocation of powers between the legislative and executive branches (grants of power and procedures), and rights. A grammar appropriate for each type can at least help identify the problem and in some cases lead toward a solution.

Take grants of power. Article I, Section 8, Clauses 12, 13, and 14 empower Congress to raise an army and navy and to make rules for each. But what about an air force? A strict interpretation would have to conclude that because these clauses deal only with "land and naval Forces" (from Clause 14), the constitutionality of an air force, if indeed it is constitutional, could only be based on the general need for "common defence," expressed in the preamble and Article 1, Section 8, Clause 1. Proponents of strict interpretation, though, are generally reluctant to depend on such broad principles, for fear that more questionable acts might also sneak in under "common defence." Yet if we treat the grants of power in Clauses 12, 13, and 14 in terms of their clear purpose, we can view "army" and "navy" as placeholders that denote the means of providing national defense known at that time. An air force is therefore covered under these provisions.

Similarly, in Article I, Section 8, Clause 11, we can read "declare war" as signifying a nation's extended commitment to the expenditure of blood and treasure. (An earlier version of the clause gave Congress the sole authority to "make war," but at the Federal Convention, on August 17, that was changed to allow the president, if Congress was not sitting, to repel an invasion. The president could "make war" for a short time, and when Congress reconvened, it could decide whether to "declare war" or not.) According to this reading, the president still would need to consult Congress when committing the nation's armed forces to extended military conflicts, a core principle behind the Constitution and all republican thinking that buttressed it. With respect to grants of power, looking at words and phrases in terms of their function allows meanings to change in accordance with the Constitution, not in opposition to it.

Interpreting rights will always be tricky. By their very nature, rights limit government, yet the government must retain sufficient powers to govern effectively. No rights are absolute, particularly when exercised in a manner threatening the normal operations or even the existence of the government. Free speech and the right to keep and bear arms do not permit making death threats against the president or pointing guns at him or her. At the least, distinguishing the various types of constitutional provisions can help us evaluate the trade-offs, certainly a first step in arriving at any decision.

44. Scalia, *Matter of Interpretation*, 145.

45. Nor did the Fourteenth Amendment, as interpreted by contemporaries, specifically negate coverture laws, despite its guarantee that no person could be deprived of "life, liberty, or property without due process of law." In 1872 Supreme Court Justice Joseph P. Bradley argued in his concurring opinion in *Bradwell v. Illinois* that the Fourteenth Amendment did not alter traditional legal definitions of a woman's place in society: "The claim that, under the fourteenth amendment of the Constitution, which declares that no State shall make or enforce any law which shall abridge the privileges and immunities of citizens of the United States, the statute law of Illinois, or the common law prevailing in that State, can no longer be set up as a barrier against the right of females to pursue any lawful employment for a livelihood (the practice of law included), assumes that it is one of the privileges and immunities of women as citizens to engage in any and every profession, occupation, or employment in civil life. It certainly cannot be affirmed, as an historical fact, that this has ever been established as one of the fundamental privileges and immunities of the sex. On the contrary, the civil law, as well as nature herself, has always recognized a wide difference in the respective spheres and destinies of man and woman. Man is, or should be, woman's protector and defender. The natural and proper timidity and delicacy which belongs to the female sex evidently unfits it for many of the occupations of civil life.

The constitution of the family organization, which is founded in the divine ordinance, as well as in the nature of things, indicates the domestic sphere as that which properly belongs to the domain and functions of womanhood. The harmony, not to say identity, of interest and views which belong, or should belong, to the family institution is repugnant to the idea of a woman adopting a distinct and independent career from that of her husband. *So firmly fixed was this sentiment in the founders of the common law that it became a maxim of that system of jurisprudence that a woman had no legal existence separate from her husband, who was regarded as her head and representative in the social state; and, notwithstanding some recent modifications of this civil status, many of the special rules of law flowing from and dependent upon this cardinal principle still exist in full force in most States. One of these is, that a married woman is incapable, without her husband's consent, of making contracts which shall be binding on her or him."* (Emphasis added.) The Court upheld the decision by the Illinois Supreme Court denying Myra Bradwell admission to the Illinois bar because she was a woman. FindLaw.com, http://caselaw.lp.findlaw.com/scripts/getcase.pl?court=US&vol=83&invol=130.

To see how coverture could creep into constitutional litigation, imagine that the federal government, to extend an interstate highway, confiscated the best fields of Mrs. X's farm, which has been in her family for generations. Under the Fifth Amendment, she has a right to compensation, so the federal government sends her money. As interpreted by the values of 1791, however, the government should have sent the money to Mr. X, her ne'er-do-well husband, estranged but not divorced, who lives a debauched life in the city. When he files suit to receive his due, basing his case on the founders' view of property rights, a truly originalist judge should overturn subsequent anticoverture legislation, which undermined the way property was perceived when the Fifth Amendment was ratified, and award the money to Mr. X. Coverture was not simply a legal doctrine, Mr. X's lawyers could argue, but a "moral perception" of the founding generation.

This argument can be and has been challenged. In 1866, when the House of Representatives was debating what would soon become the Fourteenth Amendment, opponents protested by claiming that coverture statutes might be nullified inadvertently by the clause that prohibited states from depriving "any person of life, liberty, or property without due process of law." They did not want to pass a constitutional amendment that went that far, prohibiting coverture. Supporters of the amendment countered that the word "property," in the similar clause within the Fifth Amendment, referred to property as granted by state and local law, and those jurisdictions would be free to keep or abandon coverture as they saw fit, without reference to either the Fifth Amendment or the proposed one.

Imagine, then, nine originalist justices in the year 2015, when they hear Mr. X's case. They must decide the case on several obscure points of history. Did the framers and ratifiers of the Fifth Amendment define "property" according to the "moral perceptions" of the time, which demanded coverture and must be honored, or according to local and state law, which could be changed? Or perhaps both, not noticing that these might come into conflict? In that case, which definition should trump the other? Then, once a justice had made his or her peace with the founders of 1789 and 1791, he or she would need to repeat the investigation for 1866–68, asking the same questions with respect to the framers and ratifiers of the Fourteenth Amendment. On the answers to this complex set of arcane questions their decision would hinge, and depending on their historical interpretations, married women in 2015 either will or will not be constitutionally entitled to own their own property.

46. Jack M. Balkin, *Living Originalism* (Cambridge: Belknap Press, 2001), 7, 23.

47. Scalia, *Matter of Interpretation*, 46, 145.

48. Scalia, "Originalism: The Lesser Evil," 861.

49. Justices Thomas and Scalia pick and choose when to apply originalism to the Fourteenth Amendment, and when not to do so. They oppose affirmative action policies because they claim the Constitution (including and especially the Fourteenth Amendment) is color-blind, but if they applied their originalist method to the adoption of the Fourteenth Amendment, they should probaby conclude otherwise. Eric Schnapper, in his study of the congressional action on the Fourteenth Amendment and concurrent civil rights legislation at the height of Reconstruction ("Affirmative Action and the Legislative History of the Fourteenth Amendment," *Virginia Law Review* 71 [1985]: 753–98), concludes: "From the closing days of the Civil War until the end of civilian Reconstruction some five years later, Congress adopted a series of social welfare programs whose benefits were expressly limited to blacks. These programs were generally open to all blacks, not only to recently freed slaves, and were adopted over repeatedly expressed objections that such racially exclusive measures were unfair to whites. The race-conscious Reconstruction programs were enacted concurrently with the fourteenth amendment and were supported by the same legislators who favored the constitutional guarantee of equal protection. This history strongly suggests that the framers of the amendment could not have intended it generally to prohibit affirmative action for blacks or other disadvantaged groups" (Ibid., 754). Debates on the both the legislation and the Fourteenth Amendment presaged the debate over affirmative action in the late twentieth and early twenty-first centuries, as we see in President Andrew Johnson's veto of the Civil Rights Act of 1866. Measures within the bill, he argued, "establish for the security of the colored race safeguards which go infinitely beyond any that the General Government has ever provided for the white race. In fact, the distinction of race and color is by the bill made to operate in favor of the colored and against the white race." Despite his complaints about preferential treatment, Congress passed the bill over his veto. Emboldened, it then passed a Freedmen's Bureau bill with several race-conscious provisions offering special assistance to blacks. This color-conscious treatment was furiously debated, but in the end Congress enacted them. President Johnson then vetoed the new bill because he opposed favorable treatment for "any favored class of citizens," but the House voted to override his veto by 104 to 33, and the Senate did likewise, 33 to 12. Overwhelmingly, Congress voted in favor of what today we would call affirmative action measures. Further, at the time that Congress debated particular provisions entailing special treatment for blacks, it debated and approved the Fourteenth Amendment; the votes on the legislation and the amendment were largely along identical lines. The expected application of the Fourteenth Amendment, historically speaking, is clear: the Reconstruction Congress did not take a color-blind approach but approved race-conscious measures intended to address past injustices. Today, we do not necessarily have to abide by Congress's expected application of the amendment that it proposed and sent on to the states, but originalists, to be true to their method, should. Because the historical evidence would not support the conclusion they wish to draw, however, they don't.

50. Scalia, *Matter of Interpretation*, 40.

51. Balkin, *Living Originalism*, 24, 29. Balkin distinguishes between two forms of originalism: "framework originalism," which he accepts, and "skyscraper originalism," which he rejects: "These two types of originalism differ in the degree of constitutional construction and implementation that later generations may engage in. Skyscraper originalism views the Constitution as more or less a finished product, albeit always subject to Article V amendment. It allows ample room for democratic lawmaking to meet future demands of governance; however, this lawmaking is not constitutional construction. It is ordinary law that is permissible withion the bounds of the Constitution. Framework originalism, by contrast, views the Constitution as an initial framework for governance that sets politics in motion and must be filled out over time through constitutional construction. The goal is to get politics started and keep it going (and stable) so that it can solve future problems of governance. Later generations have a lot to do to build up and implement the Constitution, but when they do, they must always remain faithful to the basic framework" (21–22). If presented with these two alternatives, James Madison, for one, would have leaned toward the latter, or at least he did in *The Federalist No. 37*, while arguing for a flexible approach to the Constitution: "Experience has instructed us that no skill in the science of government has yet been able to discriminate and define, with sufficient certainty, its three great provinces—the legislative, executive, and judiciary; or even the privileges and powers of the different legislative branches. Questions daily occur in the course of practice, which prove the obscurity which reins in these subjects, and which puzzle the greatest adepts in political science." No constitution can function as a fully completed edifice; instead, it needs to be filled in within the contexts of real-world experiences. "All new laws, though penned with the greatest technical skill, and passed on the fullest and most mature deliberation, are considered as more or less obscure and equivocal, until their meaning be liquidated and ascertained by a series of particular discussions and adjudications." This, in fact, is what happened, starting with the tumultuous constitutional debates of the 1790s, in which Madison was an active participant. Benjamin Franklin, a true scientist, likewise would have preferred the framework approach, which allows for empirical input (see note 55 below).

52. Madison, *Notes of Debates*, September 17.

53. This story comes from James McHenry, a delegate to the Federal Convention from Maryland: "A lady asked Dr. Franklin Well Doctor what have we got a republic or a monarchy— A republic replied the Doctor if you can keep it." James McHenry, "Anecdotes," in Farrand, *Records*, 3:85. McHenry's document does not bear a date.

54. Patrick J. Buchanan, "A Republic, Not a Democracy," March 2, 2005, http://antiwar .com/pat/?articleid=5015.

55. The first reading treats Franklin as a bureaucrat: we write the rules, he supposedly meant, and your job is simply to follow them. The second reading, more historically astute, sees him as an open-minded scientist devoted to experimentation. For Franklin, the framers' proposed Constitution was the latest and grandest experiment in forming republican governments. After independence, eleven states had experimented with new constitutions, but two of these soon dropped their recently minted constitutions to form even newer ones, and a third state constitution, Pennsylvania's, was being seriously challenged even as the framers met within the Pennsylvania State House. For at least thirty-seven years prior to 1787, Franklin had entertained an

interest in constitution making. In 1750 he offered ideas for a continental federation, which four years later evolved into his famous Albany Plan of Union. In 1775, after the outbreak of the Revolutionary War but a year before the United States declared its independence, he revamped those ideas, this time proposing a central authority with the power to pass "general ordinances as tho' [thought] necessary to the general welfare." Following independence, Franklin served on the congressional committee charged with drawing up "a plan of confederation." John Dickinson, the committee member who prepared the first draft, drew on Franklin's earlier ideas. The final version of that agreement, the Articles of Confederation, proved weaker than Franklin would have preferred, and now, in September of 1787, the Federal Convention was proposing to supplant the Articles with a new set of rules that Franklin and others hoped would "form a more perfect union." Would Doctor Franklin, the great scientist, really proclaim with absolute certainty that the latest in this series of experiments was the final solution, before the new plan had even been tried out in real life? Like other framers, he wanted first and foremost to get the experiment started by putting *something* in place; improvements could be made later, as in fact they were (Franklin, *Papers*, 4:119 for the 1750 plan and 22:122–23 for the 1775 plan).

INDEX

Page numbers in **boldface** indicate document texts.

CELEBRATING INDEPENDENT PUBLISHING

Thank you for reading this book published by The New Press. The New Press is a nonprofit, public interest publisher. New Press books and authors play a crucial role in sparking conversations about the key political and social issues of our day.

We hope you enjoyed this book and that you will stay in touch with The New Press. Here are a few ways to stay up to date with our books, events, and the issues we cover:

- Sign up at www.thenewpress.com/subscribe to receive updates on New Press authors and issues and to be notified about local events

- Like us on Facebook: www.facebook.com/newpressbooks

- Follow us on Twitter: www.twitter.com/thenewpress

Please consider buying New Press books for yourself; for friends and family; or to donate to schools, libraries, community centers, prison libraries, and other organizations involved with the issues our authors write about.

The New Press is a 501(c)(3) nonprofit organization. You can also support our work with a tax-deductible gift by visiting www.thenewpress.com/donate.